Theater of
War and Exile

Also by Domnica Radulescu

Women's Comedic Art as Social Revolution: Five Performers and the Lessons of Their Subversive Humor (2012, McFarland)

Theater of War and Exile

Twelve Playwrights, Directors and Performers from Eastern Europe and Israel

DOMNICA RADULESCU

Foreword by MAYA E. ROTH

McFarland & Company, Inc., Publishers
Jefferson, North Carolina

LIBRARY OF CONGRESS CATALOGUING-IN-PUBLICATION DATA

Radulescu, Domnica, 1961–
Theater of war and exile : twelve playwrights, directors and performers from Eastern Europe and Israel / Domnica Radulescu ; foreword by Maya E. Roth.
p. cm.
Includes bibliographical references and index.

ISBN 978-0-7864-7312-0 (softcover : acid free paper) ♾
ISBN 978-1-4766-1919-4 (ebook)

1. East European drama—History and criticism. 2. Theater—Europe, Eastern—History. 3. Israeli drama—History and criticism. 4. Theater—Israel—History. 5. Politics and literature—Europe, Eastern. 6. Politics and literature—Israel. 7. Theater—Political aspects—Europe, Eastern. 8. Theater—Political aspects—Israel. I. Title.

PN849.E9R33 2015
809'.8947—dc23 2015015673

BRITISH LIBRARY CATALOGUING DATA ARE AVAILABLE

On the cover: Image from the Trap Door Theatre's production of the play *The Word* Progress *on My Mother's Lips Doesn't Ring True* by Matei Vişniec

Printed in the United States of America

McFarland & Company, Inc., Publishers
Box 611, Jefferson, North Carolina 28640
www.mcfarlandpub.com

For Henry

For all who survive war and exile and
the theater artists who tell their stories

For the memory of my father
(1926–2000)

Acknowledgments

First and foremost I wish to thank my home institution, Washington and Lee University, for the generous support of my scholarly work through sabbatical leaves, Lenfest research and travel grants, and conference funding, all of which has substantially contributed to the creation and completion of this book. In particular I want to thank my colleague, friend, and dean, Suzanne Keen, for her unrelenting support of my work and for facilitating many of my creative endeavors and projects. I also wish to thank Marc Conner for his prompt support with the funding of several components of this book and related creative projects. And I thank Victoria Blackstone for help with indexing.

I would also like to thank the theater artists included in this book who have generously shared their thoughts, ideas, unpublished works, and illustrations of their work, as well as given interviews for the completion of my study: Matei Vişniec, Saviana Stanescu, Motti Lerner, Dijana Milošević and the DAH Theater, Marcy Arlin, Pavel Zuštiak, Noa Baum, Milena Markovic, and Radmila Adamova.

Finally, I wish to thank the unknown member of the Women in Black group in Belgrade, Serbia, who welcomed me into her home and handed me a copy of the precious volume of survival stories gathered under the title *Women in Black: Women's Side of War.*

Table of Contents

Between pages 162 and 163 are 8 color plates containing 12 photographs

Foreword by Maya E. Roth

If, as Peggy Phelan distills, "trauma makes a tear in the symbolic network itself" because its scope or intensity overwhelms, trauma can simultaneously create an urgent compulsion to express what is beyond speech or pillars of meaning (*Mourning Sex: Performing Public Memories* 5). In so doing it can press survivors and witnesses of political trauma to tremendous creativity and activism. In a way, that is the backstory of Domnica Radulescu's exceptional book.

Theater of War and Exile offers an exhilarating study—and bold, multilayered argument—for theater's role in navigating and transforming traumas of exile and war. As an artist, scholar and (global) citizen, I will keep learning from this volume and the artists it highlights for years. So, I trust, will the field. An émigré Romanian scholar and artist, Domnica Radulescu interweaves activist, artistic and scholarly investments by focusing on contemporary theater works that "have emerged directly and ferociously out of wars and experiences of exile, out of violent political events and their aftermaths" in the Balkans and in Israel-and-Palestine. Radulescu avers that postmodernist modes can express traumatic ruptures and transformations in artistically revelatory, profoundly political ways, expressing the ontologies of exile and processes of war trauma. Surely this is because theater is at once social and material, creative and contingent; the liminal symbolic space of theater provides a forum for intervening at the crossroads of individual and collective experience. Indeed, through her diverse, compelling case studies and multidimensional analysis, Radulescu argues that a "conspicuous aesthetics" can best engage the psychic and physical wounds of political trauma, constellating the living and dead. Hovering nearby is Diana Taylor's articulation of *hauntology,* building on Derrida: "(P)erformance makes visible (for an instant, live, now) that which is always already there: the ghosts, the tropes, the scenarios that structure our individual and collective life" (*The Archive and the Repertoire: Performing Cultural Memory in the Americas* 143). Radulescu's inspired book reminds us that the ontologies and *hauntologies* of exile and war structure cultures and lives in ongoing ways, creating rifts and after-lives of trauma, utopic imperatives and urgent art.

Radulescu's astute interdisciplinary research is buoyed here by her sustained expertise in Eastern European culture and exile, theatrical praxis, scholarly expertise on subversive humor and feminist theory, and inventive engagement with postmodernism. The volume contributes to multiple fields, from trauma studies to Balkan Studies, from theater as social change to global performance. In so doing, it reflects on war and proliferating exile/s as well as the relationship between art and society—particularly in times of crisis, coercion and crossing cultures. When, for instance, Radulescu analyzes Romanian-French Matei Vişniec's work and his self-perceived conflict between his two different writing modes (and ethics) as playwright and as journalist responding to war atrocities, the book engages readers in the paradoxes of testimony, querying the distinctive stakes of an *aesthetic,* not only a body, of theater of war and exile. Radulescu's vivid distillations of divergent artists' work is a joy to read. Whether describing Romanian-born Saviana Stanescu's "aesthetic vortex of comedy and tragedy" for works premiered in exile in America, Czech-born Pavel Zuštiak's experimental dance theater adaptation of Polish-born Jerzy Kosinski's novel *The Painted Bird,* "mingling" "two Eastern European artists' war traumas" in a dance of spatial dislocation, or the Serbian DAH's multidisciplinary devised performances of remembrance and "rebirth" which tour internationally to witness and heal memories of atrocities perpetrated in their home/land, Radulescu listens astutely. She conjures artistic and social praxis as interlinked. And she proffers that some of the most vital, experimental theater today is the work of exiles, refugees and survivors of atrocity from Eastern Europe.

Nowhere do the artistic vitality and ethical provocations of an aesthetic of trauma in theater get more fully probed than in Radulescu's twelve case studies of writers, directors, choreographers, and performers for the stage. Drawing equally on repertory and archive, she analyzes their inventive, compelling theater of war and exile with critical precision, com/passion and creativity. She excavates focal works' potential to critique, resist, and renew social orders through the symbolic, embodied, collective work of theater. To that end, Radulescu's generative scholarship includes original interviews with nine of the twelve international artists, querying their perspectives on the relationship of form to meaning and trauma, which helps her to interrogate art's relationship to war and exile today further and to renew our understanding of political trauma *as well as* experimental theater. An émigré artist-scholar herself, Radulescu evinces an equally profound grasp of complex cultural histories and artistic means, attuned to their gripping social and psychic stakes.

Several guiding insights drive this volume. First Radulescu brings scholarship and artists in dialogue, attuned to theater practice and the real atrocities that have inspired the works. Secondly, she probes the politics of aesthetics and how postmodernist form can navigate more complex relationships to, and layers of, the material staged. Third, she brings to this book a feminist, critical and activist insight that the personal and political inter-animate. At stake for Radulescu is to rebut the strand of postmodern scholarship which rejects "the real" and, simultaneously, to counter the strand of testimonial theater that relies on realism or documentary methods to witness war and trauma.

Placing her work in conversation with Bakhtin, Said, Brecht, and Dolan, Rushdie and Kundera, among others, Radulescu develops a nuanced theoretical framework for a "conspicuous aesthetics" of theater of exile and war deployed by living artists coming from the Balkan wars, Eastern Europe's former Soviet dictatorships, and the "double exile" of Israel-and-Palestine. Indeed, she argues that this radical array of theater succeeds as resistance and transformation precisely because it refutes realism and more overt testimonial or verbatim theater prominent in Anglo-American circuits. Evocative and associative more than representational, the aesthetic she articulates grapples with the scope, scale, disorientation, and intensity of exile and war through estrangement, creative devices and formal structures of theatricality: not through equivalence and realism. "The Bakhtinian laughter and carnivalesque vision of reality are directly coordinate with a non-essentialist view and a perfect tool for the subversion of oppressive societal structures," as she succinctly observes. In that, this book connects to scholarly essays by Laura Edmondson regarding Erik Ehn's "hallucinatory realism" which fuses the "grotesque" with the "quotidian" or Australian Playwright Christine Evans' call for a political theater that works through abstract means (metaphor, doubling, form), pleasure, and "change," freeing scenarios and imagination from the logic of inevitability and literality.

Radulescu's close focus on Eastern European theater artists also helps to intervene in the use of tragedy for staging trauma, for Balkan theater carries an experimental *and populist* cultural legacy of carnival, theater of the absurd, surrealism, dance and song, ritual play, and of the "circus of life and death," as she traces with passion and lucidity, bred by the liminality and paradoxes of the Balkans. Persuasively she articulates a Balkan aesthetic—highly theatrical, carnivalesque, irreverent in its mix of tragedy and comedy, high and low cultures, game and ritual— constituted in liminal terms, morphing, and unstable. As such, *Theater of War and Exile* provides a savvy consideration of postmodernist aesthetics more broadly, of the legacies of Brecht on international political theater, on the relevance of Artaud and Ionesco, surrealism and circus to this theater of trauma, particularly for artists from Eastern Europe.

Indeed, one of the most important contributions of this book to the ever-growing field of (activist) scholarship about theater against war, genocide and political atrocities today—as pursued by colleagues such as Laurie Beth Clark, Mary Karen Dahl, Laura Edmundson, Branislav Jakovljevic, Carol Martin, Robert Skloot, and Diana Taylor, to name a significant few—comes in Radulescu's multifaceted conviction in the *artistic importance* of this theater, as well as its social urgency. She argues that these twelve case studies—frequently experimental, conspicuously theatrical, and seared with both real experience and creative transformations, rife with complex paradoxes and vivid ruptures of time/space, story and self/role—manifests a profound potential for critique, evocation of suppressed memories and truths, and multi-layered sensory impact as well as community ritual. As a child of a child survivor of the Holocaust and an artist-scholar who trained with a dissident Polish director who escaped martial law, I know the afterlife of trauma and the aesthetic Radulescu describes deep in my bones. It is not only that these artists learn to speak through abstract creative means to hoodwink censorship (although this can be true), it is also that creative activation of multiple vision, attuned to paradox, rings most fully *true*, full of complexities, performativity and living echoes.

This book's significance derives in no small part from Radulescu's expertise in contemporary Eastern European theater in diaspora, work that arises from recent decades of harrowing violence, Balkanization, and displacement. In this she builds on recent publications such as Silvija Jestrovic's *Performance, Space, Utopia: Cities of War, Cities of Exile* (Palgrave 2013). Indeed, this book fills a lacuna in scholarship about a larger web of twenty-first century Eastern European artists in diaspora, with profound artistic grasp of the exhilarating importance of their theater and its pluralist range and global contexts. The Balkans itself registers as plural, placed, and porous: a crossroads of Europe and Asia, of North and South, steeped in centuries of violent conflicts and cross-cultural alterity. Radulescu's inclusion of Israeli artists Motti Lerner and Noa Baum—adult children of Holocaust survivors from Eastern Europe—gains force, then, because she casts Israel-and-Palestine, like the Balkans, as perpetually liminal, a crossroads—now steeped in the "double exile" of Jews and Palestinians. Thus, the ethics and aesthetics this book compels moves across borders of identity, nation, and generation.

Reading this book one is reminded how profoundly twentieth century theatrical praxis, is indebted to émigré artists from the Balkans. From Ionesco, who lived in exile in France from Romania, to iconic, influential directors of the 1960s and since such as Grotowski, Jan Kott, and Andrei Serban, who have shaped generations of experimental theater in Western Europe and America, to current Eastern European artists in European, global and festival (or university) circuits such as those highlighted in this volume, these artists' praxis is profoundly shaped by their experience of war trauma, oppressive tyrannies (i.e., during Communist occupations) and exile. Radulescu underscores that not only individually but as a community, their experiences of trauma have triggered artistic innovation and expressive urgency. To that end, she artfully places the artists' work as part of a deeper continuum, alongside Kundera, Jerzy Kozinski, and Milos Foreman, for instance. It is a tribute to Radulescu's gifted writing, research, and argument that I leave this book knowing far more about the Balkans, my own theatrical praxis, and invigorated for the field by the provocative theater she shares.

If the first chapter investigates exile as an ontological mutation as expressed through theater and performance by artists from Romania, the former Czechoslovakia and Poland, Radulescu's second chapter excavates a theatrical aesthetic of war and genocide activated by traumas of the Balkan wars leading to the dissolution of the former Yugoslavia and Israeli/Palestinian crises in recent decades—understanding both regions as quintessentially liminal places, contested and haunted. Sites of contention range from bodies to borders, and the works articulate traumas across cultures, with the majority of works produced by dissident artists (Serbian and Israeli, for instance), surfacing contestations in the dominant oppressive culture and the spiraling afterlife of political traumas. Radulescu's case study chapters journey from a focus on the ontology of exile, which she recognizes as an "ontological mutation," both creative and haunted, generative and consuming, to the traumatic ruptures of war—which ripple in psychic, social, and artistic modes. Her sophisticated study of an aesthetic of exile prepares us then to grasp the dystopic theatrical aesthetics of war more fully. Importantly, she moves us inside and outside of political atrocities, shifting from evocative images to lucid analysis, from psychic to social processes, just as she sees this theater to do. The third chapter stewards readers' focus to performance as preserver of memory. In this movement, the book charts a larger trajectory from trauma's rifts to the promotion of peace and cross-cultural perspectives. If the first chapter lays out a theoretical framework, we can read her conclusion almost as a manifesto, charged by revelations about her own life experience as artist and émigré.

This book fuses Radulescu's life's work as scholar, artist, global citizen, and émigré. For beyond her scholarly books and essays to date, Radulescu is the author of two best-selling novels about Romania, escape from Ceausescu's tyranny, and exilic reinvention, *Black Sea Twilight* and *Train to Trieste*—the latter published in twelve languages. Prior to this book I knew the author best through her two recent plays *The Town with Very Nice People: A Strident Operetta* and *Exile Is My Home,* two boldly cross-cultural ensemble plays that placed highly in recent Jane Chambers Contests for feminist playwriting that I steward for the Women and Theatre Program and the Association for Theater in Higher Education (2013, 2014). Both plays model profoundly international ethics and experimental aesthetics, which make them valuable to contemporary feminist playwriting; as I write this foreword, *Exile Is My Home* has just completed a successful developmental workshop at Theaterlab, an experimental off–Broadway theater, with direction by Marcy Arlin, whose work as founding artistic director of the Immigrants' Theater Project is discussed in this book. Epic in structure, kaleidoscopic in reach, post-modern in style, and exilic in theme, her novels and plays invite detours and connections, alike, imagining transformations even as they reverberate diverse scenarios of dispossession. So too does this scholarly work. The themes that haunt and feed this monograph—exile, war, the relationship between art and activism, vivid interplay between past and present, between place, displacement and identity, and between political trauma and transformation—also inspire her fiction and plays. Thus, Radulescu is an experimental ethnographer, an informant of a circuit of internationally-engaged artists transforming traumas into art across the world.

Lucid and passionate, critical and creative, multivalent in methods, frequently poetic, highly personal, always rigorously researched, this book takes readers on unexpected journeys to pursue its ambitious scope and stakes. Scholars interested in international and formally adventurous theater—as well as in trauma studies, exile, peacemaking, and war's impact more broadly—will find inspiration and insight in this book. It is also a boon to artists. For through her persuasive, ambitious work, Radulescu reveals *how*—not only that—this radical theatrical aesthetic expresses, understands, and can transform political trauma. Borne of crisis, the artworks she excavates are profoundly unsettling and provocative, sometimes restorative, always creative; they act on our bodies and emotions, our minds and our memories, their dissent and renewal staying with us through their inventive art and stirring stakes. That too, suggests Radulescu, bears out their impact, making a profound difference in lives as they reshape cultural legacies.

Maya E. Roth is the Della Rosa Distinguished Professor of Theater and chairs the Department of Performing Arts at Georgetown University. As dramaturg-director, she specializes in gender and performance, classics revisioned, ensemble, and staging trauma.

Preface

This is a book about theater that emerges from political trauma. In it I ask such questions as these: How does writing from a place of trauma, as a witness or survivor of war, of political oppression or displacement, affect the style of the writing, the aesthetic of the theater, the sound of its voices and the shape of its performances? Does the experience of political violence influence what we write about as much as how we write about it? Are playwrights and other theater makers who bear witness or who experience the traumas of displacement and wars forming communities and bridges across cultures and countries, and are these theater makers connected not just by the topics they treat in their theater but also by the shapes of their art? Is theater aesthetic also a matter of politics? And does theater art really make a difference? Of course the weight of this study itself depends partly on the answer to this last question and on the will to believe—as do so many others who passionately engage in the making and/or exploration of political theater—that yes, of course, theater that emerges from profound political trauma such as war, genocide, and displacement in an attempt to resist and to heal, will make a difference and help create a better world.[1]

Theater and Political Trauma

In the preface to the anthology *Theater of Genocide*, Robert Skloot (2009, 24) reaffirms the necessity of "theatrical images that protest against killing, test our ethical assumptions and responsibilities and affirm a knowable, palpable communality as a basis for a humane future."[2] Skloot maintains that it is the "presentness" of theater that makes it an ideal art form and a perfect medium for social transformation and productive acts of resistance against the violence of our times. This is not a new claim, of course, as the entire twentieth century history of political theater since Bertolt Brecht has been based in various degrees on the belief that the social nature of theater endows it with great potential as a catalyst for political action and change. However, because of the proliferation of genocidal events across our planet, the perfecting of the means of destruction and killing, and the increasing displacement of millions across the globe due to wars, ecological disasters and dictatorial regimes, there seems to be an even greater urgency that compels theater artists to engage politically through their art and to become forces of social transformation and healing.

This book goes a step further in the exploration of political theater in that it focuses on aesthetics more than on ideology; on the shape of ideas and the tone of the voices heard more than on the philosophies that imbue the plays. In the building of its main argument, the stone at the center of the arch is the notion that theatrical form is also content, that aesthetics is also politics. Lane Bruner makes the cogent distinction between "the *aesthetics of politics*, or aesthetic acts that support hegemonic political fictions, and the *politics of aesthetics*, or aesthetic acts that intentionally resist hegemonic political fictions" (2012, 2).[3] My book is about the "politics of aesthetics" and the theater I focus on is an "art of resistance."[4]

The orchestration of the book is multilayered, weaving many contradictory notes and multicolored threads into one critical and creative quilt. This endeavor is meant to offer not only theoretical explorations of a kind of theater issuing from political traumas, but also creative answers, practical solutions and productive strategies for surviving, bearing witness and healing through experimental artistic products and initiatives. It is a book whose theoretical and critical frameworks are also interwoven with interviews of theater makers from countries at war or with a history of recent wars; with theater artists who write in exile or have expatriated themselves from their native countries, or who due to their historical and geographical positioning write plays that explore the traumas of war and dislocation. Of the twelve playwrights and theater projects/artists discussed in my book, I have personally interviewed nine of them about their art and the themes woven in my study. Finally, this book also includes fragments of unpublished theater pieces generously shared by the artists that illustrate the theoretical framework I am trying to establish. Just like the questions I am asking, the form of my book is troubled and unconventional, edgy and multifaceted.

The nature of trauma itself is in the realm of the un-representable, and therefore, whether dealing with the primary theatrical texts and with the devised performances inspired by the experience of war and displacement or with the second-degree critical discourse that analyzes art forms inspired by trauma, we can only reach the pain and attempt the healing while containing the memory in oblique ways that escape direct representation. "Throughout the trauma literature there seems to be an effort to differentiate the extraordinary nature of trauma from ordinary wounds, stress or distress. Trauma is 'world shattering,' 'overwhelming,' 'unrepresentable,' an experience so 'profound' that it precludes 'cognitive knowledge'" (Clarke 2010, 66). Trauma theories and studies on trauma in the twentieth century have pointed out that we live in a "catastrophic age" and that "modernity is characterized by the sign of the wound," while "the modern subject has become inseparable from the categories of shock and trauma" (Nadal and Calvo 2014, 1).[5] Discussions and studies of post-traumatic stress disorder (PTSD) have multiplied over the last decades, particularly, with entire populations of soldiers returning to their homes after debilitating war experiences. PTSD has been poignantly called by Ruth Leys (2013, 2) "a disorder of memory."[6] The theatrical works explored and presented in this book make an attempt at reorganizing such "disorder of memory" into cohesive worlds. They often veer into the "un-representable" through experimental, fractured, edgy theatrical forms that defy conventional and realistic representation and that bear exactly the "overwhelming" nature of trauma itself, precluding "cognitive knowledge" and relying more on intuitive relations and imagery. In connection to the representation of the "un-representable," Robert Skloot reaffirms what he thinks has become a commonplace that such realities need to be "managed abstractly or obliquely, poetically and symbolically on stage, because theatrical realism cannot accommodate this purpose." In response to extraordinary political traumas, theater needs to replace realistic representation "with other forms that arouse conscience and deeper understanding" (2009, 23). It is such forms that are the focus of my study.

Introduction

Defining an Aesthetic of War and Exile

"Exile is a dream of a glorious return. Exile is a vision of revolution: Elba, not St Helena. It is an endless paradox: looking forward by always looking back. The exile is a ball hurled high into the air. He hangs there frozen in time, translated into a paragraph, denied motion, suspended impossibly above his native earth" (Rushdie 2006, 212). This passage by Salmon Rushdie from his hugely controversial book *The Satanic Verses* captures in bold language part of the thematic scope of the present book. An exile from one of the former communist East European countries myself, I have never been able to overcome the "endless paradox" of "looking forward by always looking back" in my life or in my writing. Books about exile have amounted over the past several decades to an entire area of studies. In my own book *Realms of Exile: Nomadism, Diasporas and Eastern European Voices* of a decade ago, I made the following comment, referring to the verses of the Latin poet Ovid in his collection *Tristia: Ex Ponto,* while in exile on the territory of the present Romania: "In that moment of leaving one's native land for an indefinite period of exile, the most precious possession one has is, indeed, one's mind over which no tyrants, regimes, or 'Caesars' can ultimately rule. And that is both the sorrow and the bitter joy of the freedom of exile" (2002, 13). This comment was made in relation to the following Ovidian verses: "Behold me, deprived of native land, of you and my home, bereft of all that could be taken from me; my mind is nevertheless my comrade and my joy; over this Caesar could have no right" (2002, 13). This fierce sense of freedom that the exiled artist experiences once left with nothing but her or his own mind and creativity is also "the ball hurled high into the air," a bold and also painful stretch across frontiers, an impulsive embracing of the unknown in a reckless but necessary desire to make the whole world one's own by weaving two contradictory movements: that of keeping the memory of the lost native spaces alive and that of reinventing oneself in new and foreign spaces. This is also the reason why the art of exiled writers often reflects a fractured conscience, a brittle yet fierce memory and an audacious defiance of linearity and conventional realism. Having to contend with a conscience split between lost spaces and unfamiliar spaces, the mirror of the exiled writer is forever broken: reality, the self, memory, the perception and representation of space and time will always have irreparable cracks, and it is the cracks that account for the troubling beauty of their art. The poet Joseph Brodsky noted, "Exile is after all a kind of success." The art emerging from the experience of exile is one such example of "a kind of success" achieved at the expense of a profound sacrifice and loss of the self as well as from a simultaneous reinventing of the self.

It is not incidental that I have chosen to address this fascinating conundrum of the relation between trauma and theater aesthetic as it relates to playwrights and theater artists from Eastern Europe and Israel. There are of course many contemporary artists and playwrights, many of them American, some Pulitzer Prize–winners such as Lynn Nottage, or Erik Ehn, the playwright quoted several times in my study, whose theatrical work has been inspired by genocidal events in the world and that are not amply discussed in my book or not at all. Unfortunately our world and century never cease to horrify us with such examples of violence. I unapologetically admit that I have chosen works from and about this particular geographical and cultural landscape precisely because they also relate to my own personal experiences and growth as a writer and exile from the communist dictatorship of Nicolae Ceauşescu. Since the book explores the deep connections between lived experiences and the creation of theater, between historical realities and the aesthetic they engender, I have wanted to keep my explorations within the realm of art and culture that I most viscerally connect with and that I have had most direct contact with. In other words, I have wanted to speak from a place of experience and embodiment rather than from an abstracted place of mere knowledge, particularly given the nature of theater and performance as an embodied art that takes place in real space and time. Beyond the personal considerations, it is also necessary and long overdue to take a look at the contributions that various theater makers and writers from these parts of the world have made in the area of political theater during the past several decades; how they have changed our world and theater practice in response to violent events, genocidal wars, and the flood of immigration and displaced persons. Except for Israel these are all post-communist countries that before 1989 had shared various levels of subservience to the Soviet Union, had developed similar societal and political structures derived from socialist Marxist ideology and have known different political trajectories since the 1989 revolutions. The Bosnian war of ethnic cleansing of the nineties and the Israeli Palestinian wars are at the core of inspiration of the playwrights included in my study, while the experiences of immigrants, particularly from Romania, Bosnia, Serbia and Poland, inform the works gathered under the theme of exile.

One of the theses at the center of this book emerges from the philosophical premise that the experiences of exile and war, and specifically that of the political exile of no return that has marked the world in a most dramatic way during this past century, cause an ontological mutation in our psyche and in our relation to time and space. It is my contention that the writers and theater makers who have suffered this ontological mutation or who are writing about it are constantly hurling that ball high into the air; they create an aesthetic form that bears the traces of such a profound ontological experience. In other words, our dislocated sense of self and the world around us influences the forms, the structures, the style, and the voices in which we tell our stories. Given the fundamental psychological and existential dislocation at the basis of the traumas of exile and of war, the theater writings and events created by exile or expatriate writers bear the same marks of dislocation, rupture, and of simultaneous "looking forward" while "always looking back." Exile, being in the words of Edward Said "the territory of non-belonging" (2002, 139), and theater being on the other hand an art that is profoundly implanted in its social context and in a particular time and place, the clash between the two makes for splintered structures and voices, for disordered narratives and chronologies, but equally creates a drive to turn brokenness into wholeness.

This is not to say that there are not also plays and fictional works by exile writers that use realistic or more conventional narratives and linear chronologies, but rather that there is a significant body of dramatic works and of theatrical projects by artists who have left their countries or who have experienced the traumas of political oppression and war in their own countries that bear such conspicuous aesthetics. At the level of narrative, voice and structure, this aesthetic incarnates a fractured psyche in search of its wholeness while also making a virtue of its fragmentation. The purpose of such a book is both an aesthetic and an ethical one. In my search for recurring forms that reflect and testify to the traumas of exile and war, I am interested in demonstrating how art that is born out of radically traumatic experiences can become both a survival and a healing strategy for ourselves and the world we live in. And it can become a strategy of survival and healing not only because, as has been said many times with regards to past historical violence and atrocities such as the Holocaust, we have to remember the past, to keep the memory alive and to tell our stories. It is healing also because in the transfiguration of reality through art forms that are oblique, symbolic, poetic or troubling, the past and the memory of trauma can be processed and transcended into a weightless reality where reflection, laughter, contemplation and critical thinking are made possible again. I contend that it is not just the telling, the witnessing and the creation of a memory or history of trauma that can heal and restore us some of our lost wholeness, but also the alchemic processes of transformation of one reality into another that have a restorative potential. As experimental theater makers such as the Polish director Jerzy Grotowski believed, theater offers a different kind of reality, an alternative life whose creation one can control, witness and experience peacefully in a protected environment.[1] Grotowski "emphasized the use of the body and voice as means of primal communication with the audience in an intimate setting" (Whitmore 2012, 81). By entering the life that unfolds on stage, the audience has the opportunity to engage in such "primal communication" and experience the lives of other people while reflecting critically upon their own, upon the state of the world and their place in it. It is not by repeating the trauma through the telling of it that political theater can change us and the world for the better but by processing the trauma into an art form that both speaks of the trauma that inspired it and transcends it through various processes of the creative imagination. In the groundbreaking collection titled *Theater Matters: Performance and Culture in the World Stage*, Jane Plastow offers a memorable definition of the kind of political theater I am interested in, namely the theater "of social intervention"[2]; a theater that is also aesthetically engaging and of crucial importance in the lives of peoples and societies with traumatic histories:

> The theater not only examines the resultant sense of loss or self-worth but also attempts to take part in the healing process of asserting culture and identity, so that the people involved can begin to re-value and even re-invent themselves in the context of their post ore neo-colonial situation.... This does not in any sense crudely privilege message over aesthetic sensibility, but rather posits a theater where function and aesthetic importantly cohabit in the same performance arena [Boon et al. 1999, 2].

The dramatic works and the theater projects contained in this book share several common features: to various degrees they function as testimonials of traumatic political experiences involving exile, expatriation or war, and they largely tell stories of survival, while drawing their inspiration from real political and historical events and often from personal experiences of political violence. The theater artists portrayed here engage in non-realistic and unconventional theatrical forms, plot development and character creation, and even when they do engage in realistic representation they do so by overcoming the limits of traditional realism by the use of parody or strategies of the hyperreal or simulacra. They mix lived and imagined experience, historical and personal facts in a postmodernist fashion that questions the very notion of the real[3] while also paradoxically attempting to get closer to certain versions of the real and to raise awareness in audiences about historical and political happenings. The works discussed in my book are often self-subverting and self-referential, thus breaking the suspension of disbelief. I will use the terms postmodernism and postmodernist sometimes as encompassing all three dimensions described by Philip Auslander in his discussion of postmodernism and "aesthetic performance" in the sense of: "(1) A periodizing concept, (2) a way of describing the contemporary culture in which performances occur, and (3) a stylistic descriptor" (2004, 98).[4] Mostly I will use the term postmodernist as an adjective describing many of the works explored here. This term refers precisely to the "stylistic descriptor" and to the "stylistic features" that "align them with postmodernism as a structure of feeling, an episteme rather than a chronologically defined moment" (Auslander 2004, 98).

The plays and performances I have chosen engage in carnivalesque discourse and stage action, and mix tragic depictions with comic discourse in incongruous combinations reminiscent of the surrealist aesthetic, of the Theater of the Absurd or of the Theater of Cruelty envisioned by Antonin Artaud.[5] They make use of the actors' bodies in their multiple capacities as carriers of meaning and as vehicles of cathartic liberation in ways that illustrate some of Jerzy Grotowski's and Eugenio Barba's performance strategies. The aesthetic of war and exile, as I will often refer to in this book, has the function of both illustrating the psychic breakages suffered by the author (or in larger terms by the community or nation that the author belongs to) and of surviving and exorcising such psychic ruptures.[6] This is not an attempt towards establishing a simplistic correlation between biography and art, or between history and its reflections in literature, but rather an exploration of the ways in which trauma influences the form of the art that tries to express it, heal it and exorcise it. It is to say that the historic, cultural, and geographical place we create from does matter and does determine the aesthetic choices we make as artists. In turn, these choices bear on the ways in which we survive and heal from such traumas. It is not enough to just witness; it matters how we witness and in what images we package the memory of trauma. In referring to "the theater of genocide," which is a category I will widely discuss in this book, Robert Skloot notes:

> Like all engaged art, it seeks to comment on and influence public discourse through various strategies: by the description of the victims' suffering and the assertion of their essential worthiness, the discussion of the perpetrators' motivation, the presentation of images of healing and compassion, the evocation of empathy, the questioning of the proper use of historical knowledge, and even the expansion and dissemination of what the critic Susan Sontag called a "collective instruction" of culture [2009, 5].

The theater aesthetic of war and exile that I try to articulate pertains to the larger field of postmodernist aesthetic while also bearing the marks of a certain Balkan flair that evokes liminal spaces and frontiers, fragmented identities and fractured cultural landscapes, an exaggerated or deliberate self-deprecating dimension, and an exoticism and "orientalism." These elements set it apart from West European and American postmodernist works of theater and performances. In this regard, the component of the carnivalesque both at the level of stage action and of theatrical discourse, of the mixing of high and low, of the old fashioned with the modern, of the living and the dead, of the comic and the tragic in circus-like manners, is specific to Balkan and East European mythic and folkloric universes and prevalent in the theater emerging from these regions.[7]

The dramatic and performative projects gathered in this book form an artistic universe that stubbornly tries to resist the irrational and violent world around it and to keep recreating itself, just like an exile does once in a new land. The artists included in my study invent new forms of expression that act as testimonials and also as oases for survival and rebirth. It is not just that the dramatic forms and theatrical projects I chose speak of survival and rebirth, but also that they *are* the survival and the rebirth, they *are* the healing following the trauma. Many of the theater works I discuss have emerged directly and ferociously out of wars and experiences of exile, out of violent political events and their aftermath; and they not only testify to these experiences but by the very virtue of their emergence and existence almost simultaneously or very shortly after these events, they stand as a wall of resistance, a space of peace, a place of solace, truth and re-belonging.

I include war next to exile in my exploration because war is also a kind of exile for the people suffering it, and war leads to the making of refugees and to the creation of spaces of "non-belonging." I have also chosen to use the broad concept of exile to refer to émigrés, expatriates, refugees and immigrants,[8] not in a desire to obliterate the nuances and differences among all of the above terms but because I am mostly looking at the philosophical and political state of displacement of a person from their native spaces, the ontological condition and mental state of such a person that may well be a refugee from a dictatorship like myself, an expatriate from

Israel like Noa Baum, an émigré like Matei Vişniec, or in the legalistic sense an "immigrant," like many of the authors studied here and their characters: people who have left their native countries for either political or economic reasons to settle in another country. The term exile has a more definitive connotation of "terminal loss" (Said 2002, 173) and thus a more tragic dimension. War creates spaces of exile and leads thousands to take the fate of refugees, and it leads to exile "as a space of non-belonging," "where in the primitive times peoples were banished and where in the modern era immense aggregates of humanity loiter as refugees and displaced persons" (Said 2002, 177).[9] Modern wars are responsible for "the compounded misery of undocumented people, suddenly lost, without a tellable story" (Said 2002, 139–40). The theater created by artists out of a need to testify, survive and transcend historic wars and the reality of exile provides both metaphorical and real spaces of belonging that often turn the realities of those who are "suddenly lost" into "tellable" stories. These spaces acquire the double function of both refuge from the violence of war and of a home from the loneliness of exile. Such an example of a space of belonging is the DAH Theater, which emerged in 1991 as a response to the beginning of nationalist violence and the war of ethnic cleansing in the former Yugoslavia and which is both a theater group and an actual theater venue situated in the heart of Belgrade. Whether real or imaginary spaces, the theater works and projects included in my book partake of a common effort to responsibly traverse the difficult paths of the "disorder of memory" that is trauma and of a passionate crafting of safe places where such disorder can be disentangled and comforted.

Bertolt Brecht and the Aesthetic of Theater of War and Exile

In the discussion of an aesthetic of a theater of war and exile, we cannot avoid the examples, theories and theater practice of Bertold Brecht or his unparalleled innovations in the areas of theater creation, production and theory.[10] An intermittent exile himself who escaped his fascist motherland and its ravaging war to the United States only to be interrogated by the infamous House Committee on Un-American Activities during the McCarthy era, Brecht's theories and practice of theater were the first to articulate and illustrate an aesthetic of rupture, alienation and fragmentation as the only viable one for modern theater. Through his famous invention of "epic theater" and the practice of "distancing" or "estrangement" between audience and the characters they see on stage; through the creation of a stubborn connection between his characters' reactions, actions and motivations and the historical moment they represent, called "historicization"; and through his irrevocable break of the famous and infamous fourth wall that had marked millennia of Western theater, Brecht was the first theater artist to encourage an aesthetics of non-mimetic representation and of what Douglas Kellner has called a "politics of separation." In Kellner's words, "Brecht intended that epic theater show emotions, ideas, and behavior as products of, or responses to, specific social situations and not as the unfolding of the human essence" (2010, 31). Thus it was the very rejection of Western theater's essentialism and claims to universalism that gave the first blow to mimetic theatrical representation. In order to develop a critical sense in his audiences, Brecht often used montage, dance and song episodes, and combined them with dialogues and interspersed them with storytelling moments in which the actors presented their characters at a distance, aiming not towards the creation of empathy but of critical thinking. Some critics have pointed out that the success of Brecht's theater relies on the fact that he failed to fully remain true to his own theories in the theater he wrote and directed. I profoundly disagree with this position, as I believe that Brecht's fundamental contribution to Western theater, and to world theater in general, is in the area of the aesthetic and theatrical form. He was the first to realize the political nature of the aesthetic dimension itself and the need to radically renew it so that theater could have a profound impact on its society and so that theatrical form could coordinate with the emancipated ideas breathing throughout the century. He understood that it is not through the elegance of the ideas or the depth of the sentiments expressed but through the seamless and engaging way in which ideas are shaped that the art of theater can have a transformative role in society.[11]

I find it beautifully ironic that as a revolutionary artist who exiled himself to escape from the war that his own country had waged against the whole world, Brecht initiated and created a theater aesthetic that promoted the techniques of montage, collage, distancing, breaking the aesthetic continuity of the theater experience and of the fourth walls, of mimetic mirrors and of the suspension of disbelief. He imprinted on his work the marks of rupture and mismatched realities that had marked his own existence as a war survivor and exile of sorts. Trauma changes us forever, and for an artist that change takes place as well in the nature and shape of her or his art. Unity and fullness are best achieved through a mix-and-match operation of fragments and remainders of experience in the theater of trauma.[12]

The non-essentialist and materialistic representation of realities and of people in the specificity of their historical, cultural and political realities; the use of disjointed aesthetics and of techniques of montage; and the stylized interspersing of dance and song with dialogue, storytelling and multimedia episodes are very much in the same vein as the theater of war and exile discussed in this book. That it was an artist who experienced his own country's rise to fascism, who fled the horror and devastation of the war and exiled himself in the United States only to turn the "dream of a glorious return" into reality upon his repatriation in his native Germany (where he was given his own theater), who revolutionized Western theater with an aesthetic meant to awaken critical thinking and inspire to social action, is beautifully coordinate with the thesis of my book.[13]

The "Real" in Mapping Out the Aesthetic of Theater of War and Exile

In this book I also take issue with the position—found largely in theoretical works that try to articulate a postmodernist worldview, be it philosophic or aesthetic—that announces the disappearance of the real and of history in favor of layers of simulation, simulacra, and pastiche. Jean Baudrillard is the most famous theorist in this area, and although fascinating and valid to a large extent, his theoretical and philosophical stance becomes demoralizingly one-dimensional in its categorical dismissal of the real both at the level of society and in the realm of cultural products, as these are according to him replaced by the notorious "hyperreal," by copies of copies that claim to be "more real than the real" and that have completely estranged us from reality and history.[14] Baudrillard goes so far as to claim that simulacra have replaced reality altogether and that representations or signs have replaced and modified reality and nature so that "the territory" no longer precedes the map; rather it is "the map that precedes the territory" (1995, 1–2). Of course our world has suffered profound acts of estrangement in the realm of human relations, the connection to nature and to history through the exacerbated technologies, simulated or digital images, virtual realities and mass media productions that inundate us from all directions and on a daily basis. I base my study on the belief that, in Lane Bruner's words, "there often is a mappable distance between the fantasies people have about situations and the situations themselves" (2012, 13). The map and the territory do not always overlap, as in the Borges story that Baudrillard takes as a starting point in his discussion of simulacra, and the map does not always "precede the territory." My interest lies in discovering and exploring "the mappable distance" between the map and the territory and the exceptions to the terrifying layering of simulacra that marks our world. I am engaged in the lucid incursion into pockets or oases of authentic feeling, action, humanity and imagination that are still to be found in our wretched world. Live theater, and particularly theater engaged in its society, offers such an oasis.

Even though many of the plays and performances explored in my book deliberately make use of simulacra, parody, or pastiche or create a hyperreality, ultimately they all reclaim the real in two ways: (1) through their unequivocal ties to the historical moment, to historical events of their times and to their authors' own personal experiences as they reach out to connect to live audiences, and (2) through their stubborn recognition and celebration of the undeniability and sacredness of the actor's body on stage with all that that presence implies: body language, voice, breathing, color, sound, in a word an indomitable aliveness. In this book I stubbornly reclaim the real and celebrate the determined presentness of theater and of the realities it connects us to, whether these realities are outside of ourselves unfolding in real time and space or in our own psyches. I oppose the "melancholy" derived from the alleged loss of the real in favor of its imitations with an awareness of the values beautifully articulated in Albert Camus's *The Myth of Sisyphus*, namely passion, lucidity and rebellion. Baudrillard's "melancholy" is a sure way towards nihilism and indifference,[15] while passion, lucidity and rebellion endow us with a tragic stance vis-à-vis the universe and lead to action.

The theater studied in my book displays features of a postmodernist aesthetic precisely in its fierce reclaiming of the real, while making use of diverse and layered dramatic strategies that incite us to question our relation to reality and the boundaries between the real and the imagined. It disrupts the monolith of the hegemonic systems governing capitalist society that Jameson and Baudrillard rightly see as the ultimate rulers of our world. But I am interested in a different kind of postmodernity than that articulated by Baudrillard or Jameson. I agree with Kristin Schmidt who, in her book *Postmodernism in American Drama*, says, "Postmodern dramatists approach performance art as a valuable resource for their dramatic endeavors. Among others, the influence takes shape most vividly in the attempt to make the theatrical audience reconsider the traditional boundaries between performance and reality, art and life, fiction and autobiography." And Schmidt reasonably notes that even though "postmodernism has been a concept to be wrestled with" and "it has been shaped by conflicting opinions and arguments," "drama has made ample use of postmodern features that, to different degrees, express transformative practices" (2005, 14).[16] On the other hand, Mark Fortier cynically and erroneously claims, "Postmodern theory sees theatre as a quaint and marginalized activity in a wired world," and he wonders "whether live theatre even really exists anymore." He also asks us: "What is it about theater that remains compelling for you? Is it just because it's there?" (2002, 220). What remains profoundly compelling for me and for the thousands of theater artists across the world that boldly defy the views of the disappearance of live theater through compelling examples of engaging productions is not that "it's there," but that it's here. Theater is here because it is alive and because it creates communities. Even under layers of acting mannerisms, techniques, costumes and props, the live actor reminds us of the here, and that we are in a concrete here and not in an abstract "there." Jon Whitmore notes simply but poignantly, "Attending the theater means going to a place where people congregate. In the parking lot, entrance way, lobby and performance space, spectators come in contact with one another, they take part in a collective social event" (2012, 58). This is the undeniable presentness of theater. Equally well articulated is Johannes Birringer's statement about the physicality of theater, which also accounts for its inconsolable ephemerality that mimics that of life itself: "Unlike literature, film, painting, or the popular mass media, the theater must show its physical, bodily existence and its 'liveness,' the volatile progress of its human labor, the contingencies of the space in which it labors, and its schizophrenic awareness of its own unreality" (1993, 3).

In the compelling book *Wounded I Am More Awake*, which tells the wrenching and also inspiring story of a concentration camp survivor from Bosnia who is also co-author of the book, an example from the long series of unimaginable atrocities perpetrated against Muslim Bosnians in the camps held by Croats and Serbs held my attention and urged me to connect it with the present study of theater of war and exile. It jumped at me particularly because many of the plays and performances that I discuss are inspired by and have emerged in response to this genocidal war of the nineties that took place smack in the middle of Europe only half a century after the resounding worldwide "never again." I have not only researched in depth the realities of that war but have also visited reconstructed Sarajevo, the fresh cemeteries of Bosnians killed in the siege, and most wrenchingly, the camps and houses of Srebrenica where the worst genocidal events since World War II in Europe unfolded with the whole world watching and failing to understand or believe that it was real. The sinister warehouses marked with gruesome graffiti by the Serbian guards, the stark rows of simple white tombs in the cemetery that is growing with fresh graves every year across from the former camps, the broken houses of Srbrenica on the Muslim sides of the streets, some of which still have traces of blood on their inside walls, struck me as unbearably real. The author tells the story of a concentration camp fellow, who also happened to be an overly sensitive and timid professor of literature. One day, he tells us, one of the guards brought pencils and paper to the emaciated prisoners, who had been tortured, starved and kept in unspeakable squalor for months, and told them that they could write to their families but that he would read every letter and if he didn't like it, the author of the letter would be shot. The prisoners knew he wasn't bluffing, as they had seen many of their fellow prisoners beaten to death or randomly shot at the guards' whims. This is the letter that the professor, "the soft-spoken man who had never said a mean word about anyone," wrote to his wife: "Dear wife, I am in a concentration camp, the worst mother fucking camp in the world, worse than anything the fucking fascists in the SS came up with" (Boskailo and Lieblich 2012, 64). Fortunately for the professor, the guard actually came back with the letter, laughing and saying he found it really funny, but he ordered him to rewrite it. His friend, who is the camp survivor co-author of the book, Esad Boskailo, saw that the professor's second letter was even more "vituperative than the first," and before Lieblich had a chance to hand it to the guard he wrote this letter in its stead: "Dear wife, we're all fine. Love to you and the children." This happened in actual reality and was not reconstructed on a stage. Yet it is the kind of reality that has inspired and informed many of the theater artists gathered in this study. This story is about the "world-shattering" nature of trauma, about the limits of desperation when one no longer cares for one's life, and about the courage and the dark humor that can emerge even in the worst situations of hopelessness to resist the irrational use of brutal force.

The plays of Matei Vişniec, Saviana Stanescu, Biljana Srbljanović, the devised productions of the DAH Theater, and the storytelling of performance artist Noa Baum push us to the limits of reality testing, as they bring in characters and stories recreated from the accounts of real people and events, from real traumas and brave testimonials of trauma survivors, while also creating the possibility for healing and closure through exquisite layers of artistic strategies. The theater artists whose work I celebrate in my book engage in what Esad Boskailo has referred to as "tragic optimism," that is, finding "hope in the midst of sadness" (Boskailo and Lieblich 2012, 120, quoting Frankl 2006, 137–138). The cohort of artists quoted, analyzed, explored here are all searching for meaning and producing meaning through the workings of live theater that engages and moves us beyond the postmodern apathy vis-à-vis reality to a postmodernist reclaiming of reality.

These playwrights and theater artists illustrate to various degrees Brechtian techniques and aesthetics. All the works explored here break the fourth wall; they engage in the "separation of elements" that often comment on one another or are in contradiction with one another to "provoke thought and insight" (Kellner 2010, 33); they use stylized episodes that blend carnivalesque elements and disjointed narratives with the complete use of the actor's presence and body on stage as simultaneously performer, storyteller, and commentator of her/his own stories. All are meant to function simultaneously as testimonials, as spaces of belonging and as furnaces for critical thinking and revolutionary action. All challenge the spectators' comfort zones and attempt to turn the very process of spectating into one of acting. The theater of war and exile is merciless vis-à-vis its audiences as it does not allow us to indulge for too long in cathartic experiences and the all-too-comforting suspension of disbelief; it jolts us from one reality and from one aesthetic mode to another with the ultimate goal of making us take a harder look at our own lives and historical moment rather than escaping from them. And if it creates any empathy towards the characters presented on stage, it is to inspire us to social action towards their counterparts in actual reality rather than to make us feel better about ourselves for having emoted at their stories. As it is a theater of the unsettled, it causes unsettling emotions, thoughts and reactions.

In her seminal study *Empathy and the Novel,* Suzanne Keen eloquently articulates a theory of healthy skepticism at the long held notion that reading novels leads to empathy, which leads to "altruistic action," which leads to better individuals. She challenges the "contemporary truism that novel reading cultivates empathy that produces good citizens of the world" (2010, xv). I embark on my treacherous critical journey with a comparable skepticism towards the notion that going to the theater will make us better people and incite us to change the world. But because going to the theater is *not* like reading a novel and because the theater I focus on constantly breaks its own illusions in disruptive meta-theatrical and self-referential detours, I dare to persist in my belief that at least it awakens certain instincts of goodness, generosity and most importantly a questioning spirit that might have been dormant for a while. Such a spirit would bring us closer to Brecht's utopian audience who "knows how to observe, and gets its enjoyment from setting its reason to work" (1964, 14). Quite opposed to creating empathy in spectators, Brecht chose reason over feelings for the reason that "feelings are private and limited" (15). A cautionary note might be necessary, though, with regard to Brecht's preference for reason over feelings, because his own plays and most plays discussed here do elicit a variety of feelings in the spectators together with an awakening of political consciousness and critical thinking. The difference between the Brechtian type of theatrical event and traditional or classical plays that lead to a cathartic ending or to the arousal of empathy in the spectators is that in the former we are guided towards a distancing from our own emotions and possibly made to engage in self-analysis, to increase our self-awareness and to take a sharper critical look at the reality around us. Keen notes, "The most commonly nominated feature of narrative fiction to be associated with empathy is character identification" (2010, 93). And, as she eloquently argues in her study, empathy created in readers of novels has rarely lead to significant social action or changes in legislation. However, even if scarce, examples such as the closing of the abusive orphanages and educational institutions in Charles Dickens' times, possibly as a result of the scathing criticism found in novels such as *Oliver Twist* or *Nicholas Nickleby* (Keen 2010, 52–53), do speak at least of the potential for socially engaged narratives and masterfully created characters to create some ripples and disturb the arrogant stillness of the status quo of social inequity. From the point of view of all the theater artists featured in my book, those ripples alone are worth the effort and the belief in the socially transformative power of characters and actions unfolding on the world's stages, as one ripple may lead to another and by an effect of reverberation entire structures and seas of complacency may be moved and disturbed in surreptitious, subtle ways that in turn may lead to larger and more radical waves of change. Many examples of such ripples of social disturbance, of raising of consciousness and waves of social or political change created by various theatrical events, are later offered in this book. Ultimately, though, I am not particularly interested in demonstrating whether the theater I analyze makes us better people or not, or leads to the creation of more responsible citizens. I am interested in how and why it engages us at a variety of levels: our critical thinking, our emotions, our senses, our moral standing. By engaging us, we might be inspired to produce change—or we might not. But in either case, the door has been opened for that possibility and unconventional paths towards change may have been drawn.

The Carnivalesque and Political Trauma

The element of the carnivalesque is conspicuously present throughout the works discussed in my study. By the term *carnivalesque* I encompass the Bakhtinian notions of reversals of hierarchies, of the laughter derived from references to and images of the "lower bodily stratum" or of the aesthetics of the banquet, and the actual elements of carnival (or even circus) that endow these works with their Balkan color and specificities (1984, 28–30). Why does so much of the theater of war and exile from Brecht to the authors explored here use an aesthetic of the carnivalesque, the merging of the tragic and the comic reminiscent of the circus clown's twin faces, the Bakhtinian reversals of the high and the low, vaudeville songs and dance that break the continuity of the dramatic structures and the narrative lines? From Motti Lerner's assassination drama to Saviana Stanescu's "Hairy Tale" of a mail order bride and her carnivalesque journey from Romania to New York, and even to the DAH Theater's devised testimonial performances, they all resort to the use of grotesque imagery, moments of humor or irony, reversals of conventional hierarchies, and banquet and festival aesthetic.

Lane Bruner argues that the "carnivalesque is a resource for political action ... because it destabilizes the kinds of certainties that lead to political illness especially as manifested in 'forms' of the humorless state" (2005, 143). He argues as well that the carnivalesque, parody and satire are healthy forms of dissent that contradict and often oppose the unhealthy seriousness of conservativism, oppression and essentialism. War, oppression, dictatorship, and genocides are indeed all frighteningly humorless events and situations. The restless carnivalesque roller-coaster of high and low, laughter and tears, spiritual and carnal, opposes the static seriousness of oppressive states and the monolithic architecture of essentialist worldviews, just as the nomadic existence of traveling circuses or acting troupes opposes the dreary solidity of nationalistic boundaries and the traditional conventions of established societies. Furthermore, the liminal spaces and broken frontiers of Balkan regions, and of other divided, fragmented, torn national and political spaces such as East and West Germany, the countries of Eastern Europe and the ultimate liminal space of the gathering of exiles that is Israel, are contoured in the overlapping of multiple realities of which none is more or less real than the other. Bruner describes several episodes of public carnivalesque behavior as political action against oppression and state humorlessness that took place in the eighties in the former Soviet Union and Poland. For instance, combining their street action with the painting of Solidarity graffiti, thousands of Polish citizens in the late eighties took to the streets dressed as elves and created a movement called the Orange Alternative. "Orange Alternative 'happenings'" were "places to learn opposition" and to "discover more political forms of protest" (Bruner 2005, 145).[17]

The Bakhtinian laughter and carnivalesque vision of reality are directly coordinate with a non-essentialist view and are a perfect tool for the subversion of oppressive societal structures. The mismatch of the parts, the fragmented plot and narrative structures, the stridency reminiscent of Jean François Lyotard's notion of postmodernity that emerges from a crisis of modern subjectivity[18] seem to be not only inevitable in the representation of realities of war and exile but also necessary. As the very realities of modern wars and exile are conducive to a ruptured psyche and consciousness, it is not surprising that the theater treating these realities will reflect them in broken images and sequences. But moreover, beyond a direct causal relation, such representations and their "stridence" are apt to break the suspension of disbelief of the audiences, force them out of their comfort zones and provoke them to critical thinking and social action. The theater activist Augusto Boal once famously said: "Perhaps the theater is not revolutionary in itself; but have no doubts, it is a rehearsal of Revolution" (1985, 155).[19] While I appreciate the extraordinary work that Boal has done in the area of revolutionizing societies and even changing policies through theater, a cautionary note about revolutions would be appropriate for anyone who might get too excited about the idea of them. Often revolutions are violent and in the process victims become oppressors; or a revolution might change one oppressive system for another. The French Revolution and the Bolshevik Revolution are glowing examples of such dynamics. And often theater activism alone, without an acute sense of artistry and textured creativity, might not really make much of a difference or might even turn off people from the ideas that it tries to forcefully feed them. The eighteenth century playwright, feminist writer and revolutionary Olympe de Gouges, the first French woman to earn a living through playwriting, warned against the violent actions and practices that the great Robespierre and the other French revolutionaries were engaging in. She is also, unbeknownst to many, the author of "The Declaration of the Rights of Women," written in response to "The Declaration of the Rights of Man." She was recompensed for her peace activism and feminism by execution through hanging. Her plays, which create complex, emancipated female characters, endure even though they are very little known by other than French literature specialists.

The feminist performance theorist Jill Dolan noted that the art of performance can offer us "fleeting intimations of a better world" (2005, 2). Such intimations may be found in the theater of Olympe de Gouges in the form of revolutionary women characters who carved their destiny, resisted the practice of forced marriages and followed their heart. From the perspective of the theater of war and exile the "intimations of a better world" could be glimpses of peace and rootedness, of safe places and integration, or on the contrary a criticism of dystopian universes created in the aftermath of wars. Such "utopian performatives," as Dolan has called a certain kind of political theater, do not aim toward a unified vision of the world and of reality but attempt to find comfort in plurality and diversity of vision, in dark humor, carnivalesque reversals and nuanced characters. Theater that is truly revolutionary is theater that through innovative craft motivates us to question everything, even revolutions.

Postmodernism, Plurality and Balkan Hybridity

The aesthetics of a theater of war and exile displays a plurality of forms, voices, discourses and even genres within the same play or performance. Jon Whitmore states, "Postmodernism is defined broadly and loosely to encompass performances that are primarily nonlinear, nonliterary, nonrealistic, non-discursive, and non-closure oriented" (2012, 4).

Indeed the plays and performances analyzed in this book display all or most of the traits enumerated here. Whitmore also distinguishes between "playscripts" and performances that are either recreated by directors from the texts or altogether created or devised by theater directors, and he refers largely to the latter ones as exhibiting the characteristics of postmodernist theater (1–3). In this study I deal with both "playscripts" that are created by their authors with postmodernist performances in mind, and performances that display postmodernist features in their execution.

In the discussion of political theater in the postmodernist vein, a cautionary note is necessary. Philip Auslander has expressed his disbelief in the idea that "postmodern art can, or need, escape representation, though it must always deconstruct its own representational means." However, he concludes, "This challenging of representation through representation is a crucial postmodernist strategy of resistance" (2007, 31). It is equally important to take in the distinction that "different kinds of art and performance are intended for different kinds of audiences" and that "discourse on the politics of art ... and especially on performance, does indeed generally assume an idealized audience that responds the way the critic or theorist responds" (2007, 30). I am equally sensitive to Lyotard's cautionary note that "to hang the meaning of the work of art upon its subsequent political effect is once again not to take it seriously, to take it for an instrument, useful for something else" (quoted in Auslander 2007, 30).[20] This is not in the least my intention in the exploration of theater of war and exile; mine is rather the reverse: to unravel the aesthetic workings of theater inspired by wars and exile experiences and demonstrate that it is *because* of these aesthetic complexities that such art has a potential to transform diverse audiences. Nevertheless, I maintain the necessary awareness of the fact that when we speak of audiences we often refer to an idealized group. I also bring in concrete examples of specific audiences and their responses to a performance and the theater artists' own testimonials of audience response and interaction with their works.

I would like to go so far in my study as to propose that the postmodern theater aesthetic itself emerged precisely as a by-product of a century and period in which the historical realities of war and the masses of exiles and refugees it engendered had reached the highest pitch, the most wrenching and unprecedented stridency. Following World War II some of the most influential intellectuals and artists were émigrés to Western Europe or to the United States. Most had witnessed or had been directly affected by fascism or Stalinism. Thinkers and writers such as Theodor Adorno, Hannah Arendt, Vladimir Nabokov or Eugène Ionesco questioned the very meaning and usefulness of art in a world that had endured unparalleled horrors. Yet playwrights such as Eugene Ionesco and Samuel Beckett continued to write and to create unprecedented theatrical forms in a world of unprecedented realities. In *Westward Ho* Beckett says cryptically: "Nothing else ever. Ever tried. Ever failed. No matter. Try again. Fail again. Fail better" (1984, 1). Theater was for him the art of failing better, and for many post–World War II artists and philosophers continuing to write was an exercise in "failing better," yet an exercise they could not stop doing. Much postmodernist art displays the traits of skepticism at its own need for existence and yet a fierce desire to exist at all odds and to speak of that failure and of that distrust in itself, in the world, in humanity.

More sophisticated patterns of evil, more elaborate forms of torture, genocidal events and wars spread and modeled themselves one after another, and they have been made more ingenious by the new technologies and the digital world. Entire societies have been desensitized to war, and to the sight of atrocity, by virtual universes and a world of simulation in constant confusion about the "real" yet in desperate search for it. Most of "our genocides"[21] have arisen from ethnic hatred, a will to erase the Other and to annihilate difference. As Erik Ehn has noted, genocides attempt to "forbid history—to forbid the making of meaning by barring our real and imaginative abilities to gather history" (2012, 248). Yet, hard as it may be as a playwright to match an art form to an unexplainable content (or, as he calls it, an "irresolvable object"), he stresses that "theater's loose ends" are most apt to attempt such a matching just as "sometimes it takes a broken shoe to fit a broken foot" (5). When speaking of his own theater cycle about genocides, *Soulographie*, Ehn admits that he does not wish for his plays to "contain the history or repeat the history," but to "provoke a memory of history even if you haven't remembered it" and to create "a space for remembering" (2012, 68).[22] Such admission is coordinate with my argument that it is not enough for theater art to tell or recount the trauma; it needs to reshape it in the creative cauldron of memory. The theater discussed here does the very opposite of "forbidding history" in its strenuous attempts to recapture histories, to make meaning, to tell stories and to place the stories in their spatial, cultural, historic, geographical and personal specificities, all while breaking them down to interrogations and rearranging them in rhythmic, colorful patterns.[23] As it does that it also creates "spaces of memory" for victims, witnesses, bystanders or any other audience groups who wish to enter such spaces and are open to being transformed by them.

Three elements seem to persist and to form something of a triangular paradigm: (1) The theater of war and exile evokes or resonates with the rupture and dissonance of the very experiences of war and exile as spaces of "non-belonging" and of multiple coexisting realities; (2) The theater of war and exile that has emerged either as theater of witness or as theater of "social intervention" (Silberman 1993, 1) creates safe spaces that are spaces of questioning and paradoxically are safe *because* they take us out of our comfort zones, as if warning us about the dangers of the world and forcing us either to take action or run for cover; (3) The theater of war and exile discussed here displays some of what critics have referred to as the postmodern condition and a postmodernist aesthetic with the added elements of the carnivalesque.

Could it be that the plurality of definitions of the postmodern, its refusal of representation and the impossibility of pinning down a coherent theory or aesthetics derive precisely from the fact that postmodernism and postmodernity[24] emerged in a time when the realities of war and exile were prevalent in the Western World and were added later on in the century to the false unification of cultures under the umbrella of global economies, cultural hegemonies and the destabilizing realities of postcolonialism? Could it be that the very plurality of definitions and the resistance to definitions of the postmodern is precisely what makes it postmodern? And that postmodernism emerges precisely in the moving sands of coexisting realities, that the postmodernist aesthetic exists, much like the aesthetic I am trying to articulate in this study, in liminal spaces, margins and locations that escape any stable or stabilizing characterizations? Edward Said noted boldly, "Modern Western Culture is in large part the work of exiles, émigrés, refugees" (2002, 137), and the critic George Steiner asserted that a certain genre of twentieth century Western literature is written by exiles about exiles, "wanderers across language. Eccentric, aloof, nostalgic..." (Steiner, quoted in Said 2002, 137). In this vein it would not be too presumptuous to claim that a significant portion of postmodernity is the product of exile writers, artists, intellectuals—survivors of wars, genocides, dictatorships of the left and the right whose creations emerged out of hopelessness and unassuaged yearnings to create meaning, or simply to prove that art is still possible even after events like the Holocaust, or the Bosnian war of the nineties. As "wanderers across language," cultures, and spaces, such artists are rooted in the historic moment more than in any particular geography, and they remind us that "we live today within the general socio-economic and political condition of postmodernity," "for postmodernity is not an ideology of position we can choose or subscribe to or not, postmodernity is precisely our condition" (Jenkins 1997, 3). Paradoxically, the wandering condition of the exile, because of its multiplicity of perspectives on the world, may just be an emancipatory condition that, while nostalgic for a lost past, is recklessly riding that "ball hurled high in the air" towards a fresh future that it desperately wants to bring into the present and make its home.

I propose also bell hooks' beautiful articulation of homelessness and margins as another clue to the questions posed above and as a productive direction for my study with regards to the issue of liminal spaces, fragmented identities and the search for an authentic home:

> At times home is nowhere. At times, one knows only extreme estrangement and alienation. Then home is no longer just one place. It is locations. Home is that place which promotes varied and ever changing perspectives, a place where one discovers new ways of seeing reality, frontiers of difference. One confronts and accepts dispersal and fragmentation as part of the construction of a new world order that reveals more fully where we are, who we can become, an order that does not demand forgetting. Our struggle is also a struggle of memory against forgetting [2002, 148].

Such embracing of margins, liminal spaces and homelessness is in tune with the definition of postmodern identities as capable of transformation and ready to resist uniformity: "Identities are layered upon differences that overlap each other as opposed to the search for similarities and homogeneity" (Petrunic 2005, 2).[25] And now a connection can be made between the very idea of the postmodern and that of the Balkans:

> Were postmodern identities to call upon the notions of plurality, difference, and heterogeneity, a web of interconnectedness between the Balkan peoples would be expected whereby peace and harmony would reign instead of war and disunity. Due to the lack of progress in developing a politically-stable multicultural society and due to a history of imperial oppression in the Balkans ... the ambiguity of determining a Balkan identity is in fact the essence of a hybrid identity. Hybridity is not only an effect of the cyclical oppression of groups of people in the Balkans but also a cause of the present crisis in identity [Petrunic 2005, 3].

The Balkans is already a place of exile and liminality, a space of strife and indefinite identities in search of a definition. Cheryl Robson reminds us, "The definition of the word to *balkanize* is: to divide an area into small antagonistic states" and points to "the history of political double-dealing in a troubled region within southern Europe, surrounded by the Adriatic, Aegean and Black Seas" (2002, 6).[26] It is at the confluence of such Balkan liminality and spatial parceling, of exilic homelessness and postmodernist plurality, that the theater discussed in this book lives and thrives. There is an intriguing overlap between the theoretical notion of the Balkans, the actual realities of Balkan regions, and postmodern inquiry and aesthetic. While postmodern theory even across its most diverse and disunified articulations promotes multiculturalism, diversity and bringing the margins to the center, Balkan strife and "disunity" emerges from the fierce rejection of heterogeneity and multiculturalism and aspires towards a utopian and destructive vision of homogeneity as demonstrated in the virulent wars of ethnic cleansing in the nineties. Thus a postmodern worldview can be seen also as a form of healing ethnic hatred by turning fragmentation, heterogeneity and difference into a virtue to be celebrated rather than a stigma to be brutally eliminated.

I set myself the very ambitious task of tying the postmodern and the Balkans, the carnivalesque and the experience of exile and war, into one kaleidoscopic knot in which fractured aesthetics meets fractured identities, in which the high and the low, the tragic and the comic are indestructibly tied, in which essentialism is consistently disarmed by critical questioning and cultural specificity. This thick knot of glowing contradictions is also the one of hybridity, beautifully articulated by Homi Bhaba: he sees "hybridity" as emerging in "the interstices" where "intersubjective and collective experiences of nationness, community interest or cultural value are negotiated" (Bhaba, cited in Petrunic 2005, 2).[27] Ana-Marija Petrunic develops the provocative argument of the need for "Balkan hybriditiy as art" as a way of bursting the all-too-self-important bubble of cultural essentialism. It is in the specificity of place with its myriads of details and intersections that the meaning of the theater of war and exile is being fabricated and gelled, where identities emerge as embodied selves and not as disembodied ideas.

Hybridity and the ever-moving sands of postmodern/postmodernist theory and aesthetic are productively protected within the umbrella of the carnivalesque as a life-affirming circle of resistance to violence and humorless oppression. The unabashed laughter of the carnival creates a necessary airiness in both actual social situations and in the representation of serious or tragic realities. The circus within the tragic is a fertile oasis where contradictory and conflicting perspectives coexist and have dialogue with one another, where "tragic optimism" can thrive and help us in our efforts toward the production of meaning in our lives.

Erik Ehn refers to his body of work in the cycle *Soulographie: Our Genocides* as "a ruined body," a series that is "pieced by the will of a network, and presented impossibly (a landscape that can't be taken in, entirely, from any one point of view)." Ehn speaks in startling terms of a shattered, broken form, and of "inadequate language" as the only way to break the "immobility" of genocide. "When we accept events to be inconceivable or inexplicable and leave it at that, we buy into a political lie and submit our heads to the truncheons of uselessness." "To invade reality," he also says, "we have to shatter a pane, to reach through and unlock the windows.... Engaging is stripped, fragmentary, splintered description—engaging—is resistance" (2012, 10). The broken form, the "splintered description," the coexistence of a multiplicity of points of view and the disruption of ordinary language are imposed by the subject itself. The unseemly realities of war, genocide and the splintered identity of the exile demand the "hybridity" of perspectives, the postmodern resistance to definition, the carnivalesque irreverence towards fixity and authority of any kind. In the tragic circus of disrupted lives and ruptured identities, in the desperate and relentless attempts of the artist to make sense of the shards of reality, the Balkan specificity adds its special flair, its bittersweet flavors of the margins of Europe, of Orientalism gone bad and incongruously gelled in the hodge-podge of globalism.[28]

Often perceived as the "Orient of Europe" or "the Barbarians at Europe's gate" in Western eyes, East European and Balkan peoples have often developed a sense of inferiority vis-à-vis Western values and commodities while simultaneously seeing themselves as "the guardian of European values" and internalizing the negative connotations of Balkan and Balkanization as "fragmented" and "unstable." As Vesna Goldsworthy has noted, "Balkan" has come to "always refer to someone other than ourselves" (1998, ix).[29] I will show how the artists included here manage to overturn these "othering" processes and from their positions of both insiders and outsiders to Balkan realities establish a critical and aesthetic platform from where they observe and resist essentializing practices that are both coming from or are directed at the liminal spaces of Eastern Europe.

Chapter Outlines

The many theoretical and analytic layers of this book unfold in a simple and clear-cut structure. In the first chapter, "Exile as Ontological Mutation: Theater and Performance about Post-Communist Regions," I look at playwrights from Romania, Poland, and the Czech Republic in light of the critical framework I have laid out so far. Some are refugees to Western Europe such as Aglaja Veteranyi or expatriates to the United States such as Saviana Stanescu or Pavel Zuštiak. Others such as Radmila Adamova or Dorota Maslowska are not exiles per se and still live in their native countries but have experienced certain epiphanies with regards to the alienation and condition of modern refugees, immigrants or nomads that have imposed themselves as subjects of their theater. I also include myself in a section of personal testimonials about my journey as a writer and political refugee from the former communist dictatorship of Romania, trying to share firsthand how my fiction and theater writings bear the marks of my exilic experience. I trace the shreds of melancholy and yearning, the confusion of nomadic experiences and the chase after the American Dream through specific theatrical architectures. I look at the blending of dramatic styles from naturalistic to surrealist to absurdist (Stanescu, Veteranyi) as well as at dramatic languages and their many incarnations in lyrical escapades (Veteranyi), pungent slang (Maslowska), stark enunciations (Adamova), languages that become stage action and actors' bodies that produce cryptic text (Zuštiak).

The second chapter, "Theater of War and Genocide and Theater Dystopias" moves to discussions of theatrical works by East European and Israeli playwrights who have lived or continue to live in countries at war or in postwar societies, such as Motti Lerner (Israel) Biljana Srbljanović and Milena Markovic (Serbia) or expatriate playwrights from Eastern Europe who were profoundly affected by the Balkan war of the nineties such as Matei Vişniec. In this chapter I ponder over the theater forms that evoke the destruction and devastation of wars at the level of individual experience. I look at shocking combinations of violent images and language with dark humor and parody, the creation of dystopian theatrical universes that incorporate in ironic manner ancient archetypes derived from Greek myths (Vişniec), Western fairytales (Srbljanović and Markovic) or the device of theater within theater and madness (Lerner) to give shape to inexpressible realities of war and genocide. Here I also analyze in some detail the ways in which postmodernist devices such as simulation and pastiche are used by these playwrights in reverse fashion to that theorized by Jean Baudrillard; namely, rather than obscuring, diluting or even annihilating the reality of war, they bring it out in sharp colors. If according to Baudrillard our age and its cultural and artistic products are complicit in "a liquidation of all referentials" (1994, 2), the authors studied here keep stubborn ties with the referential and bring its refractions onto stages of the world. They use what Baudrillard has referred to in passing as "dissimulation" (namely, pretending "not to have what one has") as opposed to "simulation," which is feigning "to have what one doesn't have" (1994, 3). They perform the artistic acrobatics of making use of games, simulacra, and theater devices of simulation in order to dissimulate the hard realities of war and the dystopian worlds it creates, thus rendering them more accessible to audiences. In a way they trick us into seeing hard truths in their game of hide-and-seek with such truths.

The third chapter is concerned with theater projects, performers and groups that have emerged as a direct response to the realities of war in their native countries or to the realities of immigration in America. I explore the performance art or storytelling of Noa Baum in her production of a show that boldly looks at the Israeli-Palestinian conflicts and wars through personal stories from both sides. I focus on the ways in which her narrative and performative strategies break the barriers between the self and the Other in this endless political quagmire. I interview Marcy Arlin, the artistic director of the Immigrants Theater Project in New York City, to offer an example of the meeting between the ethical necessity of tackling the realities of immigration and diversity and the diverse aesthetic shapes that such realities are housed in by foreign or exile artists. I close the chapter with the inspiring theater and performance art of the DAH Theater in Serbia and virtually wander through several of their devised works that have emerged from personal stories of war survivors and families of disappeared victims. Here I draw attention to their devising strategies and the delicate balance the director and actors keep between the act of testifying to trauma and creating art inspired by trauma, between respectful testimonials and powerful art that may bring healing.

Theater of War and Exile in the Larger Context of Theater of Margins

It is certainly not only the theater of war and exile that makes abundant use of Brechtian, carnivalesque or postmodernist aesthetic strategies. Much of feminist theater and performance makes use of Brechtian alienation or breaking of the fourth wall and finds a fertile ground in the Bakhtinian theories of carnivalesque reversals, in particular at the level of gender roles.[30] The many intersections between feminism and postmodernism in terms of theory and practice, ideology and aesthetic have been discussed widely by critics.[31] What I am interested in showing, however, is how and why the theater of war and exile lives at the intersection of all these aesthetic strategies, largely developed out of an anxiety of margins, with the deliberate purpose of turning margins into places "of radical openness" and fearlessly tackling stories of human suffering or political injustice or staring in the face of the tragedy of the human condition in general. I am interested in the shapes taken by theater art that grows on the fault lines between historical periods and national or international catastrophes and that is meticulously condensed in the territories of the personal and the specific.

Historically, the margins have often been fertile producers of innovation in the theater. The *commedia dell'arte* of the early Renaissance, which many scholars including myself consider as the beginning of modern Western theater and which emerged from the carnival and street performance of late Middle Ages, broke all frames and rules of conventional classical theater, often parodying ancient texts, making use of cross-dressing, theater within theater, disguise, stage games and entertaining acrobatics called *lazzi*. This theater was created by, about and for those living in the margins of the bourgeois and aristocratic societies of their times. Female performers in particular had a crucial role in developing the art of improvisation that became the signature mark of the *commedia*. The heroes of the performances were servants, middle class women, and desperate young lovers in conflict with and mocking the authoritarian seriousness of old husbands and stingy masters. The troupes' modus vivendi was the precursor of the traveling circus troupes of today: actors travelled in wagons between cities and even countries with all their accessories and families, thus living a nomadic life in the in-between spaces of cultural, economic and class lines. Their theater had huge success with the masses across ethnic, social and gender lines as it disrupted and ridiculed the status quo of established and well-off societies.[32]

Mainstream theater has until today almost always supported the status quo or offered only timid criticism of society within the limits of good taste and accepted conventions, be it neoclassical French theater, Restoration British theater, nineteenth century European drama, twentieth century realist theater, boulevard theater, melodrama or Broadway musicals. It has always been supported by rich benefactors, performed in lush spaces with expensive sets and costumes. On the contrary, the theater emerging from the margins about the margins, by itinerant actors, exile writers, and immigrant artists, has been produced and performed in the street, in unconventional spaces, in tiny theaters on side streets with small or nonexistent budgets, and acted by poorly paid actors. But it is these exiles and marginal artistic populations that have disrupted the status quo and the seriousness or superficial humor of the center and its conventional productions. Exile artists of the twentieth and twenty-first centuries continue in some way—across the arc of all classical, traditional, realist theater—the journey of innovation and experimentation started by the first nomadic theater artists making of the margins places where life and art meet and transform into one another in sensuous and surprising incarnations.

The theater artists with whom I dialogue in this book do not hold any claims that their art would be more real than the real. On the contrary, they approach the realities they try to understand and capture in their theatrical works with great deference and humility. Neither are these artists caught in an obsessive focus on intertextuality and "writing the body," nor are they stuck on "the authority of the text" or "the fetishization of the body" (Birringer 1993, 46–47). They are acutely aware that all art falls short of fully expressing or soothing the horror of genocides and the irrevocable sadness of displacement. There is no one theory that could frame the theater I am talking about, nor should there be. These artists consciously and madly persist in this noble failure of art because they cannot do otherwise and because they hope against hope, in their "tragic optimism," that the theater they create can at least slice through layers of simulation. And because they hope that in that magical moment of togetherness, as audience and actors are gathered in the presentness of the theatrical performance, we might form communities of authentic thought and feeling that restore some of our lost humanity and through refracted images of the real facilitate a reclaiming of history and of our lost selves.

One

Exile as Ontological Mutation

Theater and Performance about Post-Communist Regions

In this chapter I discuss plays by authors and theater makers from East European countries whose works emerge from and/or treat the experience of exile and displacement. I claim that given the ontological nature of the experience of exile, immigration, expatriation or displacement from one's native country, the theater aesthetics forged in the furnace of the creative imagination haunted by this experience will bear the marks of rupture, fragmentation, existential alienation. Edward Said articulated it best: "[Exile] is the unhealable rift between being and a native place, between the self and its true home. Its sadness can never be surmounted" (2002, 172). It may seem too simplistically deterministic to connect the fractured aesthetic of what I have referred to as the theater of exile to the actual experience of exile or displacement of the artist creating such works. Yet aesthetic form is not an arbitrary phenomenon fabricated with no connection to the cultural, geographical, psychological, or linguistic circumstance in which it has emerged. Maybe more than any other art form, theater bears the marks of its surroundings, the conditions of its conception in its very structure and stylistic flesh. The theater of exile is soaked in the sadness of loss that "can never be surmounted," yet it tries to surmount it through the carnivalesque, through the alchemic transformations of the tragic into the comic, and through polyphonic voices that speak of different and often conflicting experiences of the world. The "exilic authors" discussed in this chapter "employ hybrid transnational styles" both from a desire to "make their experiences comprehensible on the new markets" (Manole 2009, 66) and to embody artistically the balancing act of straddling different cultural, linguistic, geographical and psychological realities.

The plays discussed in this chapter cross diverse and contrasting spaces in unpredictable ways, moving between native places to utopian places of various adoptive countries, from lost spaces to landscapes of the American Dream or the Western European dream, in no logical order other than that of memory or of a fractured psyche always searching for wholeness, home, or something that can never be recovered. At other times the spaces are vague, elliptical or altogether inexistent as actual locations, but they are cultural, psychological or imaginary spaces. Because of the troubled relations with space as either a locus of trauma, a locus of refuge, or a disappointing utopia, the voices are often strident and the plot lines broken between realistic representations and dream, surreal or hyperreal images and occurrences.

Aglaja Veteranyi: The Tragi-Comedy of Nomadism

I choose to start this chapter with the dramatic or epic poem by the Romanian writer of German expression Aglaja Veteranyi. At the height of her writing career, with several literary prizes to her credit, among them the 1999 Swiss Prize for Best Book of the year for the work *Warum das Kind in der Polenta kocht* (*Why Is the Child Cooking in the Polenta?*), Aglaja Veteranyi committed suicide in the year 2002 just after submitting her last novel to a German publisher. She was also an actress, a circus performer, the creator of a theater group in Zurich and a successful poet. Like the playwright Sarah Kane before her, like the poet Sylvia Plath before Sarah Kane, she staged and prepared her death with meticulous care, leaving behind a small but powerful body of work that is as edgy as it is startling in the honest and sharply ironic documentation of displacement, abuse and grief. She was a refugee from Romania and for years, she travelled and lived with her family—all circus performers from the Bucharest National Circus—the nomadic life of circus people moving from place to place, from country to country.

Why Is the Child Cooking in the Polenta? is a cross-genre novel, epic poem, and monologue that tells the wrenching story of a young girl traveling with her family of circus actors across the world after having escaped or been thrown out of their native Romania. The story emerges from the author's own life as a child in a family of circus people who escaped

Ceaușescu's Romania, taking with them circus paraphernalia. The image of the itinerant circus performers becomes an aggregate symbol of all loitering refugees.[1] Her dramatic poem is written from the perspective of a young girl terrified of the possibility of the death of her mother, whose circus act is to hang by her hair from the trapeze. I consider Veteranyi the emblematic exile writer to the point of flagrant literality; she documents in a puzzled and fractured voice a nomadic and terror-filled existence, telling, living and recreating a story of displacement and homelessness. The fractured and dreamy narrative is held together by the crystal clear and perky voice of the young girl. The discourse is like a hopelessly foreign language: in the Romanian translation it sounds foreign, in the English translation it sounds like it should have been Romanian. Foreign words and particularly proper names are thrown in once in a while, together with a metalinguistic layer of description of the languages spoken in the family of nomadic circus performers. Mostly the bulk of the story is narrated in the language of stark, uncompromisingly ironic and honest poetry. Since this is the story of a circus family, the carnivalesque is not just a theatrical or poetic device for the construction of the plot, it *is* the plot, both the form and the content of the poem. The book is not written as a play, yet from its publication this work has been translated into the language of the stage and produced in theaters in Switzerland, Germany, and Romania as if it were written as a play. It is as if the form of the book itself follows a nomadic pattern and becomes a poem, a novel, or a theater play depending on its readership or audience.

"Does God speak other languages? Can he understand foreigners too? Or are there angels sitting in little glass booths and translating? AND IS THERE REALLY A CIRCUS IN HEAVEN?" (Veteranyi 2012, 7). To Veteranyi as for most exile writers language is a space, a world, an entire universe of living. The dislocation, or what I have called earlier the ontological mutation caused by exile, is both experienced through the loss of the native language and of the universe enclosed in it and partly recovered through the adoption of a new language. But because new, adopted and recovered, the new language is fractured and points to a fractured existence in which the basic, existential concepts and experiences—God, mother, life, death—are perceived and felt in the second degree, through translation. The voice of Veteranyi's child protagonist cuts through the core of this life in translation and from the honesty of the voice comes a certain sad irony, a melancholy humor almost like the cliché face of clowns, half laughing, half crying. The circus is her literal home, her education, her entire universe. It is for Aglaja the closest thing to a universal language that crosses cultures and idioms and even gets to heaven. This strident and terrified child's voice telling a biography in syncopated rhythms and cinematic imagery[2] is the running thread through a world of broken images and experiences away from home in a dizzying and often cruel carnival. "This house is a home, my sister says. Here you have to put on a lot of weight, or else you'll be crushed by the mountains. And you need lots of skin to get warm" (80). And then, "I left my skin fall to the ground" (81). Burning alive, being skinned alive and other forms of torture and dismemberment run as terrifying metaphors through the book as imaginary deterrents from or palliatives to the pain of homelessness and the fear of the loss of the mother's hanging down in the circus cupola by her hair or the absence of the mother when the children are left in someone else's care. Cannibalism is the central metaphor of the dramatic poem and also, terrifyingly, the plot of the story.

"THE STORIES I LIKE BEST ARE ABOUT PEOPLE EATING OR BEING COOKED." And when the fear of the mother's dying in her circus act becomes unbearable, the torment of the child increases. "I DREAM THAT MY MOTHER DIES. SHE LEAVES ME A BOX WITH HER HEARTBEAT INSIDE. The child is cooking in the polenta because it's tortured other children. It catches hold of orphans, ties them to a tree and sucks the flesh off their bones" (89). Veteranyi's carnival takes the Bakhtinian notion of the banquet and indulgence in the lower bodily stratum to its most extreme form of cannibalism; this is reminiscent also of Artaud's Theater of Cruelty, in which the act of performance has to become a complete purging, a supreme burning and transformation similar to a plague. Caught in the extreme form of a nomadic existence and mixed with the extreme form of performative terror, namely living as a traveling circus family, fearing death and dismemberment of the mother, as well as living in a confused state of constant ethnic, cultural and domestic instability, the young girl's character and voice partake of the postmodernist discourse of broken consciousness, and lack of wholeness.

"IN A FOREIGN COUNTRY MY FAMILY IS LIKE SHATTERED GLASS" (124). "WE MUST NEVER GROW FOND OF ANYTHING" (15). "HOW MANY PLACES ARE FOREIGN COUNTRIES?" (87). If the state of exile is the ultimate lack of wholeness, the condition of exile might just be the perfect example of the postmodern condition. Veteranyi's discourse has no reverence for logical syntax, chronology or continuity of space, as it is the product of a life on the road and a consciousness in translation. Languages, relation to spaces, relation to self—all are "like shattered glass" and are made even more haunting as the story is told in the voice and from the perspective of a child. The chaotic journey of the circus performers is stunning in both its literality and symbolism as the reader/spectator sees the world reflected in pieces that are often all mangled up, upside down and inside out as if seen through the shattered glass of a mirror. Here the aesthetic of exile is made palpable through the fracturing of narrative line, syntax, and perspective yet is always kept hanging by the thread of the fierce voice, just like the narrator's mother hanging from her hair in the trapeze.

The foreigner is the ultimate outsider. But living in a constant state of margins can also take us to what bell hooks considered to be the quality of "a place of radical openness." The serial homelessness of the protagonist and her family in Veteranyi's play/poem/novel illustrates hooks' notion that "one confronts and accepts dispersal and fragmentation as part of the construction of a new world order that reveals more fully where we are, who we can become." The interpretation by bell hooks of "dispersal and fragmentation" as a productive way of resisting social inequity, marginalization and displacement is pushed to the limit in Veteranyi's discourse. The storytelling itself is a nomadic experience about nomadic lives and mixed ethnicities told in absurd contradictions: "OUR STORY SOUNDS DIFFERENT EVERY TIME MY MOTHER TELLS IT. We're Orthodox, We're Jewish, we're international! My grandfather owned a circus arena, he was a salesman, a captain, travelled from country to country, never left his own village and was a locomotive engineer. He was a Greek, a Romanian, a farmer, a Turk, an aristocrat, a Gypsy, an Orthodox believer" (53). The Balkan fragmentation and exilic disorientation soar to unmatched heights of ironic poetry in Veteranyi's discourse, mixing categories and superimposing contradicting realities onto one another to a delicious multiplication of identity.

In this cruel carnival of eating and being eaten, of constructing oneself on the road and mirroring oneself in the shards of glass that construct the foreigner's identity, the narrator or the protagonist of *Why Is the Child Cooking in the Polenta?* is at home only in the cocoon of her own poetic ironic language, in the linguistic equivalent of the clown's sad and happy face. She reconstructs the world through playing and through the bitter carnival of her homeless circus existence, and the reconstruction takes place with the means of writing. Yet the writing is itself an experience of loss and recovery, of uprooting and failed re-rootings, mostly of an existence in the second degree, as it is an existence in translation or in an adopted language. "Before I saw my father for the last time, he made a movie in which God was one of the characters. My mother played God's grandmother and I played the Guardian angel.... GOD IS SAD. HE IS PLAYING A HUNGARIAN SONG ON THE VIOLIN." The linguistic carnival of Veteranyi's childlike but not childish voice becomes her one and only home away from home, in restless search for a home. Her linguistic carnival is the more poignant since she is writing in German, therefore not in her native language, and contending with a history of family illiteracy as well as her own past illiteracy. Vincent Kling, the translator of *Polenta* into English, has noted:

> Creative ambivalence and anomaly reign everywhere in *Polenta*, both on content and technique. As one example, the very appearance of the text on the page ... presents wide gaps of space, pages almost blank, and aphoristic or summary passages in capitals, as if the narrator's attempts to arrange the words were burdened by uncertainty, irresolution, hesitancy, and the need for anchoring points, all arising in turn from the struggle to achieve basic aptitude in written expression.... She's writing to find a place of her own, not to claim authority or climb the career ladder..., writing essentially for self-exploration, to define herself and the world [Veteranyi 2012, 191].

Veteranyi's style is a superb illustration of exilic writing that tells the story of a wildly nomadic and disrupted existence in disjointed syntax and narrative that in turn seem to attempt and simultaneously fail at making sense of language and the world it contains. From the dolls that "don't speak any foreign languages" to a God playing Hungarian songs, to the children who don't speak her and her sister's language, to the naive question, "HOW MANY PLACES ARE FOREIGN COUNTRIES?" the creation of Veteranyi's voice and narrative thread are as deliciously and bitterly free as they are fractured, as funny in their literality as they are melancholy in their poetic innuendos. They represent the narrative of a self that is lost in translation, thief of languages and cultural landscapes, a self that is perpetually in search of a familiar place that she can call home all the while striving to be her own home in a life of perpetual vagrancy. For the foreigner having to adjust to a new country or countries in Veteranyi's case, the basic human experiences, yearnings and notions of family, love, God, and the world are all mediated through the foreign language and therefore poised on an abyss between the yearning for a former, unmediated yet terrifying existence under a dictatorship, and the phony gloss of foreign languages in foreign countries in an ever rootles and illusive present. This present is often wrought with a nostalgia for a pathetic past and regret for the action of defection, as ironically expressed by the mother: "If I had known what democracy is doing to us I would never have left home! My mother says" (123).

The circus existence and traveling is, ironically, the only grounding that Veteranyi's child protagonist has, in a series of foster care, boarding schools, and caravan ramblings that give her the maturity of a distanced look at all the realities she crosses, the relief of unrelenting irony at stable, un-displaced existence and an unsentimental perspective of her own initial home. In the words of translator Vincent Kling, "The picaresque and carnivalesque shape the narrative approach and plot structure of *Polenta*: both the overall narrative viewpoint and the specific linguistic formulations preclude any romance or indulgence in nostalgic yearning for an idyllically evoked homeland or any sense of adventure about carefree life on the road" (199). Because this is literally a story of life on the road, told on the road, at times from a Gypsy *vardo*, at times in between her mother's formidable and terrifying acts of hanging by her hair from the circus cupola or during short respites of charitable housing and interrupted schooling, the reader almost hears the bumps and jolts in the road as they are made audible and palpable in Veteranyi's disrupted style and syntax, and in her mutated or synesthetic experiences. This is the priceless description of the food in one of the boarding schools where she and her sister live for a brief period: "THE FOOD HERE TASTES LIKE BREAKING DOWN THE TENT" (91). The tent being one of her only temporary homes, other than the traveling caravan or the *vardo*, its dismantling would reduce their existence to nothingness. And since food has the taste of nothingness and breakage, no wonder that in the terrifyingly brittle existence that Veteranyi's heroine experiences, cannibalism seems almost like a desirable option: at least the food might actually taste of something instead of nothing. This wrenching yet unsentimental ballad to life on the road, to the sadness of circus life, and the cynical laugh of rootlessness that is Veteranyi's poetic and dramatic work, is also a testimonial and a beautiful illustration of an aesthetic that is equally flesh, blood, politics and nourishment: in the brittle voice, in the shards of glass, in the spikes of irony lies also the survival of the heroine.

"At the end the grandmother stands at the door and waves," tells the narrator in Veteranyi's poem/play/novel. This is the description of the end of the movie that one of the characters in the novel has made and not the ending of the story in the first degree. We never know how that story ends, but the image of the grandmother waving evokes endings, departures, separations, as well as new beginnings, a sense of nostalgia and yearning, all in a layering of fictional universes. Recently Veteranyi's dramatic poem was made into a widely acclaimed indie movie of Hungarian production called *Aglaja*, directed by Krisztina Deákt. It as if from the glitter of the circus and the dust clouds raised by the circus caravan on foreign roads, the protagonist/author had envisioned such a prestigious future for her work in a sadly yet ironically postmortem immortality: "I'm only going to die in the movies," says the little girl. "Then when I die the light will go out and I'll be alive again. I'm never going to die completely" (65). From wherever she may be rambling in her otherworldly exile from our wretched world, hopefully Aglaja Veteranyi rejoices in her dream come true, for indeed she is never going "to die completely."[3]

Saviana Stanescu: Balkan Roots, Western Wings

It might be best to start the discussion of Saviana Stanescu's theater with her own self characterization:

> I am a Romanian-born playwright with Balkan roots. Back in Romania I used to write surreal and absurd plays and to create interdisciplinary performances. Here in the USA ... I became concerned with issues of identity and immigration, content-wise, and with character development and innovative dramatic structure, form-wise. At this point I work on integrating my 12-year American experience and newly developed craft with my bold Balkan inventiveness and imagination, while tackling meaningful/global issues [Stanescu 2013].

It would be pertinent at this point to complement Stanescu's statement with the note that Romanian theater and literature have a long history if not a clear tradition of embracing and/or innovating in surrealist and absurdist aesthetics forms. Stanescu falls well within that tradition of anti-traditionalists. A few facts are worthy of note at this point in the discussion of Romanian contemporary theater makers: Tristan Tzara, a Romanian Jewish writer at the turn of the last century, initiated the Dada movement, which is considered a precursor of the surrealist movement. The Romanian playwright Eugène Ionesco started "the theater of the absurd" (a term coined by Martin Eslin) with his play *The Bald Soprano*. During the long period of the communist dictatorship of Nicolae Ceauşescu a group of Romanian writers created the movement called "oneirism," which resisted the state-imposed socialist realist aesthetics with poetic and narrative forms that made abundant use of dreams, the fantastical, and the absurd as a form of resistance and a way of exercising their freedom of expression in codified ways that would escape censorship.[4] Theater makers who made a name for themselves outside the Romanian borders, such as the former artistic director of the Guthrie Theater, Liviu Ciulei, or the theater director and Columbia University professor Andrei Serban, have excelled at creating innovative and experimental productions of both classical plays and contemporary works and at breaking the barriers of realistic representation and traditional staging. I have often wondered, with all the necessary and cautionary notes to myself to avoid lapsing into nationalistic sentimentality, why it is that Romanian literature and art—and recently what has been coined by the *New York Times* as the "new wave of Romanian film"—have offered such an abundance of experimental and often radically rebellious aesthetic forms. In my musings and searches I have not been able to come up with anything other than the fact that in its history, cultural and geographical make-up, Romania has been and continues to remain a country of crossroads and liminal spaces, a palimpsest of overlapping languages and ethnicities starting with the proverbial first inhabitants, the Dacians, and including the notorious invaders, the Romans, the further Slavic, Greek, Ottoman, Habsburg, Hungarian and German invasions/rules/influences. More recently, the country has been torn between a fierce embracing of Western values and a self-hating Balkan disintegration. Maybe the earlier reference to Balkan identity as one of "hybridity" and as "living between two" fits Romanian cultural and artistic identity to perfection. Recent cultural studies have revalorized and reconsidered the tensions between margins and centers, "core" and "periphery" in European literary and intellectual history, with a view to demonstrating the "unfixidness" of these notions while equally proving that "some centers *are* centers and some margins *are* margins and the only way to acknowledge the value of their encounter—or indeed, their clash—is to perceive them as such" (Radunovic and Pourgouris 2006, xv–xiv). Romania and the Balkans "*are* margins" in the "periphery" of Western Europe and the wider Western World including the United States. Aesthetic and cultural "hybridities" are born either out of encounters and clashes between centers and margins, or between different margins. But as bell hooks has noted, such margins that remain margins also have the advantage, precarious as that may be, of having a wider view of the center and of other margins and of opening into "spaces of radical openness." The reality of hybridity, the encounters between margins and the clashes between margins and centers, is explored to its fullest in Stanescu's plays and boldly developed in the delightful incongruities of her plays' structures.

Stanescu (2013) refers to her work as an immigrant writer in the United States in the following way, mentioning her fascination and interest precisely in hybrid realities and identities:

> In my American plays I explore topics of displacement and reinvention, of cultural clashes and power dynamics between countries, groups and individuals. I am interested in that *in-between* space where migrants dwell, living in the "hyphen" between two cultures or communities. That hyphenated/hybrid identity fascinates me. I'm always ready to analyze and dramatize ways in which the American Dream turns into a nightmare for many people while remaining an idealized Paradise for others.

Stanescu's plays have known significant success in the United States, France, and Romania, where they have been staged in bold productions. Her play *Waxing West* was staged at La MaMa ETC in New York City and was the 2007 winner of the Innovative Theater Award. One of the directors who developed the award-winning play *Waxing West: A Hairy Tale in Two Acts and Four Seasons* noted that she mixes genres, combining dark absurdism in the vein of Beckett and Ionesco with scenes that employ a contemporary, psychologically-oriented American sensibility (Eisner 2010, 28–30). Stanescu herself has noted that she uses "dark humor and an absurd yet socially relevant contemporary sensibility combined with a more realistic/naturalistic approach" (2013). Diana Manole has aptly noted, "Saviana Stanescu attempts to change the stereotypical view of immigrating to twenty first century United States and implicitly, of America and the American way of life" (Manole 2009, 66–7). Stanescu's theater offers a superb illustration of the aesthetics of exile that I have tried to theorize in this book. The characters, voices, images and dramatic actions of her plays emerge from that liminal zone of the hyphen in between cultures, countries, ethnicities and languages. The Balkan carnivalesque approach of unmitigated and unforgiving humor that sweeps everything in its way—political correctness, cultural difference and clashes, the American Dream, marriage and even death—throbs throughout Stanescu's play, leaving us properly unsettled and troubled. A review of *Waxing West* noted, "Saviana's play is a perfect example of the subversion of pain with jokes, parody, and irony," as well as that she "has been able to mix her aesthetics in this play that traverses two continents[5] (*Brooklyn Rail*, April 2, 2007).

The interplay of dream sequences and naturalistic scenes, the mixing of chronologies as they flow out of the characters' conscience and subconscious realities with no regard for historical time, and the juxtaposition of Romanian and American landscapes and realities create a sense of simultaneity of fractured experiences. The experience of immigration of the protagonist, Daniela, a cosmetologist who comes to New York in order to marry an American computer engineer with kinky sexual habits, emerges in truncated clips that move between the before and the after of her American experience and are woven with nightmarish sequences of the former Romanian dictators Elena and Nicolae Ceaușescu. They have become vampires "sucking capitalist blood in a socialist, democratic way" (Stanescu 2007, 180). They follow Daniela's progress and actions everywhere and subject her to cruel tests. There is also a constant rotation of images of America as chronotope,[6] an interplay between exilic imaginaries that collapse time and space in disorderly ways: what it would be like to be there in the American Dream with magic plastic cards that can buy everything, and the actual reality of Daniela's American Dream in which she steals bottles of chewable vitamin C and books from Barnes and Noble, pretends to eat her soon-to-be-husband as a Thanksgiving turkey, and reads self-help books with no visible benefit. A similar sliding out of existence, a slipping in the space of the hyphen, the in-between cultures, countries, languages, cuisines that Veteranyi's protagonist goes through, are also present in Stanescu's play in the surreal dance between Daniela's American life, her yearning to go back to Romania and the cruel tortures inflicted upon her by Elena and Nicolae-turned-dictator:

> **Daniela:** Given the existence of something beyond existence, I have ceased to exist. (*She starts licking Ceaușescu's hand.*)
> **Daniela:** I am your ashtray. Your tomb. Your Disneyland. Your past. Your present. Your future. You can do with me whatever you want. I am here to stay. I am here to endure. I am here to live...
> **Ceaușescu:** She's sick!
> Enough, pet! Wait in front of the door!
> Ruins. I'm an earthworm crawling among wrecks. Eating the dust... (*She starts licking Elena's hand.*)
> **Ceaușescu:** Send her home. She'll ruin our party...
> **Daniela:** Dust. Rust. Blood. Champagne. Wedding. Funeral. Birth. Death. Cut. Grow. Wax. Grow. Hair. Hair. Hair. Everywhere hair [232].

The wrenching sense of a meaningless universe and an even more wrenching sense of a disjointed self in Stanescu's play sends me to the poignant words about the irreversible and death-like nature of exile so beautifully articulated by Edward Said:

> Exile cannot be made to serve notions of humanism. On the twentieth-century scale, exile is neither aesthetically nor humanistically comprehensible: at most the literature about exile objectifies an anguish and predicament most people rarely experience at first hand; but to think of the exile informing this literature as beneficially humanistic is to banalize its mutilations, the losses it inflicts on those who suffer them, the muteness with which it responds to any attempt to understand it as "good for us." Is it not true that ... like death, but without death's ultimate mercy, it has torn millions of people from traditions, family and geography? [2002, 138].

I have often compared the trauma of exile to a form of death or amputation, but to Said death is in fact merciful compared to the cruel uprooting of exile, understood in the modern twentieth and twenty-first century sense of abrupt and irreversible dislocation from one's native geography due to political reasons and profoundly caught in the historical moment. Daniela's journey from Romania to New York is caught, if not trapped, in her own historical moment, in the Romanian polenta cooking she hates, the vampiric dictators and past that torment her, the dysfunctional relation with Charlie Aronson, the melancholy relation with the homeless man Uros, and the emotionally fraught and sexually ambiguous relationship with Charlie's sister Gloria. Yet because she is forever trapped in an ethnic, national, political and personal dysfunctionality, the specifics are also instruments of torture. Indeed, it is hard to think of anything in Daniela's experience as "beneficially humanistic."[7]

It is not humanistic and neither is it beneficial, because the protagonist of this play, coming from that "no man's land" that is the Balkans into her version of an American nightmare, has forever lost what Pierre Bourdieu has called the original *habitus*, or "the coherent amalgam of practices linking habit with inhabitance" (Said 2002, 140) and has thrown herself into an alienated and alienating universe of consumerism, emotional paralysis and layers of stereotypes. All that being said, since I walk the tightrope of many paradoxes in this book, I also claim that the critical look that Stanescu and other artists cast at such breaks between "habit" and "inhabitance" and the empathy shown in their writings towards individuals suspended in the abyss of no-man's lands and hyphenated realities, is in itself a humanist act in the larger sense defined also by Said, who said he would "continue to use [it] stubbornly despite the scornful dismissal of the term by postmodern critics." Said understands humanism as being "able to use one's mind historically and rationally for the purposes of reflective understanding and genuine disclosure. Moreover humanism is sustained by a sense of community with other interpreters and other societies and periods" (1979, xxiii). Being lucid and critical of the loss of humanism in this sense acquires a humanist dimension.

Stanescu's theater has a profound humanist core precisely because it tries to find the lost tenderness, humanity and meaning that the "large aggregates" of immigrants are still desperately yearning for. Daniela's only true friend is a homeless survivor of the Bosnian war of the nineties obsessed with the epic of Gilgamesh and Enkidu and actually the only truly profound and humanly enriching relation she has in her immigrant journey. The interplay of the American dream before Daniela's coming to America and the actual depressing reality of her life in America as Charlie Aronson's soon-to-be but never-to-be wife, the chronological spiraling of going forward, backwards and forward again in the twisted chronology of the narrative, and the shifting of spaces between Bucharest and New York obliterate any sense of belonging and of successful settling, re-rooting or reacquiring a *habitus*. To use Stanescu's own words, her character is caught in the "hyphen" between past and future, Romania and America, communism and capitalism, fantasy and reality, life and death, and in Romanian style, the living, the dead and the undead. The coveted and cliché dream of an America with "a nice house, two floors, four bedrooms, two cars, one for you and one for your husband ... breakfast and dinner with all the family.... Three main courses. Two desserts! Everybody smiling! A coffee filter, a washing machine, a microwave ... those microwaves cook everything by themselves, don't they?" (195) turns to a hateful existence of unwanted chores to satisfy the exotic needs of her future husband: "I don't want to remind you what I do for you for FREE. I don't' smoke here. I cook for you. Romanian food! ... I hate Romanian food, Charlie, I hate 'sarmale' and 'mamaliga' and the Romanian traditional smell, and the Romanian exotic flavors, and the Romanian claustrophobic kitchens" (183). The conversation with Charlie appears before the fantasy of the American house in reverse chronological order. Daniela's monologue about the self-help books she has been reading in America is placed before a scene with her brother Elvis in University Square in Bucharest as they talk about the masquerade of Romanian revolutions. Scenes from 2000 unfold after scenes happening in 2001. Instead of following the known style of flashbacks, Stanescu uses "flashforwards" in a constant scrambling of past future and present. These chronological reversals reflect, as well, what I have been referring to as the dislocated relation between space and time that the exiled person/writer experiences. In an article about the Bakhtinian theory of chronotope "applied to the organizing process," Philippe Lorino and Benoît Tricard note that "organizational time," which is the time by which societies function both at the micro and macro levels, involves this temporal three-dimensionality: "past as real, present as negotiated, future as constructed"; "it is the locus of individual and collective emotions linked with memory, events and expectations" (2012, 110). Because the past is no longer real for the exile who has lost her ties to the space in which that past unfolded, the negotiations of the present and the construction of the future are forever compromised, and the order of these three temporal elements is often confused and jumbled up.

"Dammit, this is gonna be difficult," says Daniela in America, trying to make sense of her American life and overdosing on self-help books that she has stolen from Barnes and Noble. "You don't have the references to our complicated Romanian Dacian Tracian Roman Ottoman Byzantine Balkan communist post-communist anti-communist pro–American history, all you know about us is Dracula-the vampire, Ceauşescu-the-dictator, and Nadia Comaneci-the-gymnast!" (208). In the next act, back in Romania, a year earlier, disgusted with Romania's corrupt politics, she dreams of being in America: "I'm not gonna vote for anyone. I've had enough of all of them. I've had enough! I'll be in America before the elections" (210). She is disaffected in her native space because of the "joke" that Romanian politics and parties seem to be, and she is alienated in her adoptive space because of the thin layer of understanding and one-dimensional perspective that the natives project on foreigners, in this case on refugees from Romania, applying a few disconnected facts as an identity marker to all refugees coming from that part of the world. For a Romanian exile in any of the world's diasporas, Daniela's line, "all you know about us is Dracula-the vampire, Ceauşescu-the-dictator, and Nadia Comaneci-the-gymnast!" strikes a real chord and incites both frustration and alienation. In my own 2008 novel *Train to Trieste*,[8] the protagonist Mona notes in her first months in Chicago: "Once in a while someone has heard of Nadia Comaneci or Dracula, or someone says they know another Romanian.... I understand that my country is known for its gymnasts and vampires" (193). Having lost forever the initial, native "locus of individual and collective emotions linked with memory, events and expectations," the exiled protagonist moves through time as if it were space, going forward and backwards in rambling, circular or spiraling meanders.

The interludes in Times Square and the conversations with Uros, the homeless war survivor, seem like the most authentic and, ironically, grounded moments in the play. The allusions to Gilgamesh and his search for his beloved friend Enkidu in the underworld create a beautiful subtext to both of their searches for love, meaning and a form of immortality, a bridge across the hyphen or the abyss of cultural differences, historical chasms and economic gaps through the thin, shimmering line of the reflection on the human condition.

> **Uros:** It was dangerous in Ghilgamesh's time. It's dangerous today. It will be dangerous tomorrow. I don't need to watch the news to find out such a simple truth....
>
> **Daniela** *(sitting on the wheelchair's arm)*: Your obsession with Gilgamesh's story.... What's so special? A guy and his friend....
>
> **Uros:** A king and his friend Enkidu....
>
> **Daniela:** ... traveling in search of....
>
> **Uros:** Immortality!
>
> **Daniela:** You cannot believe in immortality!
>
> **Uros:** Of course, not.... Mrs. Death and I are old pals. She follows me like a shadow. She clings to me like a spider She's the tie around my neck.... I want to take her with me on Gilgamesh's traces. To see her grimace there, on the land where she was defeated.
>
> **Daniela:** She was never defeated, Uros.
>
> **Uros:** Yes, she was.
>
> **Daniela:** You saw her in your war, in Yugoslavia.
>
> **Uros:** Of course I saw her. She gulped my left leg. Gulped my wife Jasna. Gulped my son Andrej. Gulped my daughter Tanja. But she spewed me out. I was too much for her bowels. That's why I want to take her on a "honeymoon." To Iraq [201–02].

Uros, who is Daniela's only American friend, is a tragic illustration of what Said has called those "immense aggregates of humanity" who "loiter as refugees and displaced persons," "undocumented people, suddenly lost, without a tellable history" (2000, 201–02). We should indeed mind Said's urging that "we must set aside Joyce and Nabokov and think instead of the unaccountable masses for whom UN agencies have been created" (139). Just as for Veteranyi's circus-nomad protagonist, her only home was in her words and in her voice, for Daniela, her only home and zone of comfort is in the fragile tie with one who is even more of a homeless person than she is and in the eternal story of the search for love and meaning on a long, lonely journey across real and imaginary landscapes, among the living and the dead. Gilgamesh's story is also one of exile, as is Ulysses's story, Ovid's, Eneas's, the homeless war survivor Uros's, and the Romanian cosmetologist Daniela's. In this aesthetic of loss, uprootedness and displacement, home is in the story. Daniela's story is her only home. "Here is the story," she claims loud and clear at the beginning of the play: "The whole story. Nothing but the story. My story. Yes. Everything that happened.... Tell the story, the story.... My story. My story" (242). In the abyss of that hyphen between worlds, continents, languages, and histories, her personal story singles her out of the large "aggregates" "without a tellable history" and gives her a space, precarious as that may be, in the book of immigrant stories, in the journeys of perpetual return.[9] Beneath the dark humor and carnivalesque reversals, underneath the scrambling of dream sequences with reality and the macabre "Balkan" humor, there is a profound, wrenching sadness that oozes throughout Stanescu's play and that dictates the dislocated form to match a dislocated self. The "eternal return" takes place in the nightmares with Elena and Nicolae Ceaușescu as cruel vampires who abuse and mock Daniela, in the dream/nightmare "Good-bye, America (Another End)," in the conversations with her dead father and in the actual desire and attempt to go back to Romania.

The refrain of the return that precedes, in the structure of the play, the initial leaving from Romania with "five suitcases" in the scene "Good-bye, Romania (An End)," which in turn precedes the scene of the attempted return with only three suitcases in a scene titled "9/11. Flash Back, Flash Forward," gives the latter part of the play a melancholy sentimentality despite itself, the hopeless circularity of nostalgia: "I'm thinking of going back./ Back./ To Romania. Back home." Or "I should go back Charlie.... I do horrible things here, Charlie, I'm a thief" (218). And then another departure, another good-bye, a new uprooting is layered on the story of an already uprooted individual: "Bye-bye, New York, that's all (*violin music goes louder*)" (240). In the scene of the first attempt at return to Romania, Uros, the homeless war survivor who wants to go to Iraq to find his soul, dies on a bench in the subway after Daniela has used Charlie's credit card to buy plane tickets for herself and him, one to Romania, one to Iraq. Reality is as much a nightmare as are nightmares, and the lines between the two are blurred in the same structural confusion as the reversal of beginning and end. At the conclusion of the play the words "end/beginning" are written on a screen. Nostalgia is a failed return, the suffering caused by a desire to return. In Daniela's case the return is a failed return, and the settling in the American Dream is a failed settling. If the initial departure was somewhat hopeful, with five suitcases, the attempted return is shameful and pathetic, with only three suitcases and violin music. The dilution and mixing of past and present, beginning and end, echoes what a postmodern critic has called "Nostalgia for the Future, Waiting for the Past (Lang 1986, 209)." And Svetlana Boym calls nostalgia "the incurable modern condition," as she points out, "The twentieth century started with a futuristic utopia and ended with nostalgia. Optimistic belief in the future was discarded like an outmoded spaceship sometime in the 1960s" (2001, xiv). The American Dream itself is nostalgia for the future, which mixed with the nostalgia/anticipation for the past creates in Daniela's case a centrifugal motion that ultimately leads to a weightless immobility or a disconcerted set of back-and-forth motions. These movements cancel each other out and place her and her story in the spatial and temporal limbo of a perpetual wait, not unlike that of the notorious vagabonds Vladimir and Estragon from Beckett's *Waiting for Godot*.

Yet unlike the maddening immobility of Vladimir and Estragon, Stanescu's character Daniela is ultimately a person of action who time and again manages miraculously to emerge from the burdens of her past, present, nightmares, or hellish realities and grasp the present with all its urgent and sometimes unbearable demands on her conscience and psyche. We see her at the end of the play addressing the audience with Charlie's photograph, following the September 11 events and inquiring about him, since he worked at "the sixty-sixth floor." Stanescu's own personal history is marked by the September 11 events, as she had only arrived in New York on a Fulbright scholarship on August 25, 2001, which is also the date marked for the ninth scene of the play, "Red Wine and White Sheets. August 25, 2001: New York." The play ends on September 11, 2001, which marks Stanescu's beginnings in the United States. The beautifully ironic and deliberate reinvention of biography into art also encapsulates at its best the immigrant experience, which is the coexistence in the same overwrought present of beginnings and ends, unfolding not necessarily in this exact order. John Clinton Eisner, who wrote the introduction to Stanescu's volume *The New York Plays*, notes, "She is part of Romania's bridge generation: a group of outspoken artists who participated in the 1989 Revolution and began laying the groundwork for alternative arts and culture in a democratic society." The bridges that Stanescu builds through her theater work, connecting two languages, cultures, physical landscapes, "ideas and action," and the "surreal and the very real," are, in Esner's inspired words "very like the immigrant experience; no matter where in the world one travels to escape impossible circumstances, one relies on vision and imagination to transform it into a true home" (2010, 23). As I have pointed out earlier, Daniela's home is her own "tellable" story, as Stanescu's home is her body of plays, as Veteranyi's home is her voice with all its stridencies or shards of glass piercing through the ragged edges. The chronotopes are shattered, as time becomes space and space starts being measured in time. New kinds of homes are being built in immigrant theater such as Veteranyi's and Stanescu's—homes that inhabit you as much as you inhabit them, portable homes of thought, voice and imagination. These new voices claim theater itself as an ever-evolving home for all those who have lost theirs and are yearning for one.

Lawrence Samuel has noted in his book *The American Dream: A Cultural History* that while this dream "is the guiding mythology of the most powerful civilization in history," "the problem is that it does not exist" (2012, 1). Saviana's "New York plays," *Waxing West, Lenin's Shoe* and *Aliens with Extraordinary Skills*, are all about the chase after the elusive American Dream of fresh immigrants to the United States and really more about the American nightmare, which Samuel has called appropriately the "evil twin always lurking in the shadows" (9). The reversed chronologies of the narrative lines, the gliding in and out of realistic and dream/nightmare sequences in *Waxing West*, or the dreamscapes and "Incisions in Nadia's Mind" in *Aliens with Extraordinary Skills* emerge from the very elusive nature of the American Dream-turned-nightmare and the experience of fracture and displacement of immigrants chasing after the dream and inevitably falling into the "evil twin."

In *Aliens with Extraordinary Skills*, Nadia, a professional clown from Moldova who earns money by twisting rubber balloons into animals, follows the American Dream of working as a clown at McDonalds and moves to New York, where she shares an apartment with the Dominican Lupita. In her chase for jobs, money, happiness, and love she ends up being gang raped while being followed and interrogated by INS officers and being threatened with deportation. The circus and clowning elements, much like in Veteranyi's dramatic poem of the circus family, crackle with dark humor and are heavy with layers of sadness, desperation, and "nostalgia for the future," yet they become, as for Veteranyi's protagonist, a portable home where Nadia can find solace, refuge, and occasionally money.

The aesthetics of carnival combined with the mixing of naturalistic and dream scenes titled "Dreamscapes" in *Aliens with Extraordinary Skills* and dream scenes of Elena and Nicolae Ceaușescu as vampires in *Waxing West* reflect both the elusive nature of the American Dream and the disjointed nature of the immigrant existence always caught in dangerous, sad and sometimes funny acrobatics of survival, mastery of fear, the ghosts of a past they often cannot escape and utopian plunges into an uncertain future. "You gotta talk to yourself," the Dominican Lupita advises the Moldovan Nadia: "Stuff like I'm gonna make it. I will ... such and such, whatever you dream to be" (2010, 312). The interactions between the immigrants in this play, balanced between ironic bantering, matter-of-fact affection, or support of one another, and the terrifying interactions with the INS officers who taunt Nadia with the menace of constant deportation in the "Dreamscapes," seem to echo the words of the Slovan-American author Louis Adamic, himself an immigrant and passionate advocate of the diversity of America: "The American Dream is a lovely thing but to keep it alive, to keep it from turning into a nightmare, every once in a while we've got to wake up" (quoted in Samuel 2012, 30). For the characters in Stanescu's plays, the tensions between the nightmare that their own reality is turning into in the chase after the dream and brief moments of waking up create a constant aesthetic vortex of comedy and tragedy, tears and laughter, sadness and hopefulness, exacerbated of course in *Aliens with Extraordinary Skills* by the very literality of the circus in Nadia's line of work as a "professional clown." The uses of carnival as a form of political dissent, as "a resource for political action" and as a necessary destabilizing of the "humorless state" ring true in the discussion of Stanescu's works. Be it the humorlessness of the communist state and its vampiric dictators, or the cruel and humorless INS officers, their oppressive hold on the characters' minds is subverted time and again by the merciless laugh, the clowning, the balloon animals that are the source of Nadia's precarious income. We could almost think that the play ends with an uplifting image of the American Dream come true, a fairy tale of sorts in which Nadia and her American husband Bob, who saved her from deportation, now "own a Birthday-Parties business!" They have "extraordinary skills in making people laugh" and they and their children "all have American wings" (368).

The balloon animals that take Nadia on her flight towards the American Dream are a delightful symbol as they are also a puzzling non-symbol, a reality that actually lifts her up above her terrors, traumas and past. The humor and carnival in Stanescu's dramatic texts about immigrants are not just vehicles or strategies used for the illustration of politically charged content; they are part of the substance of the plot and of the characters themselves. They are what lifts the plot, characters and the audience to a state of psychological lightness not unlike what Milan Kundera has brilliantly coined "the unbearable lightness of being": a state of existence in which uprootedness and laughter, carnivalesque reversals of social hierarchies, overturning or obliterating traditional moral and aesthetic binary categories such as beginning and end, body and spirit, and good and evil, lead to freer and highly imaginative dramatic structures, linguistic uses and semiotic experiments. The bitter freedom of exile also leads to the sweet freedom of expression in a roller-coaster of shapes, colors, and images.

Despite the airy, happy ending in Stanescu's *Aliens with Extraordinary*

Skills, the last staging direction of the play is that "INS1 and INS2 enter wearing scary-clown masks." The party is never over in this aesthetic of the open-ended work dealing with themes of exile and rupture, just as for the immigrant chasing the American Dream and torn between "nostalgias for the future" and a constant re-imagining of the past, any beginning is also an end and no end is final, often triggering with it other happy or miserable beginnings/endings. The postmodern, the carnival, the Balkan are caught together in an unholy dance of dizzying creation, destruction and recreation of meaning that is not unlike the turns, tours and detours, beginnings and endings, spatial muddle and temporal confusion of the experience of exile itself. In Stanescu's plays the leaps from one fictional universe to another create an aesthetic vertigo similar to the flying on the trapeze of the mother hanging from her hair in Veteranyi's dramatic poem. She boldly creates for the stage with all the spatial and visual markers that endow the texts of her plays with a concrete and often troubling physical existence. Stanescu's precise stage directions of sound, image, and tone, from violins playing in the background of Daniela's farewell to the America scene to the frightening clown masks of the INS officers in *Aliens*, are perfect complements to the linguistic diversity and structural playfulness of her playscripts. They may verge on ironic sentimentality, nightmarish unreality or gripping realism, but they always create a vibrant sense of place, of the spatial and psychological detours of her nomadic characters.

The immigrant theater discussed here infuses the aesthetic workings of the text and the potentialities of its performance with a nomadic quality of indeterminacy and constant movement, as if fleeing from all that is stable, settled, and rooted while grabbing for roots. The aesthetic form is a manner of literary nomadism in which the play rambles through different genres, styles, and temporal and spatial frames and thus mimics the nomadic experience itself. In the interview mentioned earlier, Stanescu says she is interested in:

> outsiders as un/documented aliens, global foreigners, nerds, disoriented/misunderstood teens, loners, rebels, revolutionaries, or just regular people who felt like an "outsider" at some point in their lives. The need to belong/conform versus the need to rebel/stand out. For whatever reasons, any person's mind could become a battlefield for those two needs at any given moment. That internal conflict is a rich theatrical mine [2013].

In the confrontation between the need to belong and the need to rebel, between settling and fleeing, emerge splintered and troubling dramatic forms that encourage us to reconsider all presumptions of identity, home, or any version of the American Dream. These forms equally move us to reconsider the role of theater itself, not just as repository of memory and

Saviana Stanescu, *Aliens with Extraordinary Skills*: Women's Project Production; October 2008; directed by Tea Alagić. Gian Murray Gianino (INS officer, left), Natalia Payne (center), and Shirine Babb (INS officer, right). "Dreamscape," or nightmarish scene, in which Nadia is being tormented with threats of deportation and cruel questioning by INS officers (photograph: Carol Rosegg).

witness but also as a necessary experience and alternative reality in the production of meaning about the reality of displacement and about our "modern era" of "immense aggregates of humanity" who "loiter as refugees and displaced persons." In this "rich theatrical mine," authors such as Stanescu and Veteranyi fuse the postmodern edge with the carnivalesque grin and with the Balkan liminality in a tireless "avoidance of closure" and undecidability of meaning,"[10] in a relentless Artaudian purging and burning from which we might just come out more eager to reevaluate the notions of margins and home and see them as spaces of "radical openness."

I will close this section with one of Stanescu's unpublished plays, titled *Bechnya*. It is in regard to her writing of this play that she notes the importance of one's past and place of birth:

> Why did I start to write this play? Because I wanted to remind people how arbitrary are the crossroad moments of our lives. How everything can change in a moment. [...] But most of all, I started to write Bechnya because I needed a chance to invent a country. That's probably because I still like those stories of violence, humor and imagination called fairy-tales [2013].

A lot of immigrant writing is about inventing new countries. Veteranyi's circus odyssey is all about creating a transnational, carnivalesque country carried around the world in the circus tent and wagon. Stanescu's Bechnya is an invented country possibly deriving from a combination of Bosnia, Chechnya and Romania, as she revealed to me. The references to war and genocide, the Muslim first names of the sisters sent to the Bosnian war, and the references to adoptions of orphans remind one of Romania's troubled adoption history following the 1989 revolution, as do the references to Dracula and "blood-sucking dictators." Stanescu even uses an invented language, Bechnyan, which increases the outlandish foreignness of the play while adding a sliver of comic relief. This country is a Balkan dystopia whose stories unfold more grimly than the darkest of the Grimms' fairy tales.

Stanescu's *Bechnya* is a dark story about two "Bechnyan" sisters, one of whom was adopted by an American couple while the other stayed in Bechnya, though she also wanted to be adopted. The story is woven within several fairy tales, and the play unfolds in parallel acts and movements that interlace the dialogue of an American couple on the cusp of their adoption with the interaction between the two sisters at different points in their adult lives. The plot moves from the most recent time in the present to various points in the past, and back to the present. Throughout the play the sisters take turns falling into a fairy tale scenario starting with *Snow White*, moving to *Snow Queen*, to *Hansel and Gretel* and ending with *The Little Girl with Matches*. The play is as startlingly violent as it is poetic, and the overlap of the lines of four characters with known fairy tales and archetypal situations creates a startling palimpsest of cultural and ethnic realities. Through the wild leaps into fairy-tale and fantastical situations, we can get powerful glimpses of harsh realities of war and displacement and of a fierce and relentless fight for a slice of the American Dream. In this case the dream is a beautiful house with lots of teddy bears, in which one of the sisters, Vicky/Fatma, moves confidently as an accomplished writer with children and a husband and earlier, as a PhD student writing her doctoral dissertation on the violence against women in Bechnya and in particular on the stories brought to her by Shari/Madonna/Thelma. The latter character also happens to be the forgotten/un-adopted sister, now seeking revenge. The postmodernist mingling of genres and the use of quotation and pastiche, the overlapping dialogues meant to give a sense of simultaneity and of experiences unfolding in synchronicity with one another, the unleashed mixture of violence and humor, desperation and poetry, take us to the very raw pain of displacement and scratch our psyche with the sharp edges of unforgiving realities of war, countrylessness, and American nightmares. In the following scene one sister's dream is the other's nightmare:

Vicky: You can have a nice life too. You're a pretty woman. You can have fun. You can date someone! You can marry a nice guy, have kids, go on vacations...

Shari (*sticking the gun in VICKY's mouth*): Don't try to sell me the American Dream apple-pie! I'm not buying it anymore. Have no money for it. Have no time. What do you know about me? Nothing. Let me tell you something: I have been living in the shelter next to your church for the last three months. I was there every Sunday, staring at you. You don't remember me. You don't know me. But I know everything about you. And a lot about shelters. I'm an expert. I can write a book on shelters, wars and orphanages. A survival guide.

In parallel with the violent scene of the Bechnyan sister attacking the American one takes place the scene between the adoptive parents trying to choose a name for their adoptive child. We are being thrown into the past and then back to the present again in Vicky's apartment in jittery shifts of time and place. One moment Shari is threatening and attacking Vicky; the next, Alex and Leslie, the adoptive parents, are searching for a name—Mary is "too common," Leo is "a fish name," Cleopatra is "too exotic." The intertwining of two dialogues brings us as close as is possible in real time to the experience of simultaneous occurrences. The present of the immigrant is always layered with slices of the past and anxieties about the future. The ending of the play does not bring it all together as often endings tend to do, nor does it conclude the story; rather, it unfolds new worlds, new identities, new fairy tales, and awakens a feeling of the end of the world. Stanescu uses fairy-tale structures and archetypes only to overturn them and burst the balloon of their happily-ever-after.

Once upon a time, in a poor village of a small country torn by wars, a country where people had birthdays every day, so they could invent new names and new lives for themselves ... *(whispering)* Katoni avi? Katoni avi? *(shouting)* In a cold cell dwelt a woman named Shari.... Katona Anglika! Katona Anglika! I speak English! Good English! I know the best stories! In English! They are all true! *(whispering: lies, lies)* Baliga.... Baliga.... *(She lights the last match)*.

What if there are no more stories to be told. To be invented. Nothing. Just a cold reality. A silent cemetery of dreams...

(*Silence. She's lying on the floor.*)

Vicky appears, dancing in red shoes. Swirling. Laughing like a child.

Vicky: Zaka! Zaka!

They look at each other.

Shari: Zaka ... yes ... da ... why not? I am Zaka, snow, memory, past ... yes, that's good, I'm ZAKA, that's all I am. *(beat)* Thank you.

Lights fade. A noise, the cell's door gets opened. Light. Snow. Blackout. Spotlight on the word END written on the wall. And snow. More snow.

The space that Stanescu creates through her suggestions of sound and visual cues is threatening and does not offer the comfort of home or the coziness of a settled existence. Her humor is unforgiving and cutting as it blends the uncompromising violence of fairy tales with the real violence of our modern wars and displacements of citizens. One cannot take comfort or refuge from life's vicissitudes in immigrant literature as one would in actual fairy tales or fantasy writings, but one can certainly find plenty of occasions for questioning and reconsidering our world, shaking presumptions about what is home, what is identity, what is happiness, and one can certainly experience the unsettling yet exciting adventures of discovering new countries, real or imaginary, utopian or dystopian.

Pavel Zuštiak: All Movement, No Words

> There is no such thing as a safe answer to the gnawing question of home. Arriving to the U.S., I was first a foreigner in this land, only to become a foreigner in subsequent returns to my birthplace. Born and raised under Communist Czechoslovakia but now as an American citizen and longtime NYC resident, I understand that one is always changing/being changed, one's kindred may see only a phantom or disguise, the idea of home too becomes this false fantasy of a romantic stasis, a lost Eden.
>
> —Pavel Zuštiak, 2013

The choreographer and director Pavel Zuštiak takes no prisoners in his dance rendition of the novel *The Painted Bird* by Polish writer Jerzy Kosinski, about a boy wandering through World War II Europe and experiencing grave mistreatment as a foreigner. The production took place at La MaMa Theater in the summer of 2013. The *New York Times* review of the show notes, "Among the awful things the boy sees is a painted bird, released back into its flock, being ripped apart because it is perceived as foreign. This image does not appear in Mr. Zuštiak's work, but the sense of threat is ever-present" (July 2, 2013). Zuštiak relinquishes words and verbal communication altogether and tells stories of loss, estrangement, violence and foreignness through breathtaking physicality and the use of bodies on stage all while literally taking the audience on this unsettling yet satisfying journey. I have chosen to discuss this performance in this chapter rather than in the last one dealing with live theater projects because Zuštiak walks the tight rope of using actors' bodies to produce texts and aggregates of meaning with exquisite choreographic inventiveness. Though not created with dialogue except for the very ending, when the suicide letter of the author of the novel is read out loud as a voice-over, the *Painted Bird Trilogy* can also be seen as a "playscript" beautifully translated into performance.

Part of the show unfolds with the audience moving and following the dancers across the performance space of La MaMa Theater in a dream-like or rather nightmare-like fashion. The combination of eerie lighting, video projections that come and go unexpectedly at different points in the performance space and the hypnotic movement of the dancers/actors in and out of the rows of spectators, across the entire theater area, subverts any sense of spatial stability and belonging. Zuštiak's words (quoted above) about the illusion and instability that is the notion of home for the exile-artist become flesh, movement and rhythm in this production, constructed only to be continuously self-deconstructed. The relentless and tireless creation of shapes and scenes by the actors/dancers turns into a vertigo of spatial fluctuations and visual sensations. The sense of foreignness is imprinted on the spectators' conscience with unforgiving precision and wrenching accuracy as dancers' bodies flee, conglomerate, and move between crowded moments of contact improvisation, the bird-like fight of one dancer crossing the stage, and many dancers moving like one body

Pavel Zuštiak, *Painted Bird Trilogy*: La Mama Theater; June–July 2013; directed by Pavel Zuštiak. Jaro Vinarsky, lead dancer/actor in the first of the three-part performance ("Bastard"), in a solo piece evoking the loneliness and alienation of crossing foreign lands and being treated as a foreigner (photograph: David Kamerman).

disintegrating and coming together again and again. Foreignness, alienation, and the loss of and search for home are again themes and states of existence that demand an instability of forms and a fluctuation of structures. Zuštiak guides his actors' movements and trajectories on stage with a stunning awareness of that need.

If there were such a thing as the postmodern body, Zuštiak would have found it in this arresting production in which moods become bodies and bodies travel in a relentless arc of production and destruction. And I do not mean postmodern body in the sense of bodies refashioned by means of body art, tattooing and piercings, but in the more philosophical sense of bodies as texts that move and act in a process of producing meaning, while honoring their carnal and physical reality and while flowing on stage in a perpetual expression of mind, thought, emotion and desire. This theater/dance production illustrates the postmodern utopia of bringing disparate parts together and allowing them to co-exist in a disorderly yet provocative manner; in the words of Tobin Siebers, it reflects the attempt of postmodernism to "create a picture with emphasis on all the parts, while avoiding conflictual dualism" and creating a "grand narrative," based "on the rejection of grand narratives" (1994, 8).

Zuštiak's show is an overlapping of exile narratives as the director/choreographer superimposes his own experience of exile and of former life in communist Czechoslovakia onto Kosinski's haunting novel about World War II–torn Eastern Europe, ethnic prejudice and cruelty. As the *New York Times* review notes, "'*The Painted Bird*' may have been about World War II, but you can also sense the 40-year-old Zuštiak's impressions of Czechoslovakia after, and during the Prague Spring and Soviet repression" (Brian Seibert, July 2, 2013). From the overlap and mingling of two East European artists' war traumas and exiles emerged a work of art that moves beyond words and chooses the haunting physicality of human bodies as a medium for the expression of foreignness, spatial confusion, uprooting and the ever-daunting question of home.

The show is divided in three parts titled "Bastard," "Amidst" and "Strange Cargo," which vary quite a bit in tempo, choreography and overall mood. The first section is mostly a solo dance by Jaro Vinarsky that evokes a search for something across open spaces, confusion and the torments of an outcast's journey. Towards the end of this section, however, dancers in street and casual clothing invade the stage from among the audience, and the piece radically changes into a contact improvisation dance that may evoke crowd mentality, thinking and acting in unison, as bodies mirror and mimic each other's movements, or mass suffering and extermination as they droop and fall to the ground like a house of cards. The second section, "Amidst," brings the audience on stage, in fact closing off the audience section so that we do not have the choice of sitting down but are made to wander around among the dancers' bodies, in foggy, dim lighting with troubling video images projected above our heads. We are indeed "amidst" dancers/characters/individuals on a journey through unchartered and foreign territories. The dancers surprise us at any moment as they appear and disappear in unpredictable moves and pirouettes from all directions, from behind screens, from behind clouds of fog, creating a constant spatial confusion and sense of being irreversibly lost. The audience is forced into presentness and the creation of meaning as we are taken into the itinerary of the dancers almost against our choice, as if to suggest the experience of exile in its tormented physicality of being "here" while wanting to be "there," while remembering lost faraway places and yet rambling across time that is taking the shape of indefinite spaces. The last piece changes aesthetic and mood entirely and is a large ensemble piece. The audience is seated on stage in opposing rows, mirroring each other. This section is more theatrical, is acted in pantomime and reminiscent of spaces and situations possibly from Nazi camps or past communist bureaucracies, interrogatories, threatening scenarios. There are intimations of torture performed at the limit of the tragic and comic, the stage is occupied by office furniture and anxious bodies and the pantomime follows a rushed rhythm infused with anxiety. Throughout all three sections a sense of threat, torture, brutality and loss permeates the spectacle and the theater space either through the actors' movements or in video projections.

In my interview with Zuštiak, he eloquently explained some of his aesthetic choices and creative processes while pointing out the organic blending of form and content and the role of the audience members in creating meaning and finding their own multiple interpretations of the show.

Domnica Radulescu: Do you believe that the experience of exile influences not only the content of your art and of the stories you choose but also the form and the aesthetic of your theatrical work and performance art? If so, in what ways?

Pavel Zuštiak: The content, form and overall theatrical experience that I am creating and proposing to the spectator are all considered and interrelated. The form stems from the content often to support it or create a theatrical tension. For example with *The Painted Bird Trilogy*, which I conceived as three independent evening-length shows presented individually were eventually presented as a four hour cycle. Hopefully adding up to more than just a sum of its parts.

The little boy who is the protagonist of Kosinski's novel keeps encountering new environments at every turn of his journey. I attempted to create a similar sense of unknown, displacement, disorientation and unpredictability in the audience by changing the theatrical framing for

Pavel Zuštiak, *Painted Bird Trilogy*: La Mama Theater; June–July 2013; directed by Pavel Zuštiak; Pallisimo Ensemble. This scene offers a sharp contrast with the "Bastard" part of this trilogy as the stage is being invaded by people dressed in street clothes coming on the stage from all parts of the theater, including from amidst the audience (photograph: David Kamerman).

each of the three segments of the cycle. "Bastard" (part 1) is presented on a proscenium stage where the audience is seated in the safety of a theatre seat. This is challenged and the table turned allegorically toward its finale in a moment where a mass of 50 plus performers floods the stage and eventually face the audience. Who is looking at whom? "Amidst" (part 2) is performed in a black box with no seating, audiences move freely within the live installation with three performers and three musicians, surrounded also by five video projection surfaces. In "Strange Cargo" (part 3) the audience is seated on two sides of the stage, tennis court style, facing the other half of the audience, audience facing audience, audience facing itself. At the beginning of each part the audience does not know what the rules of the space are and is discovering them throughout the show. This also creates a sense of unpredictability that contributes, hopefully, to a heightened state of the spectators' senses and their heightened awareness.

DR: Do you connect fractured or fragmented theatrical form, nonlinear structures and chronologies, overlapping narratives to the form of your stories and the orchestration of your theater/dance pieces on stage?

PZ: What thrills me about live performance is the meeting—communion—that takes place in real time between performers onstage and the audience. In an ideal situation the energy between the two loops. Both ends grapple with the content that is being proposed. There are myriads of entry points and interpretations into this work. I desire for the work to become like a prism that when hit with audience's awareness, attention and personal histories will expand and be enriched by what the audience brings to it. They co-create the theatrical event.

In "Bastard," during the ensemble scene towards its end an image emerges of a mass of bodies lying prone on the floor. We refer to the scene as the "body carpet" scene. Although the source material deals with World War II specifically I attempted to create a scene of abstracted atrocity that could be read within any cultural or historical context thus creating an open image.

Just like in life where we experience and witness multiple narratives all at the same time and fragmented, I want the work to offer a rich landscape that would satisfy narratively yet provide no absolutes or singular interpretation.

DR: Could you point to specific moments or directorial choices in the *Painted Bird Trilogy* that you made with the intention of underlying the sadness of exile, loss and political trauma?

PZ: "There is no essential difference between war and any other traumatic experience," said Jerzy Kosiński in an often-cited interview given to *Paris Review* in 1972. In "Bastard," Jaro Vinarsky, is the outsider, the "other," silently witnessing atrocities surrounding him. At first, he fears his "otherness" is the cause of it or his deserved punishment, eventually finding it to be his strength.

In "Strange Cargo," the final, most physically intense part of the trilogy, conceived for five performers of strikingly different physiques, the dancers shift between confrontational scenes in which they threaten one another to moments of alienation and disconnect; none of the meeting of outsiders concludes in community-forming unity. The audience, arranged on either side of the theater, seems encouraged to take sides as brutal and intense episodes unfurl on stage.

Zuštiak's challenging of the audience, playing with our gaze, our sense of place and the relation to the performers, the unpredictability of the actors' movements, their various positions in the space of the stage, and their relation to the audience indeed awaken our senses and keep us in a state of troubled alertness. In the anxiety of displacement and spatial confusion, the startling comings and goings of the actors and their unpredictable interactions with each other and the audience keep us on edge and urge us towards meaning-making as if our lives depended on it. We are to some degree, as he pointed out in the interview, co-creators of the show, and that is both a thrilling and a terrifying task.

The *New York Times* review noted, "The instability of outsider and insider is the trilogy's strongest through line. Its most common action is people looking at other people. Again and again, interchangeability is enacted, as sequences are repeated with the roles of perpetrator and victim swapped. Yet the work continually draws attention to particular individuals, particular faces, either with a literal spotlight or through stillness amid motion" (July 2, 2013). In the end the reviewer, though, finds that the production lacks coherence, saying the show is "a profusion of ideas that don't cohere." Indeed they don't, and I do not believe Zuštiak intended to make his ideas fully cohere or for the pieces to form a unitary whole. Rather, it is in the controlled incoherence of the show and in the quilting of unhinged sections that I find the troubling and provocative nature of the production, as it tries to evoke through the movement of bodies and the creation of image the disjointed experiences of exile, atrocity, and war. It is in the frustrated expectation of coherence and logic that the troubling nature and beauty of the show reside.

In contrast with this slightly tepid *New York Times* review, Kayt MacMaster offers an enlightening and perceptive review in BWW Danceworld.com (2013) and praises precisely the indefinite and fragmented nature of the production, noting that it "travels through realms of transformation and bravely confronts the manipulative qualities of time and distance. It is raw and interrogational, yet the information produced is organized meticulously to uncover a sensation that is uncomfortably intimate and intentionally well hidden." The reviewer stresses the sense of a "post-apocalyptic world" and the "overarching, ear-to-the-ground nervousness," noting, "Zuštiak's trilogy *The Painted Bird* is rare in the sense that it is as intimate as a personal narrative and as authentic as historical nonfiction." He concludes that the "full experience is accessed because of the multi-dimensional approach to dance theater production—superb lighting, brilliant musical composition, skillful and straightforward performers, and authentic costuming. Essentially, Zuštiak conveys many visions as one vision. He tells many stories in few words." It is indeed the almost kaleidoscopic nature of the show and its many overlapping layers of performance and meaning-production that make it a powerful theater art piece about displacement, loneliness, atrocity, and—in tandem with all that—our own responsibility as audience or witnesses.

The dancers' bodies on stage look for homes and spaces of rest, just as the audience is made to follow them and look for spaces where they can rest, see, have a glimpse of the movement on stage or simply just stand in a corner and wait for the next image, sound or movement. The audience members are literally taken out of their spaces of comfort and made to wait, ramble, or wander; to experience a sense of loss and discomfort as they follow the dancers' unpredictable steps and turns through foggy and ever changing spatial configurations or as they sit mirroring one another across the stage with the actors' bodies in between the two rows. Both the loneliness and togetherness of bodies is incarnated on stage through a tireless flow of movement, joining, separating and rejoining in the rhythms of music that is often as strident as the lights, as haunting as the video images projected in various spots above the audiences heads. The interrupted and resumed flow of movements and bodies together with the stridency of sound and light effects echo what I have traced so far as a certain postmodernist aesthetic of rupture and disjointedness, of overlapping styles and realities. In the exile zone of no man's land that the *Painted Bird Trilogy* successfully manages to evoke, words have lost their grounding, their weight or their hold on reality, as they have changed into pure form. The aesthetic of this work that incorporates dance, video projection, theater and pantomime is in itself a freeing form of exile from the trappings of linguistic communication. The form of this work is simultaneously its content and reflects what Siebers has considered to be the center of the postmodern desire: an utopia that desires "what lies beyond the present moment" (1994, 3). Exile, being an existential state that is suspended between an irrecoverable past, an uncertain present and an unfathomable future, in between real spaces and lost spaces of nostalgia and yearning, also fuels the postmodern utopia as it desires always what lies beyond the present moment and the inhabited space.

Exile Is My Home: Personal Testimonies on Creativity and Exile

It is rarely part of conventional scholarly books to blend critical analysis of certain bodies of work with the critic's testimonies about or analysis of their own creative endeavors. But the present study does not claim or attempt to be such a conventional study. Feminist performance studies, in particular, often offer refreshing personal testimonials of the critic herself in an attempt to enhance the relevance of the theory and the urgency of the practice, to personalize and give an edge of authenticity to it, and to stress the importance of the personal experience vis-à-vis the political gesture. In this section I, too, will cross this severe academic frontier of would-be objectivity and offer several insights and testimonial evidence about my own creative and theatrical endeavors as an exile-writer in the United States. Having moved with some consistency in the course of my career between the critical and the creative, between analyzing works of literature critically and writing my own fiction and theater, I have drawn several useful conclusions and insights about the creative struggles and aesthetic thrills of writing across languages, cultures, and geographies, from a place of margins and displacement. Like bell hooks, who often theorizes on margins, otherness and the experience of race from her own personal experience of growing up and living "behind the tracks" in the margins of a small Kentucky town, as an African American woman in the segregated society of the fifties and sixties, so dare I also theorize from my particular place of displacement and yearning as a creative artist working in the United States. As for hooks,

> The effort to speak about issues of space and location evoked pain. The questions raised compelled difficult explorations of Silences—unaddressed places within my personal political and artistic evolution. Before I could consider answers I had to face ways these issues were intimately connected to intense personal emotional upheaval regarding place, identity, desire [2002, 203].

From the day I set foot on the gritty streets of Chicago, my first American home, as an ambitious, scared and penniless refugee, I identified with the "huddled masses" of different races and many yearnings a lot more than with any of the suburban white women in expensive furs strolling on Michigan Avenue. As Mona, the heroine of my novel *Train to Trieste*, explains on her first day in Chicago, "This is a city fit for my hunger."

I come from a country of margins and of liminal spaces, a crossroads at the top of the Balkan peninsula, from a region neither here nor there, a country with a bloody history, some truly infamous episodes such as the extermination of almost half a million Jews during the Nazi genocide and the grave mistreatments of the Roma people. I also come from the home of some important innovators and initiators in the areas of the arts and intellectual inquiry, some of whom I mentioned earlier—Tristan Tzara, the founder of the Dada movement; Eugène Ionesco, the initiator of the Theater of the Absurd; Constantin Brancusi, the initiator of conceptual sculpture; Paul Celan and his haunting poetry; and the list could go on. However, like many Romanian intellectuals both in the country and spread in the many diasporas across the world, I am acutely aware that, as a country of margins in the "periphery" of Europe, "Romania is frequently perceived in the West as weighing on the lower end of a well-defined hierarchical relationship between the receiver and the producer of knowledge"[11] (Minjares 2006, 3). On the other hand, such was the "self-effacing internalized provincialism" (2) of Romanian intellectuals at the beginning of the nineteenth century that according to an anecdote, a group of writers and philosophers wrote a joint letter to Napoleon asking him to invade, Romania. Obviously Napoleon must not have found Romania too much of a profitable country to invade, even though he showed much interest in neighboring Poland. Though not in the least as illustrious as the coveted French language, the mellifluous kin language I come from is formed largely of the Latin grammatical structures and vocabulary, yet also tapestried with many Slavic, Greek, and Turkish additions, just as its cultural landscapes are tapestried; and a country of some stunning physical sites that have imprinted themselves in my psyche irrevocably, as one's native spaces tend to do. As someone who has lived at crossroads and comes from a country of crossroads, as someone who has chosen to throw herself into the larger unknown crossroads of the world, I have created heroines who choose to live at crossroads and who are equally enriched and torn by the experience of living in the spaces between cultures, languages, and geographies. This is what my heroine says towards the end of my novel *Train to Trieste*, in the chapter titled "Indiana, Crossroads of America":

> I have chosen to live in the flattest, most boring landscape of the American Midwest. I love the flat, flat, wide endless cornfields, where the sun rises and sets with a vengeance every day, having no mountains, no valleys, no undulating earth to hide behind. This space soothes my heart. I have the illusion, in its straight immensity that my native land is just over the horizon. Just beyond the stretch of cornfield is the backyard of my aunt and uncle's house in the Carpathians [2008b, 261].

At the very end of my play titled *The Romanian Reunion: A Country That Devours Its Own*, the protagonist, a Romanian refugee woman torn between the different spaces and cultures she straddles, says: "I choose America, I choose *my* America. I choose graffiti. I choose people of all colors. I choose highways across the Blue Ridge Mountains. I choose my tapestry of wounds to a clean slate. I choose my constantly breaking heart instead of an un-broken, un-breaking heart" (Manuscript, 27). This play treats another reality of the exile, which has recently been termed "trauma tourism" by exile critics. While most people travel abroad and use their summers for relaxing journeys, my heroines and I go abroad to get trauma. We return to the countries that had once hurt and destroyed us in many irreparable ways and from which we once ran for dear life, in order to get hurt again and have our old wounds reopened. Thousands of my compatriots, myself included, return to our native land summer after summer, with renewed illusions that maybe we were wrong about our country, that maybe things have changed so much that we will be able to find a utopian Romania, only to reopen old wounds and carve new ones on top of the old ones. If anything, a consolidation and palimpsest of wounds may be achieved in this mad game of "trauma tourism," something like a picture of scars tattooed on our homeless souls and bodies. Consequently, very much in keeping with my overall thesis of this book, my own theater and fiction bear the profound marks precisely of this "tapestry of wounds" and palimpsest of scars carved onto my homeless, wandering soul. It was largely as a result of questions I had received from reporters, journalists, readers and audience members during interviews, readings and performances of my fiction or dramatic works over the years and in different parts of the world that the very idea of this book emerged and that I developed the notion that the experience of displacement reflects itself not only in the choice of topics but also in the stylistic form of my works and of the works of many expatriate artists.

Having worked in the theater for over three decades and having studied, researched, and directed the works of many expatriate playwrights or artists, particularly from Eastern Europe and Romania, the reflection upon my own creative processes sparked this idea and catalyzed it to unfold into a theorizing need with some urgency. Following the fall of communism in 1989, waves of exciting new works by expatriate playwrights and artists made their way onto American and West European bookstands and theater stages. While the works of poetry and fiction by widely known and even Nobel Prize–winning exile authors from Eastern Europe such as Joseph Brodsky, Czeslaw Milosw, Milan Kundera or Herta Muller were already drawing international attention with their bold aesthetics and revolutionary political stands, theater artists from these parts of the world burst onto Western stages mostly following the 1989 revolutions. Theater directors such as Andrei Serban, with his wildly innovative and experimental productions of plays from the classical repertoire such as Chekov's *Uncle Vanya* (nominee for the Golden Mask for best director award)[12] or *The Cherry Orchard*, or contemporary playwrights in the line of Eugène Ionesco's absurdist and surreal aesthetics such as Matei Vişniec or the new generation of Romanian playwrights such as Saviana Stanescu, Stefan Peca or Gianina Carbunariu, have straddled with panache the frontiers between their native country of Romania and their adoptive Western countries, whether the United States, France, or England. Such artists have learned to function in restless artistic negotiations between several cultural and linguistic landscapes and have produced bold theatrical products that (as already shown in the earlier discussion of Stanescu's theater) bear the profound marks of an aesthetic of rupture, carnival and postmodernist stridencies and incongruities.

When asked about my own work and its various temporal or aesthetic incongruities, autobiographical echoes, stylistic stridencies, or anachronisms, I often felt compelled to explain various aesthetic choices in terms of my experiences as an immigrant in the United States. By examining my own creative processes and the artistic products derived from them, I came to realize that the experience of having survived a dictatorship and uprooted myself from my native country has profoundly affected the ways in which I write, orchestrate my plots, develop my characters and craft my authorial voices. I will first give an example derived from the creation of my novel *Train to Trieste.* It is not without relevance that I bring up narrative in a book about theater, first because the story of my novel is orchestrated in scenes, tableaux, and vignettes similar to the structure of a play or the unfolding of a film, and second because storytelling and voice are components that cross over between genres. Thus certain insightful conclusions can be drawn about theater while looking at narrative, and vice versa: interesting thoughts can derive in the analysis of narrative by comparison with theater. In the introduction I compared the creation of empathetic characters in novels versus theater and the eliciting of empathy in readers versus spectators via Suzanne Keen's explorations of this phenomenon at the level of narrative. Plays also tell stories, and narratives are also dramatic. Exiled novelists and playwrights quite often mix genres and create hybrid narrative/poetic/theatrical works in what I earlier called a nomadism of genres and aesthetic forms.

In *Train to Trieste* the first half of the novel, which takes place in the heroine's native country of Romania, stretches over three years, while the second part, which takes place after her escape and settling in America, stretches over twenty years. The two parts are almost equal in terms of narrative space and page numbers. Whenever asked about this seeming incongruity, my answer has been always the same: due to the abrupt and traumatic break with her native space, language, culture, the perception of time becomes distorted and fluid for my heroine, as she has no more stable or recognizable connections with a particular space. Having to recreate her sense of self in the new adoptive spaces, while also living with the nostalgia of the lost spaces, the passing of time is perceived in irregular and uneven blocks or stretches. As opposed to the time spent in her native geography, where despite the hardships and the dictatorial oppression, she was well rooted in a culture, family history, familiar spaces and traditions and therefore time was rolling in a more steady and condensed flow, in the new country she is focused on establishing the basic connection with unknown spaces, customs, people and culture while longing for her lost self in the old country.[13] She is now living in an in-between space; she carries out a "hyphenated" existence. This inner fragmentation leads to an often confused and irregular perception of days, months, years, for she has to live and catch up in days what the natives took a lifetime to acquire: the knowledge, understanding and rooting in what for her are new and unfamiliar surroundings. According to a reviewer, *Train to Trieste* "powerfully combines the intensity of first love, the confusion of politics, and the melancholy of exile" (Fisher 2008).

The same is true for my dramatic works, which I developed following my works of fiction: my heroines move in disjointed leaps through histories, expanses of space and chronologies, and have patchy identities. Generally the construction of my plays reflects the same disrupted relation between my characters' selves and the perception of time and space, often with multiple endings or reversals between endings and beginnings, not unlike Saviana Stanescu's plays. For instance, the plot of one of my most recent plays, *The Town with Very Nice People*,[14] is driven by the heroine Roxana, an immigrant from Romania who has settled in a small Southern town where she has been the subject of various forms of discrimination and marginalization at the hands of the town's people. The tableaux move between scenes of the town and the townspeople talking about the heroine Roxana in the present, scenes of Roxana in the past and scenes in a utopian future in which she reconstructs the bigoted town into a place of vibrant diversity called the Town of Multicolor. The heroine moves between the dystopian world of the small Southern town and the utopian universes of real or imagined places across the world, driven by the hunger for diverse and multicultural worlds and always searching for a home. In the creation of my play, the mangled chronologies and fractured narratives imposed themselves with an imperative and urgent force. It seemed to me the only way in which to deal aesthetically with the heroine's broken sense of self and belonging, with her experience of straddling cultures, cities, geographies and languages and trying to make sense of, or develop some sense of unity out of, the chaos caused by displacement and the alienation of exile. The different endings, some of which consist of the heroine's death after which she comes back to life in the next tableau, illustrate in an almost hyperreal manner the idea of starting over as an immigrant again and again and again in search of an ever-elusive and never-to-be-grasped American Dream. Breaking the suspension of disbelief by having the characters refer directly to the play and its multiple endings and even begging for an ending arose both from my own resistance to closure and my embracing of multilayered cultural identities that I keep reinventing as I go along the tenuous paths of my own search for a home, or rather, for homes.

In my first play, *Naturalized Woman*,[15] the protagonist Nina, a Romanian immigrant who is going through a grueling naturalization interview in the immigration offices in Chicago in the eighties, is confronted on stage by her double—an actual character—who embodies her alter ego. Between the two of them, one carries the memories of home and of the adventure of the escape from Romania while the other is implanted in the unfolding of the naturalizing interview and its urgency. Unlike narrative, theater offers the delicious opportunity of embodying concepts and using the actor's body on stage to incarnate otherwise abstract notions, revolutionary ideas and ineffable realities. It also offers the possibility for those of us whose identities are splintered across countries and languages to re-embody and play with our diverse selves and bring them all together in a cathartic manner on stage. For artists such as myself, Saviana Stanescu or Aglaja Veteranyi, who have experienced oppressive regimes and their various stifling strategies of thought control and censorship, followed by the radical psychological jolt and the excitement of starting all over again in a situation of freedom of expression, playing with form, developing non-linear, non-realistic and unabashedly revolutionary aesthetics is both an opportunity and a necessity, a utopian experimentation with the freedom to invent and a political necessity. State-sanctioned art in former communist countries such as Romania, Bulgaria, Poland or Hungary, the so-called socialist realism, lacked depth and inventiveness; it was humorless and uninspired precisely because it had to offer a one-sided, flat image of only one acceptable view of humanity: the party line perspective. That party line, much like the universe described in Orwell's *1984*, imposed itself on every aspect of our physical and spiritual lives so that artistic inventiveness and the flight of the imagination were precious strategies of survival and resistance, of finding freedom within oppression and keeping our individuality despite the regime-imposed uniformity of thought and language.

In one of her statements about writing the immigrant experience, Saviana Stanescu talks about her own past, growing up under the Romanian communist dictatorship: "The fact that I was born and raised in Romania means nothing and means everything.... Your past is inscribed under your skin and you cannot erase it" (2013). This statement ties in with the aim of this book, which is to delve into the ways that the past "inscribed under your skin" translates into our art and diverse forms of expression. To illustrate the point about how the experience of dictatorship and exile has influenced her art, she says:

> I am a product of communism—or so I once believed. I spent my formative years under the totalitarian regime of Ceauşescu. I learned that all people are equal but—as the joke goes—some are "more" equal than others.... Growing up, I realized that words were not always telling the truth even if they were declaimed with conviction on the National TV.... I became convinced that that was the role of the artist in society: to be able to think and express what other people couldn't. To awaken their sleepy consciousnesses through her/his creative power and imagination. To be subversive. I believed (and I still believe) in the arts as our means of redemption and tool for creating a healthier society [2013].

With regards to the form of modern political theater, she proclaims with Nietzschean rebelliousness, "It ceased to be only about unity of time, place and motivation long time ago. Aristotle is dead." In the quilting, nonconventional manner I promised at the beginning of the book, I will use some of Stanescu's statements as a lens through which to look at my own theatrical creativity as an artist writing the immigrant experience. At the end of my play *The Romanian Reunion: A Country That Devours Its Own*, the heroine cries out to the world about her conflicted identity and the fact that she cannot erase her past out of her blood, hard as she tries:

> I can't undo having been born here, I can't undo having left here. I have to live with it all. I have to make it all one cohesive painting even if it has holes and rough edges and dark corners and fuzzy spots that no one and not even I will ever understand. I have to carry my countries on my back like the snail, like the tortoise, like the sea turtles.
>
> ...It's all such a bloody mess! Like a bleeding kaleidoscope of shapes and smells, like an unfinished love story botched and cut to pieces and still breathing and still crying and still whispering broken words and sighs. Like an unfinished comparison, an unrealized metaphor. Neither here nor there, and yet everywhere [Manuscript, 24].

The structure of the play itself displays this kaleidoscopic nature of the heroine's divided psyche as it moves in rushed sequences from dialogues to monologues and from realistic scenes to dream moments to a collage of simulacra, music and dance that takes place in the Romanian village museum where impersonations of Romanian peasants from the different regions of the country beckon the heroine to stay in their houses. In *Naturalized Woman* I not only proclaim the death of Aristotle in the play's dialogue itself, but my heroines invoke the ghost of Mrs. Aristotle in order to find an ending to the play in a mockery of the classical concepts of *deus ex machina*, reversal of fortune, *peripeteia* or even the famous catharsis. Seen from the perspective of the female experience, the reality of immigration and naturalization imposes new and irreverent aesthetics that keep unfolding and changing under our very eyes, just as the exile experience imposes a constant recreation of the self, and overlaps genres, chronologies and spaces. This is how the conversation with Mrs. Aristotle about the ending of the play goes:

> **Nina:** Is this Mrs. Aristotle? I would like to speak to Mrs. Aristotle please.
>
> **Mrs. Aristotle:** You want to speak to *me*?
>
> **Nina:** Yes, I am very sure. Mrs. Aristotle, I am here in the United States of America with a group of friends and we are in this play about a woman who is a refugee from Romania and just got naturalized after all sorts of obstacles and now we want to find a memorable way of ending the play. How should we do it?
>
> **Mrs. Aristotle:** Well my husband would end it in *catharsis* of course, or with a *deus ex machina* device coming after the *peripeteia*, the reversal of fortune of the noble hero. Who is your noble hero?
>
> **Nina:** We have no noble heroes here, Mrs. Aristotle. This is a different kind of play, it's a modern women's play.

Mrs. Aristotle: Oh Zeus almighty I've never heard of anything like that. But you know, I've never left my house, ever! Where is this United States? Is it where old Troy was?

Nina: No, it's a whole new continent. Why don't you come down here with us to celebrate and then we can talk more about how to end this play [Performance script, 2012, 26].

After Mrs. Aristotle joins them in the present time in America, the play ends with each of the women giving birth to a new self and to a new world, a utopian world in which under the magic wand of Aretha Franklin, who joins the women at the end of the play, the very concept of refugee is being reinvented: "From now on, Refugee is going to be a good word, a word that makes you think of roaming happily across a poppy field in the summer. Refugee will mean free and gutsy, brave enough to start all over. It will be the sequel to the Natural Woman song, and it will go like this: You Make Me Feel like a Refugee Woman… (Performance script, 2012, 26)."

In *The Town with Very Nice People*, the heroine and her story make constant leaps through space and time, as the play starts in the future, moves back to the past, then to the present, and then to an ending in a utopian future. There is no unity of time, space and action; these unities are deliberately broken and even mocked as the play has four different endings, each in a different space: the French Riviera, where the heroine invents a modern paradise of glamor and joyousness; an American city to which the heroine has fled, leaving her small Southern town, and where she reunites with her woman lover; the heroine's funeral in the small Southern town, at the end of which she jumps up and is resurrected from her coffin; and finally the utopian recreation of the small Southern town into the Town of Multicolor, where each corner becomes a riveting space of diversity and imagination at work. The play ends not with an ending but with a beginning in which the tourist guide, who for years had given the historic tour of the town speaking only of its Confederate history, now has changed his tune to the description of a postmodern, futuristic town to which everyone with a creative mind and open heart can immigrate: "Yes, sure you can immigrate, find asylum, and settle in our town, the immigration process is really easy. All you have to do is choose a corner or make a corner of your own and that gives you a share of the town, a portion of ownership. It's Marxist capitalism softened with performance art" (Manuscript, 43).

Both *Naturalized Woman* and *The Town with Very Nice People* use dark humor and a festival atmosphere in which the margins are brought to the center, refugees save the day, immigration is the new cool, and quilted identities and life stories are at the forefront and are also literal storefronts in the town's new urban configuration. As someone whose work is also out there in the world being read and analyzed by other critics, in sharing my own experience as an expatriate writer I can reaffirm, in tune with my compatriot Saviana Stanescu, that indeed "the fact that I was born and raised in Romania means nothing and means everything." Furthermore, given the kaleidoscopic and ever-fluctuating nature of the immigrant experience, for many of us "Aristotle is dead" while Brecht is more alive than ever, as are surrealism, Artaud, feminist theater, political theater, or again in Stanescu's words:

> After Shakespeare, August Wilson, Brecht, Beckett, Ionesco, Lorca, Genet, Koltes, Grotowski, Pirandello, the Greeks, African performances, Balinese dancers, Japanese Noh, Chekhov, In Yer Face Theater, devised, multi-media, site-specific, cross-ethnic, feminist and queer performances, surrealism, expressionism, post-dramatic and environmental theater, etc., etc., we can't only rely on the linear cause-effect plot-driven way of telling a story [2013].

Postmodernist aesthetic and theory come in handy, with their embracing of class, ethnic, cultural, sexual, and racial diversity and their insistence on the specific against the universal, the particular against the essential, and the margins against the center. The splintering caused by displacement leads to a better understanding of the relativity of moral values, principles of beauty and goodness and of the importance of specific location and time in defining identity. I lucidly embrace Lyotard's skepticism of metanarratives and his theorized reliance on small narratives, singular events, local personal stories, and "petits récits" that are grounded in the specific and diverse human experiences rather than in any unifying discourse.[16] Maybe exile is the fundamental source or illustration of the postmodern condition, as it jolts one out of all certainty about the stability of truth and breaks any illusion of an immutable spatial, moral or cultural reality. In the utterly social and carnal art of theater, we need to recognize the importance of splintered personal stories that are told in the rhythm of the individual stream of consciousness, even though the shards and the edges may feel uncomfortable and foreign at times. But foreignness may just be that space "of radical openness."

My own novels and plays are about being one's own country, carrying one's country in a suitcase, in a bundle of memories, in one's mind and creativity, and about creating utopian worlds within, outside and around the constantly shifting yet alluring frames of the American Dream. And again, it's not just about what it's about; it's about the shape it all comes in. It's about the form. The looseness of these invented countries of immigrants, of those of us who "loiter" around the world with no country of our own, leads to loose and jumbled structures, to an art that self-subverts and is in constant contradiction with itself, all while it searches for a holistic unity. The theater of immigrant or expatriate playwrights simultaneously urges us to find new countries within ourselves and create what Saviana Stanescu refers to as the "patchwork" of our multicultural, multinational realities, always grounded in our own personal stories. Mostly one can learn about the art of being one's own country, as the heroine of my novel has learned decades into her journey of exile, self-recreation, trauma tourism and circling around the world: "And maybe I will get used to having two countries, to having no country, to being my own country, and stretching across the Atlantic, one foot in the Indiana cornfields, the other in a berry-filled meadow in the Carpathians, like a huge baobab tree" (2008b, 301). Similarly, in a memoir crossover short story titled "How I lost My Memory and Never Got It Back," about my serial episodes of "trauma tourism," I say at the end: "And perversely, you know you would do it all over again, for the thrill of leaping into that vortex of the unknown as your plane takes off and for the thrill of sprinkling your memory all over the world. And for the thrill of being your one and only suitcase. You can take it everywhere" (2014).

In line with this voracious desire of the refugee psyche to spread across the world like a baobab tree, the heroines of my latest play, *Exile Is My Home*, are intergalactic nomads in search of a home, carrying a portable home on their backs, being their own and each other's homes and exploring different planets to compare with their native planet earth. They explode and mock all notion of belonging yet are torn with yearning to be able to do just that. The plot unfolds in a perpetual present and moves across unrecognizable spaces while memories of countries, songs, a particular house, a pond, a tree, haunt and devour them with longing. On one planet they literally devour the landscapes in an attempt to quench their yearning for a home and in a desperate hope that their nomadic existence and the imaginary spaces they create will suffice. Famished for a home and a place to settle, one of the heroines in the play cries out: "I'm hungry. I'm hungry for home, I'm hungry for dirt, for earth dirt, birth dirt, native dirt. All this exile stuff is crap. I'm going to eat everything. I'll eat everybody. I'll eat you all until I have a home. I'll be everything then, like a big fat pregnant Goddess of the universe" (2014a, performance script [at Theater Lab], 19).

The eerie and fantastical style of the play is an attempt at evoking the inconsolable sadness of exile and homelessness while confirming its enormous potential for adventure, cultural and geographic richness and ultimate freedom:

> **Mina:** I was born in exile. Where were you born?
> **Lina:** I was born on the way to the market.
> **Mina:** Oh, that makes sense then, that's why we get along. Why we sort of

get along. In any case, it's better than with the others who were born somewhere precise.

Lina: Yes, those who were born somewhere precise are always such sticklers for geography. They say things like I was born in a little town in the country of Vdnsk or the country of Mantrak, in the big city in Chesterbester, in a small house, in a big house, in a house with a big yard with a cherry orchard, in a small house with no cherry orchard, in an apartment on the third floor with a cactus in the window, so on and so forth. Booring! And then they spend the rest of their lives remembering where they were born and grew up and talking about it like it's important or something.

Mina: I know what you mean, blaah, blaah, right? I was born here, I was born over there, I am the son/daughter/sister/brother of so and so in the Textile Industry, of so and so at the Factory of Paintbrushes. Good for us that we were born in the air.

Lina: Nowhere.

Mina: Out there.

Lina: In the air.

Mina: If it wasn't so damn inconvenient to spend one's life on the road I would say living in constant exile is the best home there is [2014a, 4].

Whether that is true or not is highly debatable, but one thing I know from my own negotiations with an exilic existence is that we expatriate or exiled artists make a home out of our art while being at home in a multitude of places around the world as long as there is art. If exile is your home, then the shifting nature of that home is bound to reflect itself in your art, just as the fact of being born and raised in Finland, Russia, Japan or the United States is going to leave its marks on your forms of artistic expression. What I understood about the complicated and often jumbled puzzles of the theater works I explore in this book has largely been through the processing of my own journey across margins and chasms, across geographies and cultures, and through creating art from these existential acrobatics. While there are other forms of theater and art that make use of postmodernist and fragmentary, unconventional narratives and aesthetics, the splintered art forms emerging from the experience of exile are both an attempt at wholeness and an avid search for home.

Radmila Adamová: Eastern Europe Meets Indochina

Not only in America can the American Dream germinate and grow into a driving force of action in search of happiness, freedom and a home. Czech playwright Radmila Adamová has explored a new phenomenon of immigration in her own native Czech Republic—the situation of Vietnamese refugees settling in Prague or Brno in her play *The Alluring Little Shop*. In our global society of migrations of large parts of populations due to wars, brutal regimes, economic and natural disasters, the American Dream or its equivalent in other Western countries lives in its shimmering yet irresistible elusiveness wherever there is relative freedom and a democratic system of government as well as some measure of economic prosperity. Sometimes such a dream may mean just peace and clean water, while other times it may mean the possibility to express oneself creatively; it may mean simply having a roof over one's head or having a beautiful home with a car in the driveway. All are variations of the immigrant dream. This of course is relative to where the refugees are coming from and how the lack of freedom, oppressiveness or economic disarray that they are escaping may compare with the state of the country they are emigrating to.

Marcy Arlin, the director of the Immigrants Theater Project, says the following about Radmila's newest play, which she directed at her New York–based theater:

> Based on 2010 interviews with Vietnamese living in Prague and Brno, the play is about a daughter in a family of small-store owners in a Vietnamese shopping center.... Adamová's work is theatrical, funny, and smart, yet her characters are full of a discontented sadness, interspersed with a wild hope for a better future. Adamová states that the play is inspired by true stories, characters, and ideas [2012, 53].

In the interview she gave me, Radmila Adamová talked in detail about the creative processes that went into the orchestration of this play, the only one on the theme of immigration she had ever written. Some of her techniques resemble Brechtian epic theater: the strategy of alienation as the characters tell their stories in a detached manner, address the audience, come in and out of character and also the use of collage in combining long monologues with poems and songs, with quick paced dialogues, with recurrent episodes or conversations that work like a leitmotif throughout the unfolding of the plot—the struggle of a Vietnamese family to live, work, and survive in their new country. I asked her, "Do you believe that the experiences of war, political instability or oppression and/or exile/immigration influence not only the content of your theater and the stories you choose but also the form and the aesthetic of your theater. If so, in what ways?" This is her response:

> **RA:** Until now I have written only one play that focuses on exile and immigration. It differs from my previous plays in the way that it strongly accentuates the story and the narration; it includes long monologues. The main characters talk directly to the audience—and via the content and the form they make their message much more pressing.

> While I was writing the play, I met several adult descendants of Vietnamese immigrants and I listened to their stories and the stories of their families. Moreover, I was inspired by the material created in Marcy Arlin's workshops that focused on immigration. These facts influenced content-wise my writing. My stories are not dramatized real stories, but these stories have given me a certain look at the characters' way of thinking. I was also influenced by the Vietnamese fiction and poetry I was reading at the time. In fact, that is why excerpts of Vietnamese poems are used in the play. I also searched for inspiration in Vietnamese folk culture—I viewed Youtube videos of traditional Vietnamese songs and dances [2013].

It is interesting to note, of course, Adamová's claim that the format of her play, its structuring and character creation, differ drastically from her other plays precisely because she is writing about immigrants and is exploring the cultural clashes, shocks and dislocations that her characters undergo due to their status in society. Although Adamová is not herself an expatriate playwright, she adopted and identified with the drama of expatriation, immigration, and displacement, and in turn that identification seems to have demanded a certain unevenness, an unconventional mixing of dramatic modes, and a series of breaks in the flow of its narrative that coincides with the uneven, fractured existence of the characters themselves. The play is dark and starkly written with occasional bursts of Vietnamese poetry and song and with the action unfolding like sliding plates: the slide of the Vietnamese immigrants, the mother/aunt, son and daughter who tell their stories of departure, resettling, the hopes and struggles in the new country; then the sliding plate of the two Czech characters, Svejk and Vodnik, who tell their own versions of the interaction with the young Vietnamese woman as they are all working on the production of a play and recount their attempts to marry her in order to help her with her visa and legal status in the country; the sliding plate of the broken recurrent phone conversations between the son, daughter and grandfather back in Vietnam interrupting the flow of the main story of the immigrant family; and yet another sliding plate of the gruesome character of the murderer recounting how he killed one of the kids at his school, which happens to be the same school that the young Vietnamese girl attends. The style of the play shifts between naturalistic storytelling and monologues, Czech or Vietnamese poems, and fast paced dialogue. The storytelling is unsentimental and does not avoid depictions of violence or of depressing life situations, at times using dark humor. When asked about how she deals with the representation of violence on stage, Adamová noted the following:

> The world has always been full of violence whether we admit it or not. If the violence is a part of the story, situation or a character, it is vital that it's part of the play—nothing should be hidden from the viewer. In order to

> reach catharsis, it's important to depict also the dark side of the world and it is upon the author which form he or she chooses—whether it will be realistically depicted violence or a different form of it. I tend to use the former mode of violence depiction in my plays. In this sense, I am influenced by the European coolness drama or in-yer-face theatre of the 1990s which tried to grab the audience out of their lethargy and shake them. Sarah Kane totally shattered my concept of theatre in breaking the taboo of depicting violence on stage. Thus the violence in my works is depicted explicitly via dialogues and situations but it's also hidden between the lines [2013].

Besides the more obvious violence perpetrated by the character of the murderer, Adamová treats the experience of immigration and displacement as an act of psychological violence, a powerful trauma to one's mind, spirit and status in dark and stark ways that are reminiscent of Said's powerful statement about the irreparable pain of displacement. Indeed, as Adamová reveals in her statement, the play illustrates to some degree the marks of "in-yer-face" theater in the way she treats the trauma of dislocation to a different country. The stark honesty of the characters' accounts, and the neo–Brechtian coolness in the recounting of facts, description of emotions and thoughts render the reality of exile even more poignantly. The character named He, who has left Vietnam for Prague at the expense of great sacrifices on the part of his family, relates his first reactions at the dislocation and relocation he is going through in the following monologues that are interspersed with dialogue lines of his parents, his sister, the agent who is arranging for his trip to Prague, and the phone conversation with the grandfather. The interlacing movement of stories and dialogue conjures up revolving stages on which the actors would be situated as they deliver their lines:

> **He:** I wanted to change clothes at the airport but I realized my bag got lost. I had a few things there that I definitely didn't want to lose. Outside, the bus was waiting for us. I couldn't wait for the bag and I didn't understand what they were telling me. The interpreter said there wasn't time. And I thought, I'd probably never see those few things again, ever. I got on the bus with the everyone else. I thought the worst was behind me. Only it had actually begun. On the bus.
>
> **She:** I like poetry. But I like theater the most, of all things. However, as I have already mentioned, I am a chicken. I am going to business school.... And it's because my brother is either really stupid according to everyone or really clever. You see, he draws and paints amazingly but he doesn't have a brain for studying.... But my parents see him as useless already, they don't care about the drawing....
>
> **Father:** I was so glad I had a son when he was born!
>
> **Mother:** What will happen to us?
>
> **Father:** Come on, we have to go to work.

Mother: And he was so well proportioned when he was born. He looked as if he was going to be smart. Very, very smart.
Son: Who? Who was going to be smart?
Father: What about school?
Son: I got a D in law.
Father: How is this possible? Didn't you study?
Son: I study but it doesn't make any sense.
Father: Don't look for the sense, study more!
Mother: Your grandpa is going to call on Saturday. He wants to talk to you.
He: He
We sat down and the bus left the airport. I was looking at the sky and the airplanes that were taking off. If I could, I would get on one of them and fly back home. It was a shock. Then I watched the highway and cars and the landscape. Everything was so different. I knew it would be. I had been looking forward to that. But, now, on this bus, I didn't like it. The sky was gray, a thin layer of snow was covering the earth. I was cold. I had only the wedding suit on. A man sitting next to me handed me a cotton shirt. I covered my shoulders with it. That was the last time anyone did something for me free of charge.
Grandson: Hi, Grandpa.
Grandpa: Hello, grandson. How's school?
Grandson: Not that great.
Grandpa: I heard. Your parents are desperate. All of us here, too. Grandma sends warm greetings and is asking me to ask you to get your life together finally and start studying. Our hearts hurt when we hear your mother cry. That's not good, my boy [2012, 4–6].

Even though Adamová claims realism for this play, and the epic or storytelling monologues have a realistic or even naturalistic "in-yer-face" truthfulness, the overall structure and orchestration of voices, the unfolding of the plot, and the development of the characters do not in the least fit the conventional realist dramatic style. As she herself has noted, some of the violence is felt "between the lines." There is often quite an abyss "between the lines," which coincides with the "in-between," the "hyphenated" universe where immigrants function in their adoptive countries. The staccato rhythm of the dialogues, monologues, and poems evokes with sharp edginess the interrupted existence of the characters, the jolts and bumps in their newly acquired identities, their desires to assimilate and fit in their new world, while staying imperfectly tied to their native land.

That this edgy, non-humanistic aesthetic[17] of rupture and displacement fits also within the fluid frames of postmodernist art is illustrated meta-theatrically by the characters themselves as they are rehearsing for a play and discussing the confused state of the Vietnamese refugee girl:

Svejk (*smoking*): I told her to write some kind of a comedy, finally, so that people can laugh, have fun. But she said no, not her ... she makes art.
Vodnik: I really don't know what's going on in her head.
Svejk: Post-modernism [2012, 10].

The Vietnamese girl refuses both of their offers or advances and recounts her own version of the story, the brief dating period with one of the Czech boys, in a detached alienated way, pointing delicately to cultural differences that in fact amount to a cultural abyss.

She: So I tried. He was cool. I liked that he knew how to cook and he wasn't afraid of it and had no problems with it ... no separate gender roles. He didn't distinguish between us in that sense, which is so common in our culture. But we broke up. He wanted to sleep with me—this kind of physical stuff was very important to him. It was too fast for me, so I chickened out. I also had the feeling that he wasn't only into me. Always when we were somewhere out on a date, he stared at other girls and that wasn't nice. Our boys don't do that. We are not friends anymore [2012, 11].

The Vietnamese man, the character of He and the brother of She, recounts in the same style through long monologues his ordeals of working in a factory, sleeping in a dorm, hearing the terrifying sounds of a Vietnamese woman being raped and beaten next door and finally running away towards freedom. The style of his monologue in the following quote is markedly different from the previous ones of his recounting the desperation and hopelessness of his immigrant life, as it is touched by the lyricism and poetic joyfulness of the discovery of freedom.

He: I ran and I ran and I ran. For hours. I ran and I ran. First through the city, through the streets, parks. Then I ran out of the city. I ran through the woods. For a long time I ran through those woods. It was dark, I stumbled, fell and stood up again over and I couldn't breathe, but I heard the sound of a dog barking in my ears, so I didn't stop. I don't remember what happened then. I probably fainted because I was awoken by the cold. Or maybe by the sun. I was lying on a meadow. When I opened my eyes, I was surrounded by crowns of trees and beams of light falling to the ground in an uneven angle. I felt a snowflake landing on my nose but it was just a dim and shivering feeling which disappeared in a second.... In that moment I realized I was a free man. I was a free man after a long time and I felt happy. If I could stop the time in that moment, I'd lie like that forever, looking at a sky filled with birds. I thought of my mom and my sisters. I missed them [2012, 26].

Earlier in the play, He and She sing a lyrical and melancholy song that lifts the harsh realism of their immigrant ordeal to a heightened level of utopian beauty towards the erasure of all pain in a complete state of calm and smoothness.

> **He & She:** My heart is like a sunflower blossom
> it turns around a thousand times
> to a single sun
> your heart is like woven boat
> changing thread for a thread,
> touched by none
> without a scar [2012, 24].

Adamová also cleverly uses polyglosia, namely the mixing of several languages within the same text, in this case English, Czech and Vietnamese, which adds an element of authenticity and color to the portrayal of the immigrant experience. She renders in a delicate manner the paradox of being torn between native language and culture and adopted language and culture but also enriched by the multiculturalism that the immigrant incarnates. Since there is such a wide cultural and linguistic gap between the Vietnamese and the Czech realities, the juxtaposition of the two startles and suggests the enormity of the task of assimilation that the immigrant must perform in her or his new life and country. The shifts from harsh realities of immigrant life to idyllic landscapes of moral and physical beauty; from long monologues to fast paced dialogues between the members of the immigrant family or between the Czech boys in love with the Vietnamese girl; from poetic musical sequences that lift the mood from the darkness of an inescapable reality to the ethereal world of delicate gestures and lyrical images amount to a theatrical technique of collage that breaks the suspension of disbelief periodically and that surprises us into zones of discomfort, questioning and uncertainty. The postmodern break with humanistic, universalizing aloofness and the postmodern predilection for incongruous juxtapositions of styles, tones, languages, and cultures, the mingling of different forms of marginality, the mixing of aesthetic modes and cultural constructs are at work in Adamová s troubling and strangely beautiful play that circumvents the dramas and traumas of exilic realities with a lucid and uncompromising eye.

Dorota Maslowska: Nomadism on Drugs

I close this chapter with a zany play, *A Couple of Poor, Polish Speaking Romanians*, by Polish enfant terrible playwright and writer Dorota Maslowska (2008) that matches the first play discussed, Veteranyi's *Why Is the Child Boiling in the Polenta*?, though at a much more strident octave. Both

Dorota Maslowska, *A Couple of Poor Polish Speaking Romanians*: Trap Door Theatre; June 2009; directed by Max Truax. Tiffany Bedwell (right); Kevin Cox (left).

works are road stories, tales of nomadic existences gone wrong, about people of scrambled East European identities, developed theatrically in shocking language and chaotic spatial trajectories. However, where Veteranyi's dramatic poem abounds in a certain harsh lyricism and poetic inventiveness, Maslowska's play is a roller-coaster of demented, vulgar language and outrageous actions performed by unsympathetic characters caught in a mad road race for money, drugs, sex and an unclear object of desire. This play has been produced to rave reviews—or at least to intrigued reviews—at Soho theater in London (2008), at Trap Door Theatre in Chicago (2009), and by East River Commedia at Abron Arts Center in New York (2011). Dorota Maslowska is not an expatriate or immigrant writer. She started her writing career with novels that knew immediate success in her native Poland. The first was made into a feature film and the second received Poland's highest literary prize. She started writing plays after her novelistic success, and she wrote *A Couple of Poor, Polish Speaking Romanians* (cited hereafter as *PPSR*) at the invitation of TR Warszawa.

I am including this play in my study because it creates characters who find themselves in the most extreme forms of spatial, existential, and moral confusion and social indeterminacy as they ride madly towards an unclear destination in a taxi that they apparently have hijacked.

Reviewers and directors seem to be puzzled, if not stuck, on the use of the word "Romanian" and by passing references to Romania in the play, even though the action does not takes place in Romania but Poland and it is unclear whether the characters are indeed of Romanian origins or whether they try to pass as poor Romanians. Rather, Romania, as the author herself explains, is more of a dystopian psychological location, the margins of margins of Europe even for East European Poland. More interestingly, the hyper-nomadism of the characters brings to mind the Roma people or the "Gypsies," who in the nineties invaded Poland and just like in France, Italy or Spain raised an enormous surge of xenophobia and ethnic hatred. The false cognate of Roma and Romanian, which appears to identify the official name of the Gypsies, derived from an Indian dialect, with the name of the country derived from Latin, has often led to mistaking the identities of Romanians for Gypsies. This in turn has caused much indignation, if not hatred, among many Romanians in their own country or in the Romanian diaspora. Inversely, and feeding this hate creating confusion, many French or Italian natives and obviously Polish as well use the word Romanian to also refer to Romanian Gypsies, thus collapsing nationality with ethnicity in a muddle that for most Romanians is offensive and unacceptable, particularly given the long history of discrimination and abuse suffered by Roma people across the centuries and in the present in Romania. Most likely, as the translator of the play also suggests, Maslowska has deliberately made use of the word Romanian in its most ethnically confusing way, to refer to people in the most extreme state of nomadism and homelessness yet wildly avid for gain and drunk on the unleashed consumerism of the East European countries following the fall of communism. In the nineties and early two thousands, many Western countries were flooded by Romanian immigrants and migrant workers, some of whom were of Romani origins. As one of the most prominent scholars of Roma culture, Ronald Lee has noted, "While the EU countries have been very vocal about Roma persecution in these would-be member countries..., they have been equally unwilling to accept Romani refugees fleeing this intolerance they had so vociferously condemned" (2008, 17). Now that East European countries such as Hungary, the Czech Republic, Poland, Romania and Bulgaria are also part of the EU and therefore travel between EU countries is open and unregulated, the waves of Roma and Romanian immigrants and migrant workers have increased and in turn contributed to a renewed surge in racial violence and discrimination at the hands of the citizens and authorities of many Western countries; "murders of Roma, Gypsy bashing, and the burning of Romani homes became common in many countries" (Lee 2008, 15). What makes the combination of Polish and Romanian in Maslowska's play both puzzling and humorous is the fact that it suggests a migration of poor people from one post-communist country to another, thus placing the Romanian or Roma or Romanian Roma people in the very lowest of the social and economic echelons. As the translator notes in the introduction to the English edition, "One of the toughest provocations in the play is the use of the word Romanian. Like many of Dorota's provocations it is uncomfortable. Romanian gypsies arrived in Poland in the early '90s to experience a xenophobic backlash and Dorota's vivid memory of this informs the play" (2008, 2).

Dorota Maslowska gives a riveting account of her own nomadic experience of crossing Poland in a car, which served as inspiration for the play. She claims she started creating the play "from the most surrealist ideas and characters with operetta and futuristic psychologies." Indeed her characters—Parcha and Dzina, who are driving for hours in a taxi whose driver is terrorized into obedience by this ad hoc couple, and the taxi driver himself—have "futuristic psychologies," if by that Maslowska means thick caricatures with no evolution or progression, talking and moving in incoherent swirls. Like some postmodern version of *commedia* marionettes or type characters, they are stuck in their own addictions and manipulated by the relentless rhythm of the new capitalism and the consumeristic rage that it engenders. Here is Maslowska's description of her own wild journey across Poland, which gave her the sense of being a foreigner and an exile in her own country:

> I recreated almost moment by moment an episode of my life from that time, traveling the length and breadth of Poland. At the time I wasn't especially happy and the only thing I remember was a display of petrol stations, disposable places, with plastic cutlery, condoms, false food from a microwave, where the feeling is of being no one and being nowhere, or rather a feeling of being anybody anywhere, and a feeling of being stripped of definition and mask that was realized with a unique sharpness. So Romania—in this play—is rather not a popular country in south-eastern Europe, but a state of social weightlessness, when suddenly all costumes, props, ideas definitions and honorary decorations become unverified, and unimportant life tickets.

What she describes with color and poignancy is the Balkan state of hybridity, the "hyphenated" existence and the no man's land of the edges of Europe in the post-communist era, overlapped onto other marginal spaces and catapulted into the most crass and demoralizing trappings of capitalist materialism, global transplants, food, plastic, unrecyclable remnants of human passage, indeed an orgy of simulation and scraps of simulated objects and existences. Baudrillard would be fully vindicated by the description of this amalgam of cheap simulacra of the margins of Europe invaded by American plastic and "disposable places." Maslowska delves into a scary sociological nowhere in her desire to break the entrapments of "disguising yourself as someone other," where markers of a coveted middle class existence float like plastic bottles and bags in the once-sparkling rivers of post-communist Romania and other post-communist countries. The director of the New York production of the play, Paul Bargetto, considers it "a reflection of our own mass popular consumerist culture, being reflected back in a brutal, very funny way" (Lockwood 2011).

The prologue of the play starts with "voices from nowhere" in an enumeration of real and made up drinks, cars, expensive-sounding objects, Italian- or Spanish-sounding things invented from Romanian, mock combinations of words: "Martini rose, seicento, martini bianco, martini cough. Martini rose, seicento, los trabantos, Buenos aires. Fiat uno, cinquecento, seicento, fellatio. Mirel matie, cantare, romy schneider, coffee and tea." The "voices from nowhere" further unfold into voices of witnesses reporting to the highway patrol that they had seen "these oddly behaved people" and tried to get rid of them, were disgusted by them, even tried to run them over with a car. "We're from Romania, I can show you a flag" (*PPSR* 19), the couple apparently said to introduce themselves as they were trying to get a ride from a stranger. "Me and the wife stopped at the garage, the Orlen, and this very bizarre couple approached us, one of them, a woman, she's pregnant ... and shouting that they're Polish-speaking Romanians" (*PPSR* 19). According to one of the witnesses there is no such thing as a

Polish-speaking Romanian. The entire first act consists of an alternation of the driver's report to the police about the frightening episode with the Polish speaking Romanians and the dialogue between Dzina and Parcha as they are riding in the car, trying to persuade the driver to take them to Wroclav, or Gdansk. Their identities and relation to one another change throughout the play, but at first they act as a poor Romanian couple: "We are poor, honest Polish speaking Romanians. My wife is pregnant, she is going to Wroclav to visit a doctor, a specialist, because she has these metastases, cysts, it's just a mess there in her belly. Et cetera ... so we'll all go together, then—to wherever you are going?" (*PPSR* 21). As the driver loses his cool and becomes more concerned, the verbose Parcha keeps imposing his will with an avalanche of clichés or invented clichés about Romania and Romanians, taking the art of simulation to its highest pitch and gaudiest arrangements. "We Romanians, woa! We're feisty people.... To be honest, her real name is Pyralgina, but she tells everyone to call her Dzina. Pyralgina, Codeian, Aspirina, Cafeina ... these are traditional Romanian female names. In Romania, Saint Pyralgina was the patron saint of drunk girls coming home in the dark" (*PPSR* 22). The driver gets angrier to no avail at the Romanian couple, who are trying to steal his Christmas tree car freshener, entirely suspended in their made up, con-artist world of overlapping disguises and simulations of a dystopian national identity.

> **Dzina:** Did you buy it or did you make it yourself?
> **Driver:** How made it? How: made it myself? Did I cut it out of a carpet? You can buy this anywhere, go in the garage it's full of them. What fucking planet did you drop down from?
> **Parcha:** Look at her, how pretty she is. My little rapscallion. Well, her teeth are a joke, but it was hard life that did it, isn't it darling? Romania knows no mercy. All our lives we've been eating scraps of meat, it destroys the bones. And rubies, I mean rhubarb and for sweets we liked Rennies [*PPSR*, 23].

Maslowska either knew Romanian con artists herself or did a lot of ethnographic research for this play, because as a Romanian myself who grew up during communist times, who has been returning regularly since the early nineties and has often come in contact with Romanians or Roma people in the streets or restaurants of various Western capitals from London to Paris to Madrid, I recognize bits and pieces of a certain cultural flavor and psychological twists, English equivalents of self-pitying language used for conning, a mixture of charming deceit and uncontained greed. In short I recognize that ineffable cultural *je ne sais quoi* that makes a Romanian recognize another Romanian, a Pole another Pole or a Spaniard another Spaniard from the first words uttered, from the first gestures and actions performed, together with the specific class stratification that the respective Romanian, Pole or Spaniard might belong to. Act 1 ends with the longer testimonial of the driver to the police about the violence and robbing performed by the couple of Romanians: "And, Officer, they saved the worst till last. He held his knife at my throat and demanded money and car keys. And she was pointing at me with a handgun that she took from her bag—cocked no doubt. They were out to kill and rob me. They demanded valuables, jewellery, electronic equipment and kitchen appliances, to be specific they demanded a Thermomix, which I don't even own and never have?" (*PPSR* 36). We never find out in the rest of the play whether this criminal act ever took place or if it is the imagination of the driver scared by two poor-looking, unseemly characters trying to get somewhere. In the prologue, one of the women witnesses starts her testimony by saying: "They seemed so nice, so nice, but when we saw the terrible state of their teeth, then no, I flatly refused to give them a lift" (*PPSR* 20). Maslowska deliberately allows for ambiguities in which the opinions and testimonies about the poor, Polish speaking Romanians are like floating signifiers, which could have a signified in the actual reality of the couple's behavior or could be made up from markers in their appearance that suggest poverty, promiscuity, delinquency, and criminality and lead to stereotyped images. Bargetto, who pointed out that the play presents great staging challenges, also notes "the obvious xenophobia that Maslowska is sticking her finger in, that of course plays very well here. The Driver, who's such a major character at the beginning, he's straight out of Glenn Beck—everything he says is completely paranoid but also extremely emotional" (Lockwood 2011).

In the next two acts the pace of the play picks up at a maddening speed as if the action is unfolding through the altered conscience on someone on speed or hallucinogenic drugs. The layered identities, ethnicities, disguises, and made-up realities of Parcha and Dzina keep unfolding in a delirious rhythm as the couple is catapulted into some kind of road trip gone really bad. First they are walking along the road at night, "crying, in a complete psycho-physical mess" (*PPSR* 37), next they get into a taxi driven by a completely drunk woman, after which they are "in a ditch," after which they find themselves knocking on the door of the house of an old man who is supposed to be the real Father Grzegorz, who by the way is played in "the very popular TV soap" by no other that Parcha himself, who all this time was trying to get a ride to get to Warsaw to the TV set for the filming of the next episode to play the role of this famous father. If ever Aristotle and all of classical theater with their unities of time, place and action were mashed and ground up to a pulp and then spread over centuries of theatrical tradition, this play has managed to do just that with brio. Exile doesn't even begin to describe the existential confusion of Maslowska's characters. As for postmodernist aesthetic, Baudrillard's worlds of simulated realities, they are left behind in this theatrical apocalypse of the soul that is Maslowska's play. We also find out that Dzina and Parcha are not at all a couple but had just met that night at a party, are each more drugged up than the other, and apparently not only did Parcha did not rob the driver, but he gave away five thousand dollars and his MP3 player to a "lunatic." Meanwhile Dzina has no idea what she had done with her son, whether she left him in daycare or whether her mother ever picked him up, and she obsesses about him till the end of the play. Bargetto notes, "Part of her motivation, I think, is to be saved, so they start playing that out. It's twisted, but a real core of the play that makes it universal" (Lockwood 2011). Neither of them knows exactly whether they have had sex with each other, to the great dismay of Parcha, who hates "to have casual sex with women who think of me as Father Grzegorz" (*PPSR* 61). And it also turns out that Parcha has only been pretending to be a Polish speaking Romanian:

> For the last eight hours I've been pretending to be a Polish-speaking Romanian and describing the harmful effects of eating scraps of meat, but suddenly it turns out that I'm a drugged-up Pole on a comedown, a Polish speaking Pole on a comedown and I wake up in some kind of field, in some fucking blackcurrant patch in East Bumblefuck on the border with Kazakhstan, in a Kazakhstani cardigan [*PPSR* 40].

There are echoes of Boccaccio's *Decameron* and his character Andreuccio di Pietra,[18] who in one night loses all his money to two prostitutes, falls in a pile of shit, is shut inside a tomb by robbers, and is finally saved from the tomb by other robbers trying to steal jewels from the tomb, while Andreuccio himself had stolen a big ruby off of the finger of the dead archbishop buried there. There are echoes of *King Ubu*'s mad travels and wars across real and imagined countries, always trying to get to Poland or rule over Poland, which is as much an imaginary country as Romania is in this play. Inside these two characters—crossing real and imaginary spaces, hitchhiking, running along dark roads, falling into ditches, losing money, trying to get somewhere important, having been tricked into drinking a "concoction," riding in a car with a drunk woman driver who gets into an accident and dies at the wheel "bleeding on an airbag," while "there is a wild boar lying in front of the car," getting to a house in the forest, and ending up on the "coal barge *The Ibuprofen*" that "comes through the snow" where "they are welcomed by the Romanian crew and passengers"—there is a warped amalgam of archetypes of adventurers, of picaresque heroes from old stories, plays, novels, and movies. I also see echoes of the *commedia dell'arte* characters, in particular the famous Arlecchino, always greedy for food, money, and sex, always disguising himself to get away from authorities and bad masters, duping and getting duped, a con artist and thief yet also a charmer and poet, always on the run, yet always escaping and ending on top with the last laugh. Arlecchino concentrates in his gregarious self all the bawdiness, greed and material fullness displayed in the carnival. Parcha seems like a more crass version of this fascinating *commedia* character. However, what gives the character of Parcha a postmodernist edge is his TV-actor status playing Father Grzegorz, thus his doubling up in the realm of virtual reality. Bargettto is of the opinion that in Maslowska's play, "It seems that salvation and meaning only reside in the media. I think that's part of what Dorota's going at: In the value system, there's some kind of vacuum that's happened" (Lockwood 2011). And to prove the point, he used TV screens in his production, playing sequences of the mentioned soap opera that had been filmed by the company before the show.

Dzina and Parcha are postmodern, antiheroic versions of the eternal wanderer, the reckless adventurer, the Gypsy with a great flair for inventing sensational stories such as this: "We're Polish-speaking Romanians, we're lesbians, queers, Jews, we work in an advertising agency. Like I said before we're going to Israel to plant trees and these inbred fucks out here won't even give us a lift" (*PPSR* 47). After the accident Parcha drinks "greedily" from the woman driver's bottle, takes her Seiko watch with diamonds that are "the height of fashion," and looks for cash, instead finding chewing gum and contraceptives. Towards the end he worries: "To be honest, I'm scared, deep down in my subconscious I fear that I might not be rewarded with eternal life" (55). The hodge-podge of disconnected objects, foods, places, the overlap of marginalities, of real and imagined spaces from Kazakhstan to Israel to Bumblefuck, the mixture of drug-induced hallucinations and atavistic impulses, create simultaneously a sense of hilarity and terror, of excitement and complete alienation in an inhospitable world. Picaresque heroes usually find redemption and a safe place in the end, acquiring some understanding and drawing lessons from their mad travels. Not so much for Parcha and Dzina. At the end of the play "he goes into the bathroom and sees Dzina hanging there" (64). This was the successful attempt at suicide after a previous one in which she cuts off her own cord around her neck and runs after Parcha to the barge. These characters' journey is a wild chase through forests of simulations of simulations; they are modern junkies with demented dreams of glory and richness, without any lessons learned, no safe place to get to, nobody to love, just the howling sound of irremediable loneliness and a few quick sparks of a tormented humanness. They seem to be in free fall in the cracks of what a critic has referred to, in speaking of the Balkans, as "the lands between" and the territories between "fault lines"[19] (Stokes 1999, 16).

Without being herself an immigrant or expatriate, Maslowska has captured something profoundly visceral and terrifying about the alienation of the lost wanderers of our times, "loitering" refugees, Gypsies on the run, homeless con artists, a hopeless yet imaginative humanity from the very margins of the periphery of the fragmented, mysterious Balkans, the "Orient of Europe,"[20] where the ultimate exile is the individual lost in the mirage of conglomerates of unrelated objects—the endless chaotic bazaars at the edges of Europe. She has captured these mindboggling mixtures of realities and unrealities in theatrical forms that combine pungent language with cinematic sequences, carnivalesque disguises and mistaken identities, with Brechtian-like testimonials given by different people along the road or in a sleazy diner, with raw humor and grotesque imagery, creating a sense of unstoppable movement between spaces, realities, life and death. For if anything, her characters are always on the move, even when they are hanging on a rope.

If Veteranyi takes us on a literal circus journey, with a caravan, tent, wagon, trapeze, and sensational acrobatics, and all its color, sadness, and danger, and in the process of the storytelling transforms the nomadic circus existence into a larger metaphor of the fractured condition of the exile, Maslowska shoves us inside the startling avatars of a mismatched couple that display many of the trappings and signs of a series of circus acts gone out of whack. The dizzying rapidity of movement of the two characters, the unlikely actions similar to bad circus magic (such as Dzina first hanging on a rope and then cutting off her own rope), the way in which the two keep falling and coming back up from ditches or broken cars like two clowns on a chase, and mostly the simultaneity of howling sadness and raucous humor, make of their journey also a circus on wheels. Parcha says it best when he is at the depths of despair and at the height of drug rush and remembers "this feeling of being a wizard": "And your surname is Magdalina? Dzina Bagdelina? I'm sorry, ha! You have to give me that, in the deepest shit of my life, at the lowest fucking point, my sense of humour still radiates" (*PPSR* 37). But theirs is a dark circus with a bad ending where the "heroine" actually dies and where you wouldn't want to take your children.

The theater works studied in this chapter offer a wide spectrum of perspectives on the themes of exile, the immigrant experience, and the American Dream or variations of it in theatrical languages that defy conventional, Aristotelian and strictly realist representational drama and in turn create edgy, startling and often disturbing modes of expression for the stage. While all are built around or traversed by what Said has called "the unhealable rift between being and a native place, between the self and its true home," they each stand out for their innovative aesthetic that partakes of some of the dislocated nerviness of postmodernism, some of the Balkan carnival and circus culture, and some of the outlandish mixtures of the tragic and the comic in collage-like methods that bear the specificity of the author's cultural and personal realities as expatriate or international citizen.

Two

Theater of War and Genocide, and Theater Dystopias

It is ironic that in military terms one says "the theater of war" to refer not to the kind of theater that forms the subject of this book, namely the artistic creation inspired by historical wars, but to the actual episodes, spaces and moments in history where actual war was or is being fought. The expressions "theater of war" and "theater of operations" have been used since the end of the nineteenth century to refer to episodes, spaces and moments in history where humans are killing and are being killed in real wars. "Theater of war" refers to the "entire land, sea, and air area that is or may become involved directly in war operations," while "theater of operations" refers to "the part of a theater of war in which active combat operations are conducted."[1] Both terms were first used consistently to refer to World War I and then to World War II. It makes sense, after all, for in any war, just as in any theater, there is a protagonist and an antagonist who, depending on the angle one fights or watches the war from, change places and roles; there is a stage, of course, which is the actual space where the war is being fought; there are actors who play different roles, from the generals giving the orders to the soldiers actually engaged in combat; there are directors who create the larger vision of the show, namely the leaders and governments initiating and organizing it; and there are of course "spectators": we the public, the great masses of people, some witnessing, some watching and being shaken, some traumatized, others gloating, and yet others indifferent at the sight of the war. Often the "spectators" who watch their own being killed wish to escape and become exiles for fear of being caught in the fire; other "spectators" are forced to run for cover when the house is burning down or when they feel afraid of becoming like the victims they see on the stage of the "theater of war" or the "theater of operations." Needless to say, this real theater of war is not a safe space.

The theater of war that forms the subject of my study is, on the contrary, a safe space where actors and spectators choose to live or relive, in mediated experiences, moments from actual wars. This is from a desire to remember, to bear witness, and to heal, but also to be entertained and to transcend the traumas of violence through utopian scenarios. Whether this kind of political theater has made a difference or alleviated the suffering caused by wars in the course of human history, or whether it has made the world a better place as many of us would like to believe, is highly debatable. Those of us who are engaged in the creation, production, teaching or criticism of theatrical works meant either to bear witness to wars, to function as repositories of memory, or to raise consciousness about the devastation brought about by wars, would certainly like to believe so, and we are motivated in our endeavors by the notion that art can make a difference. Atrocious wars and genocides have been going on with what seems to be an unstoppable fury for decades, centuries, millennia, and art doesn't seem to have stopped them. But this line of reasoning never turns out to be a productive one, and we will never know if the ravage of wars would have been significantly worse without the respite provided by art or whether art has really made a difference, since like war, art has always been a reality of our world. Rather, I would like to argue that a certain kind of theater that has emerged during the last several decades in several areas of the world can function as a safe space from actual wars, that it can be a place of healing and of transformation because it has the potential of making more savvy, questioning and empathetic human beings out of both the artists making it and the spectators watching and witnessing it. I would also like to argue that it is largely due to its particular aesthetics that a certain kind of theater of war that does not glorify but denounces its violence and devastation has the potential of creating safe spaces and oases of resistance. I will place this theater in the larger context of political theater initiated by Bertolt Brecht and will attempt to define its particular role and aesthetic peculiarities in tandem with the artists' own credos about the necessity of such a theater for our times.

The aesthetics of the theater of war has the functions of illustrating the psychic breakages suffered by the author or, in larger terms, the community or group or nation that the author belongs to, and of surviving and possibly healing such psychic ruptures. The theater works discussed here have emerged directly and ferociously out of wars, violent political events and their aftermath, and they not only testify to these experiences but—by the very virtue of their emergence and existence almost simultaneously or very shortly after these events—also stand as a wall of resistance, a space of peace, a place of solace, truth and re-belonging.

Matei Vişniec: Consciousness Raising Through Theater

Matei Vişniec is a Romanian playwright of French expression, as he himself likes to be considered, who had already made a name for himself as a successful author of poetry and theater in his native country before he immigrated to France two years before the Romanian Revolution of 1989. He is himself an exile from what he calls the "fabulous town of Rădăuţi" (2014c), situated in the northern part of Romania, in the province of Moldavia, "the only town in the world with a railroad track that crosses it precisely through the center, through the middle of the cemetery, through the center of people's hearts, through their memories and divides it with perfect symmetry in two completely uneven parts: the past and the future."

Matei Vişniec's theater has been received with great interest and acclaim both in his native Romania and in his adoptive France and has been translated and played all over the world, including the United States, Japan and Iran. I would like to explore first the play that has known worldwide success and that has emerged from the author's visceral and passionate attempt to respond to the war of ethnic cleansing in Bosnia and Kosovo during the nineties: *The Body of a Woman as Battlefield in the Bosnian War* (henceforth cited as *BWB*). In his interview/confessional essay titled "How I Write" he recounts his experience as journalist for the station Radio France Internationale of reporting, over the course of four years, horrifying news of the

> atrocities committed in Bosnia, the siege of Sarajevo, the shells that were massacring civilians. What was happening in the former Yugoslavia preoccupied and impressed me, it was a massacre unfolding in the direct vicinity of Romania. Even more terrifying was the thought that there were barbaric scenes taking place in the very center of Europe, two hours by plane from Paris, near what we had thought was "civilized" Europe but that proved incapable of extinguishing this fire [2014a].

He further recounts his strong desire to go over to the very sites of that "barbaric" war, right in the middle of the shells and bombs to maybe "stop one single bullet from killing an innocent civilian." He talks about his feeling of hopelessness as a journalist over the four years of reporting about the war. The play *The Body of a Woman as a Battlefield in the Bosnian War* emerged from this inner agony and in particular from what was to him the culminating point in his personal crisis, namely the news of the rape camps and of the use of sexual violence by Serbian soldiers as a weapon of war and of annihilation of the "enemy": Muslim Bosnians. Vişniec confesses he wrote the play from a desire "to understand." He also ponders with crisp lucidity and bitter sadness on the persistence of war in modern societies:

> Civil society and the modern world have never been so threatened by base nationalism of a populist and violent nature. This was the original motive for my play: to write as a way of trying to understand.... To try and understand how, in the middle of Europe at the end of the 20th century, we are having to confront, yet again the murderous folly of a war with all the ingredients of a new world war [quoted in Robson 2002, 14].

In Matei Vişniec's play, the body of a woman is the site of war and violence, as the title explicitly announces. The play gives voice to a woman, victim of multiple rapes by soldiers, who tries to survive and ultimately overcome the gruesome transformation of her body into a site of violence, revenge, ethnic hatred. It follows the attempts of Dorra to heal her seriously damaged psyche with the help of her American therapist, Kate, who has come to Bosnia to help unearth mass graves. Dorra discovers she is pregnant, and Kate tries to convince her to keep the baby, for she wants to adopt it. At first Dorra is adamantly against the idea of keeping the baby, but in the end she unexpectedly decides to do so after she has seen a sign on a tree, announcing its impending cutting, together with other trees.

It is through the power of her voice that Dorra, the protagonist, transcends the damage done to her body and psyche. The play is equally a purging of her hatred toward her aggressors and a form of resistance, subversion and denunciation of the various perversions and violence of nationalism. The play follows the cathartic movements of the woman's voice, through all the nuances of rage, despair, bitter sarcasm, depression, to the ultimate hopefulness at the end. Like the other plays explored in the book, this one, too, rejects traditional theatrical forms of representation and is marked by an aesthetic of fracturing, disjointed plot, overlapping voices and chronologies, a certain stridency of stylistic modes and tone in the sense of pushing the tragic into the zone of dark humor and carnivalesque. Furthermore, Vişniec's play is a beautiful illustration of feminist theater aesthetics that moves away from the conventional norms of classical drama in ways that subvert the status quo of oppressive patriarchal structures by placing the woman's subjectivity and voice center stage.[2] In his interview Vişniec particularly stresses that he wanted to create a play from the point of the view of the most downtrodden victims of this war, the women survivors of multiple rapes by Serbian soldiers. He says: "I felt that in my play I had to give voice not to men, not to the combatants, but to women, the victims" (2014a).

Dorra is given the powerful weapon of irony and humor in a way that illustrates what feminist critics have noted with regards to women's humor: that it is often transgressive and subversive of all forms of oppression by patriarchal structures, and that it is often different from the humor of male artists or of men in general, because it usually lacks the reconciliatory dimension of classical comedy, because it expresses anger and, in the words of Judy Little (1994, 158), because it "mocks the deepest possible norms, norms four thousand years old."[3] The discourse of Dorra in Vişniec's play reflects that which Judy Little has called "carnivalizing," or "humoring the sentence," which entails a juxtaposition of voices, in which the voice of authority is both contained and parodied. Such a comic voice, argues Little, "may not be typical of realistic drama, but in some experimental plays by women juxtaposed styles occur occasionally within a voice, and the result is carnavalized discourse" (1994, 158). Regardless of the fact that the author of the play is a man, we can see this carnivalization of discourse in the female protagonist's mockery of the psychology of "Balkan man," and of the philosophy of Balkan man, which she calls "the philosophy of 'but'" (*BWB* 25–27). The cultural realities of sexism and violence against women are concentrated by Dorra in the all-encompassing, symbolic figure of evil that looms threateningly above the lives of women and that is "Balkan man." Dorra's irony deconstructs to shreds the figure of the sentimental, macho, sexist and racist men of a culture deemed by the West as not fully European, or "barbaric," yet seen from within as both "the upholder of European values and as the ultimate locus of passionate living" (2012, ix).[4] This is how Dorra assumes the voice of Balkan man, while carnivalizing it:

> The Balkans: An emotional time-bomb. In the Balkans, we really know how to drink. So, if you go drinking every day after work, life's bearable, you can go home, spend fifteen minutes with the kids. Or with the wife. The wife who is nothing but a reproduction machine. Who only knows how to nag her husband from the minute he comes in the door. That's why he comes home late and goes out early. In the morning he has a hangover. That's the best time for her to have a go at him. In the evening she doesn't dare say too much. In the evening a sense of honor is very strong in Balkan man. In the evening, if she goes too far, he'll just get angry and have another drink. Or two. Or three. Because in the evening, having spent time with his mates, Balkan man becomes sad. His soul feels pain. Grand metaphysical questions obsess and torture him. You don't understand the first thing about history my little chicken [*BWB* 25].

Dorra continues her mocking discourse to encompass the many nuances of racism and ethnic hatred, hidden behind what she calls the convenient "philosophy of but": "As soon as he's had his first drink, a sense of history is awakened in Balkan man.... He then sees the whole world through the philosophy of but. But is the key word to the Balkan soul, the mirror of their thought, the line where banal small talk crosses over into finely nuanced dialectics" (*BWB* 26). Dorra's carnivalized discourse incorporates the banality of sexist and racist discourse of "Balkan man" in a roller-coaster of bitter comedy in which she draws her therapist, Kate, moving more and more rapidly, at the aesthetic and theatrical levels in the direction of the carnivalesque reversal of hierarchies and accepted linguistic and behavioral norms, and at the psychological level in the direction of healing, survival and the reacquiring of dignity. By impersonating "Balkan man" and parodying his racist discourse, Dorra is empowered and slowly transforms her victim status into that of a courageous survivor who laughs at her own aggressors:

> Dorra (under the skin of "Balkan man"). Gypsies, I love 'em! I've got nothing against them. Come on, gypsy, give us a song! No, gypsies are great, they go way back, there's something about them that's both mysterious and joyful.... *But* at the same time ... they're all thieves, you've got to watch them, they steal horses, sheep, chickens, children.... Enough's enough and to top it all, now they're even stealing our own sacred folklore [*BWB* 36].

Dorra goes on in a similar vein, faster and faster, in the rhythm of music that changes to illustrate each new culture, through all the Balkan nations, from the Albanians, "poor souls," to the Bulgarians, who are "good gardeners," but "a frustrated lot," to the Turks, "a force to be reckoned with, one foot in Asia, one foot in Europe," to the Jews, "good people, and what's more, wherever they settle the economy flourishes, ... But ... let's not forget that they crucified Our Lord Jesus Christ," to the Romanians, "the only Latins in the Balkans, ... it's amazing what a hit Romanian whores are now in Turkey—even ours are starting to learn Romanian now so they can pass themselves off as Romanians in Istanbul." Finally, the scene veers into the absurd, when the two women start applying the same paradigm to "the Blacks," "the Mexicans," "the Indians," "the Aztecs," "the Patagonians," with the lines getting shorter and shorter and the rhythm of the play acquiring a delirious absurdist character:

> **Kate:** Oh, I like the Aztecs...
> **Dorra:** The Aztecs are nice...
> **Kate:** Yes, but...
> **Dorra:** But...
> **Kate:** But
> **Dorra:** But they're Aztecs! There you go!

KATE: Ah yes, that's it, yes, that's fucking it, I forgot, they're fucking Aztecs... [*BWB* 45].

The parodic reversal of sexist and racist discourse of "Balkan man," the ultimate figure of authority and tyranny for Dorra, places the two women within the realm of reversals specific to the carnival as theorized by Bakhtin. The language of the carnival is impregnated, according to Bakhtin, by the logic of things "à l'envers," of the world "upside down," of "constant permutations between up and down, face and back, and by the most diverse forms of parodies, travesties, profanations and buffooneries" (1984, 9–19). Through the use of carnivalesque discourse, the protagonist of this play has produced a momentous reversal of power between the victim and the victimizer, to the extent that through the strength of her ironic voice, Dorra has turned her victim position into one of survivor and heroine.

The play's innovative and deliberately disjointed organization mimics the rhythm and structure of the classic therapy session with echoes of Freudian analysis yet reinvented to fit the psychological and socio-historical context of the heroines. The scenes are wildly uneven and lopsided, varying from short notes or diary pages written by the psychologist Kate to psychoanalysis-like dialogic structure in which Dorra is only answering with silence, to long monologues by either of the two characters, to the carnivalesque exchanges discussed above. Between Dorra's silences and her unleashed solo pieces there are heartrending exchanges between the two women who in the end need and help each other in equal measure, often interchanging the therapist and patient roles. The orchestration, progression and language of the play unfold like a blueprint of the devastation of the war on the psyche of the heroine. What Vişniec achieves also in the creation of his character is thoughtful and compassionate meandering through a wounded psyche and the tours and detours she takes in order to work through the memory of her trauma towards healing. He presents trauma as "the story of a wound that cries out, that addresses us in an attempt to tell us of a reality that is not otherwise available" (Caruth 1996, 4).

Kate's diary pages use psychoanalysis at the level of the national consciousness of the aggressor, in this case Serbian nationalists engaged in a war of ethnic cleansing against Muslim Bosnians. The language of the diary is almost clinical and scientific, cold and calculated, offering a striking contrast with the emotionally charged scenes between Kate and her patient Dorra, who is paralyzed in her post-traumatic stress disorder state and resisting all attempts at treatment or communication under stone-like silence. Vişniec creates in this play an aesthetic of trauma that serves not only as witness to the violence suffered by the war victim, Dorra, but also as a strategy of survival and furthermore of transcendence or overcoming of trauma. The diary pages and the therapy sessions are created in a very different dramatic mode than the carnivalesque, unleashed scenes analyzed earlier, but within the overall orchestration of the play they hold the very important place of testimonial, critical analysis of a historical situation and ultimately healing.

> See if the following concepts can better explain the sources of ethnic violence in Bosnia:
> Nationalistic libido.
> Libidinous nationalism.
> Infantile ethnic sadism.
> The fantasy world of a national minority. [...]
> The nationalistic imperative: the urge to dominate, the urge to threaten, the urge to destroy [Scene 1, 16].

The first therapy session between Dorra and Kate unfolds as follows:

> *Kate enters Dorra's room. Dorra sits motionless on a chair. She stares vacantly.*
> **Kate:** Hello.
> **Dorra:** ...
> **Kate:** It's me, Kate.
> **Dorra :** ...
> **Kate:** It's a beautiful day.
> **Dorra :** ...
> **Kate:** Some people are walking in the garden.
> **Dorra :** ...
> **Kate:** If you'd like to go into the garden, I'll come with you.
> **Dorra:** ... [*BWB* 16–17].

When it is by choice, the power of silence, particularly in the possession of a victimized woman, can have tremendous dramatic and psychological power. It is equally a first stage in the character's healing processes and a passive-aggressive form of resistance and rebellion against the world that has wounded and maimed her. The diary and the silent dialogue scenes alternate with Dorra's unleashed explosions of verbiage, which change the rhythm of the play. These explosions unfold first with a bitterly parodic prayer reminiscent of the Lord's Prayer and culminate in the sarcastic references to "Balkan man," analyzed earlier, that recur at various points in the play. Kate's psychoanalysis of nationalism functions as a stepping stone for the scenes in which Dorra responds only with obstinate silence. Following Dorra's first linguistic outburst there are quick repartees in which the two heroines exchange thoughts and emotions connected to the war as much as to Kate's personal situation and reasons for coming to Bosnia to unearth mass graves. By the end, the dynamics of the play moves beyond the patient-therapist protocol, and Kate becomes as much Dorra's patient as the other way around.

Vişniec's approach to the realities of the Bosnian war through the dramatic and psychological strategies of Freudian analysis is entirely unique, as words and scenes are forged from the very depths of both the personal and the national subconscious. This aesthetic of trauma and the psychoanalysis that is meant to process and heal the trauma creates an undulating dramatic rhythm that keeps the audience in suspenseful engagement and involves us in the mysterious labyrinth of a profoundly wounded psyche. In her notes, Kate wonders:

> **Kate:** Doboj Camp, Bosnia, June 1994. *(A beat.)*
> Are those ethnic groups who have never had their own nation state most vulnerable to such atrocity? Are they more at risk than others of becoming caught up in the primitive sadism?
> Amazing parallels exist between nationalistic sadism and Freud's description of infantile sadism *(a beat)....*
> And what if nationalism is nothing but a suicidal impulse? ...
> Nationalist hysteria. Mass hysteria. Ethnic defence hysteria [17–18].

The turning point in the healing process occurs when Dorra utters her anti-prayer prayer. Dark irony traverses her prayer, which anticipates the carnival of stereotype-explosion that follows shortly. This irony carries her words in a downward move towards uncompromising rage and aggression like a sharp dart piercing the earth, like the reverse, downward moving flight of a lark moving from light to darkness, from melodious song to strident cry:

> **Dorra:** I hate you.... I hate you.... I hate you....
> No, don't tell me that time heals everything. I don't believe that time can heal everything. Time can't heal wounds that are unhealable. It just can't. Time can only do what time can do; nothing more.
> No, Lord, you can't deliver us from evil.
> No, Lord, you can't give us our daily bread.
> No, Lord, you can't forgive us our trespasses because we don't ask to be forgiven, because we can't forgive you.
> No, Lord, we can't accept your will be done, because your will brings only blood and fire and madness.
> No, Lord, you are not the truth, because truth has been murdered, truth has been buried along with heaven, which is dead like you; because your house, Lord, is now a house of the dead, yes, a house of the dead.
> No, Lord, the evil doers will never be punished and what's more they will go on to inherit the earth.

No, Lord, there is no victory of good over evil, of the weak over the strong, of the poor over the rich, of the believer over the non-believer, of life over death, of beauty over ugliness....
No, Lord, I cannot describe my suffering [*BWB* 20–21].

Vişniec's play follows the mysterious logic of rebirth from the death of the soul, of jagged improbable healing out of unhealable trauma, of two women's dance of life, death, resurrection and sisterhood in a downward and upward spiral of poetic fire, rage and finally tenderness. I purposefully traced the critical exploration of this play in an uneven coming-and-going movement, starting with the middle, returning to the beginning and now reaching the end in a roundabout way. I wanted to start from the center of the play in the middle of its carnival of irony and laughter, which emerges stridently out of pain and the transcendence of hatred only to move backwards towards the origins of hate and return in the end to the reacquisition of love. There is no logic to the destruction of war, no comprehensible or acceptable meaning that can justify what the heroine of this play and thousands of other women like her had experienced. If there is no meaning then how can there be a form? Dorra's earlier silences were the only possible form, but they had to be staved off against Kate's wall of compassion. Dorra's voice emerges like the phoenix out of the ashes. It is the sound, the undulations, the tonalities, the pitches of Dorra's voice emerging from the depths of silent despair and deadening hate that give shape and rhythms to the play; it is the form that leads to the creation of meaning. The play ends with Dorra's definition of her country, a long monologue that encapsulates in the same uncompromisingly ironic mode as the earlier carnival of ethnic stereotypes, in the same refreshing style of carnivalizing the sentence, the history of the war from the perspective of a woman, a victim, a survivor who has the striking audacity to start the world over and write her own and her country's history all over again:

My country is the inscription you see all over the place in Sarajevo: PAZI! SNAJPER! BEWARE! SNIPERS! And the taste of my country is the soup handed out by the Red Cross.
My country is an 18-year-old soldier who, for a joke, writes: CUT HERE on his neck, just like on those packets of instant soup.
My country is an American TV series that nobody wants to miss in Mostar, even when the town is besieged by Serbs on one side, and by Croats on the other....
My country is a soldier writing on a door with red spray-paint: THIS IS SERBIA. Two weeks later, new words cover the old ones, saying: THIS IS CROATIA. A few days after that, even newer words say: IDIOTS, THIS IS A POST OFFICE!
My country is an inscription written on a tree in Sarajevo: HELLO! I'M STILL ALIVE! [*BWB* 1997, 44].

If the play started with resistant silence and stark hate, it ends with rich language and uncompromising love in Dorra's letter to Kate that explains why she decided to keep the baby:

> I'll tell you. One day, just after you left, I went for a walk by the lake. As I walked, I looked at the trees and the water.... All of a sudden, a notice nailed to a tree caught my eye. I went to take a closer look, and this is what I read:
>
> WE WOULD LIKE TO INFORM YOU THAT THIS TREE IS DEAD. IT WILL BE CUT DOWN WEEK COMMENCING APRIL 2ND. IN ITS PLACE, AND FOR THE ENJOYMENT OF ALL VISITORS TO THIS PARK, WE WILL BE PLANTING A SAPLING.
>
> Signed: THE DEPARTMENT OF PARKS & GARDENS.
>
> I read this once, then again, then several times more. And that's when I decided to keep my baby.
>
> Ljubim-te, Dorra [*BWB* 1997, 45].

As in some of the plays I discussed in the first chapter, this one also ends with a beginning. When asked several years ago why he chose for his heroine to keep the child that was the result of the rape, Matei Vişniec answered that after such periods of devastation and utter destruction as the genocidal war in Bosnia, there is a need to restore normality and saneness, and it is that need that motivated Dorra to ultimately keep her child. It is also, I argue, the reason why the play ends with a letter instead of the diary pages and the closed structure of the psychoanalysis sessions. The ending offers an opening and a new journey, one that has erupted out of the prison of monologic discourses and failed communications of the beginning. The ultimate purpose of psychoanalysis is its own annihilation; the patient is healed only when she no longer needs her therapist and the treatment associated with that therapist.

In his lecture "The Meaning of Working Through the Past," Theodor Adorno traces the rise of totalitarian and genocidal movements such as fascism all the way to the child's first contact with a cold, hostile, alienating world and explains it in Freudian terms of repeating and applying that first trauma of coldness, alienation, even cruelty onto others, then further creating rational strategies to justify irrational behaviors and furthermore developing such strategies to the level of nations, history and the world. He argues that the irrationality that leads to acts of violence "is the instinctual impulses and affects that are repressed—I simply must speak Freudian here—and that teem about in the darkness and emerge again in distorted, twisted, altered form as aggression, as projection, as displacement, all those things we are so familiar with, and wreak havoc" (2005, 299).[5] He further explains that he is in no way attacking the expression of emotions and passions in his criticism of irrationality, but rather appreciates them in the Nietzschean sense of expressive forces of our humanity. What he cautions us against though is "irrationality" that is "rationally prescribed" (2005, 298). It is very much the dynamics at work in the creation of ideologies that legitimize genocide, ethnic cleansing and prejudice. Kate's use of Freudian analysis to explain nationalistic "libido," the urge for aggression and sexual violence, is an attempt to denounce and deconstruct the psyche of a nation that has prescribed irrational behaviors in rational terms to justify acts of genocide.

But unlike the history that keeps repeating itself in cycles of violence and horror and unlike the patient stuck forever in the solipsistic circle of Freudian analysis and post-traumatic stress disorder, the characters of Vişniec's play break out of such circles and offer new alternatives. Theater, with its endless imaginative strategies and emotional powers, can offer safe places of healing and laughter, utopias tailored to the size of human passions and tenderness. It is why Vişniec's play follows a spiraling movement rather than a circular one, and unfolds in an open-ended structure with the traveling letter rather than the stationary diary page, with the heroine's open plans to immigrate, move, travel, resettle far away from her home country, searching for new homes, new countries, and a new self. Like so many other victims of war, she becomes a refugee and a traveler, assuming the bitter freedom of exile and accept it as her own country and her own nomadic home.[6]

Vişniec's most recent play about war, successfully produced in France, Brazil, and Japan, *Pourquoi Hécube? (Why Hecuba?)* (henceforth cited as *PH*) gives voice to the millenary suffering of mothers who have lost sons to vicious wars. This time Vişniec returns to the classics, namely to the mythic character of Hecuba, the ultimate grieving mother who lost all her twenty sons in the Trojan War, and he recreates the myth and the character with an astounding tragic depth while also placing the ancient story within modern precepts, cultural constructs and language. In the introductory statement to the play, Vişniec notes, "The fall of Troy, in our days, is rather the city of Sarajevo under siege during the Bosnian war, or the city of Grozny destroyed during the Chechen War, or Bayreuth in the seventies, or more recently, Mogadiscio in Somalia or Alep in Syria." Furthermore, he connects the woes and misery of Hecuba to the reality of present day wars:

> The pain of Hecuba is the universal pain of mothers who give birth to flesh for the cannons, to boys destined to die young, little ones who become child-soldiers at ten years old, children who at sixteen are already fanatic about but also fascinated with war, young men who at nineteen area already veterans and true war lords [*PH* 3].

While the experience of exile and uprooting is—in an ironic reverse pun—"rooted" in the cultural, geographic, historic realities of the exile and the specific circumstances of her or his displacement, the ravages of war and the inconsolable suffering of parents at the loss of their children to the carnage of wars they have not asked for, contains a universal dimension that pertains more to human nature and the experience of grief and irreparable loss than to the specifics of a time and place. However, the unleashed expression of maternal suffering for the loss of sons also attains, as in Greek tragedy, a profoundly political role. Since Vişniec's play is a postmodern recreation of a Greek tragedy/myth, it is worth looking at it also in terms of the ancient values and aesthetics. The feminist Hellenist scholar Nicole Loraux has written extensively on the subject of grieving mothers, particularly in her study *Mothers in Mourning*, in which she explores that which "in the Greek field, makes of the mourning of mothers an important political issue that defines the life of the city" (1990, 17). While in actual ancient Greek society, the expression of maternal grief and mourning was kept within certain strict parameters, it was in Greek tragedy that the figures of mothers such as Clytemnestra, Andromache, and Hecuba were allowed on stage, although interpreted by masked men, to fully vent the extent of their rage, mourning and vengeful grief. According to Loraux, such aesthetic venting served a particular expiatory function for Greek society and the *polis*, allowing the feminine expression of suffering as a form of liberation, of balancing between masculine and feminine forces and of keeping good terms with the ever-watchful and vengeful gods and goddesses.

Vişniec's play *Why Hecuba*? borrows aesthetic elements of the ancient Greek plays, such as the chorus, the elevated poetic language, the presence of the gods and goddesses as characters, and the basic myth and story line of Hecuba's unparalleled story of loss. He recreates them with modern flair and with moments of meta-theatrical distancing, Brechtian alienation and suspension of disbelief. In his introductory note he prepares us as well for this modern/post-modern transposition or reinvention of ancient characters and values. He suggests that the chorus could at times be represented as "hordes of eager journalists, filming and photographing in an exalted manner every bit of news in the series of Hecuba's miseries," while the gods can be seen as the "big financiers, the moguls responsible with international finances, that we rarely see, these elegant phantoms hiding in sophisticated spheres without ever having any contact with us ordinary mortals" (3).

In his confessional essay mentioned earlier, "Who am I?," Vişniec makes a striking and revelatory comparison between the professions of journalist and writer and discusses with wrenching lucidity the inner battle and the conflicted relation between the two approaches to reality within the same person. As both journalist and writer, he admits to finding himself more and more at odds with his own self, in a constant battle between what is supposed to be the objective observer and reporter and the creative writer who wants to sublimate the horrors of the real world into works of art. He admits that for him, being both journalist and writer at the same time is becoming harder and harder, precisely because of the incessant series of atrocities that he has to report as journalist. "Journalism," he says, "forces you to discover the lack of hope in the future, the fact that people commit the same atrocious historical errors over and over again," while "literature means hunger for nuances" and, explored with the strategies of literature, the human being may appear as a creature of "infinite potentialities." He notes that when "reunited within the same person," the two beings, that of the journalist and that of the writer, both end up in a situation of utter crisis of faith. The writer "loses faith in the human being as the image presented by the journalist is catastrophic," while the "journalist loses faith in the writer because whatever he imagines about the human being is contradicted by reality."

From this inner battle and concurrent loss of hope in the potential of literature to change or sublimate reality and in the potential of human beings to break the endless circles of violence emerge dazzling theatrical works such as *Pourquoi Hécube?* Such a work reflects in its very structure the splintered identity of the author/journalist, the postmodernist dilution and erasure of the notion of humanism and its relegation to a simple "episteme," an entity of knowledge.[7] It equally reflects a stubborn belief against all odds in the necessity of the creative imagination to create the "safe spaces" of theater as places of witness, but equally of questioning, healing and celebration of nuance, voice, ordering of chaos, creation of meaning, rough and imperfect as that may be. At the beginning and towards the end of the play, Hecuba is presented in the shape of a she dog ("une chienne") howling in pain. As we find in the latter part of the play, the gods transformed her human form into that of an animal, for they could no longer bear her endless lamentations. In the second scene of the play, however, Hecuba appears in the full and frightening magnificence of her grief, flanked by the long cortege of the chorus addressing her in startling poetic language of tragedy:

> Hecuba: Your name means mourning and grief
> Hecuba: Your name means tears, blood, despair.
> Hecuba: Your name means black night, tearing, scream in the desert, loneliness and fear
> Hecuba: Your name means tears of blood and tears of ashes...
> ...
> And here we bring you the ashes of your son Hector, fallen in battle... [*PH* 9].

In this heart-rending ritual of grief and mourning, the chorus brings Hecuba the ashes of all her sons. She places them meticulously in a circle around her, counting and addressing each pile of cinders by the son's name and describing his character and virtues.

> Is that you, Hector, my beautiful Hector, the most courageous of the Trojans?...
> And this pile of ashes can only be you, Paris.... I recognize you my youngest son, it is because of you that this disaster has happened.... You kidnapped Helen, the wife of Menelaus the king of Sparta.... Did you not know you cannot insult the Greeks? ... And here is my son Troilus.... Also killed by Achilles.... You have gone to water your horses when Achilles attacked you.... Oh my dear sons, I feel that my heart is also becoming dust and ashes... [*PH* 9–10].

Hecuba's talking tenderly to the tiny mounds of ashes that were once her sons as they are all gathered around her in a circle of death is an unparalleled image of pain. It seems that under the eyes of the spectators, death is made real and ashes are made to quiver and invoke the ghosts of the sons who once breathed in the full vibrancy of their lives. As she once nursed, cradled and cuddled her baby sons, Hecuba now tenderly nurses and cuddles the piles of ashes in an ultimate gesture of agonizing farewell. Nicole Loraux had noted in *Mothers in Mourning* that the mourning mothers' grief is made most poignant when faced with the bodies of the dead sons, as they are also the same bodies that were engendered, birthed and nursed by the mourning mothers. Hecuba is even beyond that, as all she has in front of her are the shapeless, terrifyingly light and volatile mounds of ashes.

Towards the middle of the play when Hecuba's suffering seems to have reached its apotheosis, Vişniec breaks the continuity of the dramatic text, the suspension of disbelief and the fourth wall, and introduces a meta-theatrical movement, a spectacle within the spectacle in which all the gods of Olympus arrive on stage in order to watch the show of the Sack of Troy and the grief of Hecuba. Irony and distancing fracture the tragic discourse and create a feeling of discomfort as the wrenching woes and lamentations of Hecuba are distanced and looked at in the second degree as a spectacle. In its turn, the spectacle of her grief breaks the walls within the walls, the suspension of disbelief within the theater within theater, as the gods/spectators themselves become weary of her lamentations. The gods arrive on stage wearing gigantic masks and acting like spoiled children or whimsical adults, very much like the big figures running the world from their pedestal of riches and privilege that Vişniec has mentioned in his introductory note. Obviously, the spectacle of the Sack of Troy is one that they love seeing over and over again, all lovers of tragedy as they seem to be. In fact each one of the gods and goddesses is introduced by members of the chorus as a "lover of theater, especially tragedy." This show within the show introduces not only a certain distance but a much-needed moment of relief through irony, even comedy, while also transferring the archaic mode and the elevated style of ancient tragedy to modern-day colloquial discourse that is flippant and light. Vişniec cracks any illusion of Aristotelian convention if there ever was one, but it is in the spaces between the cracks that Hecuba's tragedy is renewed and taken to its paroxistic mode.

> **Apollo:** Masters of Olympus, good evening.... *(Coughing.)* Masters of Olympus....
> **Zeus:** *(he feels compelled to intervene, since Apollo's authority is rather weak)* Silence! *(The gods become silent.)* So, what are we going to see tonight?
> **Apollo:** Tonight, we are going to see ... the destruction of the wonderful city of Troy.
> **Hephaïstos:** Oh, not again?
> **Poséidon:** But we already saw that last week, and two weeks ago...
> **Aphrodite:** Yes, yes, it's good, I love the Sack of Troy.
> **Hermès:** No, something new!
> **Hera:** I want the Sack of Troy. It's beautiful, the fall of Troy. I could watch it a thousand times without getting bored....
> **Hermès:** No....
> **Hera:** Yes....
> **Zeus:** All right, let's go for the Sack of Troy ! Let the show begin! [*PH* 25].

At the point in the spectacle of the Sack of Troy, where the gigantic Trojan wooden horse is brought in and the Trojans are all partying around it, Hecuba breaks the party and the fourth wall within the fourth wall, dismantles the continuity of the show within the show with anguished warnings, lamentations and ardent pleas to turn history back, to stop the carnage that is about to come. She addresses each of the gods individually, appealing to their sense of justice, love of mankind and of beauty to no avail. She questions their motives and speaks of her premonitions: "Have you gone mad? Oh miserable me, am I the only one to have this bad premonition, that the Gods have also been seized by folly just like the humans?" (*PH* 29).

It is no longer clear whether Hecuba is an actress playing the role of Hecuba in the show within the show or the "real" Hecuba of the primary play who is interfering and interrupting the spectacle watched by the gods. As we are made to question the "reality" or the layering of the character of Hecuba, we enter again the territory of postmodernity with its moving sands of the so-called "real," its simulacra and concentric intertextualities.

Zeus, who is a spectator in the show within the show, and who, like all the other gods and goddesses, wears the simulacrum of a huge mask, but who is also an actor vis-à-vis us, the main spectators, calls Hecuba "hysterical" and requires of Hera to silence her altogether, for she would "awaken doubt." It is what Nicole Loraux had warned us about with regards to the mourning and dirges of grieving mothers in Greek society, namely that they represented a political danger and therefore needed to be limited if not altogether eliminated so that they not awaken doubt about the necessity and political rightfulness of the wars that had killed their sons. Zeus and all the gods and goddesses are made to feel "uncomfortable" ("*gênés*") by Hecuba's cries and warnings. Vişniec creates a triangular relation between us the spectators of the entire show, the gods/spectators of the show within the show, and Hecuba, who crosses the thresholds of the dramatic convention and breaks through all the walls of these concentric imaginary realities. Zeus asks Hera to turn Hecuba silent and she is happy to oblige, by giving her to drink a magic water that from now until the end of the show within the show will entirely quiet Hecuba's voice and screams: "During the entire following scene Hecuba will continue to 'talk,' 'cry,' to address her people and even the spectators, but her words are mute, her mouth opens and screams with no voice" (*PH* 30). In Vişniec's stage directions her silent screams are projected on a large screen and in turn all the horrifying scenes of the war and the destruction of Troy will be projected against or overlapping the image of this silent cry. This earthshattering image evokes echoes of Edward Munch's painting *The Scream* in Frederic Jamesons' poetic interpretation in light of postmodern theory:

> It seems evident that *The Scream* subtly but elaborately disconnects its own aesthetic of expression, all the while remaining imprisoned within it. Its gestural content already underscores its own failure, since the realm of the sonorous, the cry, the raw vibrations of the human throat, are incompatible with its medium.... Yet the absent scream returns, as it were, in a dialectic of loops and spirals, circling ever more closely toward that even more absent experience of atrocious solitude and anxiety which the scream itself was to "express." Such loops inscribe themselves on the painted surface in the form of those great concentric circles in which sonorous vibration becomes ultimately visible ... to become the very geography of a universe in which pain itself now speaks and vibrates through the material sunset and landscape" [1991, 14].

Hecuba's silent scream also reverberates and, through its projection on a screen in a hyperreal representation, it imbues the entire space and universe around it with its terrifying void of sound and utter desolation. In this palimpsest of broken theatrical walls and dramatic layering, of hyperreal images, Hecuba's silent scream emerging from her wide open mouth pierces through all theatrical conventions as it tries to awaken in us our most primitive and visceral anguish and to get to a stable point within the realm of a perceived real. The show within the show is repeated, and some of the gods and goddesses cannot have enough of the tragedy of Hecuba, insisting that she can still suffer more, while others, particularly Aphrodite, have had enough of her lamentations. But Zeus, the ultimate god/father/patriarch, has the last word and Hecuba's tragedy keeps going on and on, widening in never-ending concentric circles like the Scream echoing throughout the entire universe. The hypnotic nature of what becomes a repetitive theatrical structure, which nevertheless opens each time in wider circles of pain, creates a feeling of vertigo and of abysmal, inescapable doom. After we witness also the murder of Hecuba's twentieth and last son, Polydorus, her youngest one, whom she had hidden from the wrath of the gods, and after we also watch the sublimated representation of the sacrifice of Hecuba's only daughter, Polyxena, on the grave of Achilles, in an apotheosis of flames, and after Hecuba launches a deafening "WHY" to the gods and the entire universe, Vişniec jolts us entirely out of the world of ancient Greece and throws us with merciless boldness in an entirely new aesthetic and human universe: "A hospital or an asylum? A

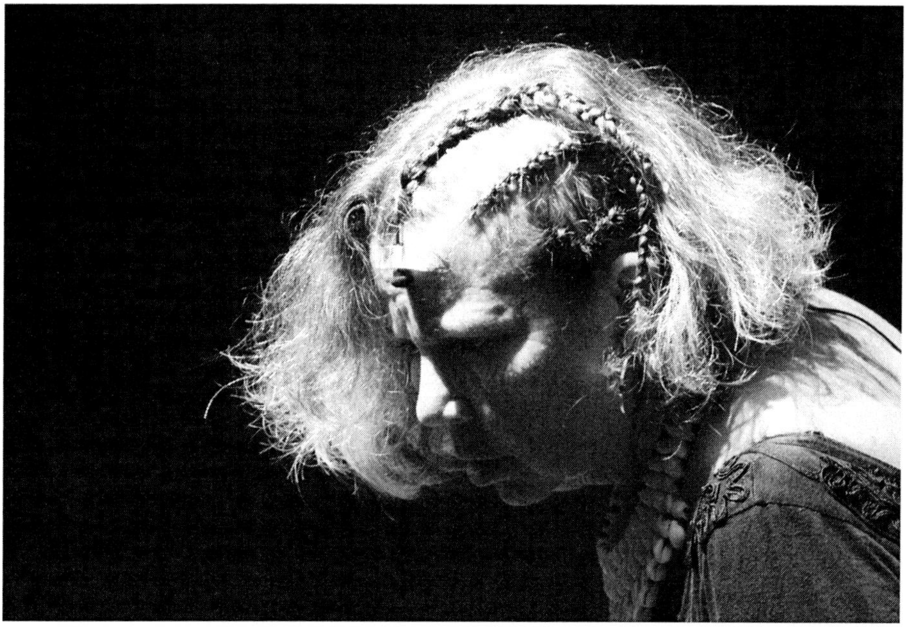

Matei Vişniec, *Why Hecuba? Por que Hecuba*: Teatro Vila Velha, Salvador di Bahia, Brazil; January 2014; directed by Márcio Meirelles. Chica Carelli as Hecuba, mourning and grieving for her lost sons (photograph: Márcio Meirelles).

shelter for homeless people or a retirement home in disastrous shape? We do not know, but we are far from Ancient Greece" (*PH* 69). The inhabitants of this insalubrious, inhospitable space of metal beds and filthy sheets, old people, homeless people and vagabonds all complain about the deafening sounds and bangs that have reached them. Vişniec has obviously displaced and relocated Hecuba's tragedy from the world of ancient tragedy, which no matter how dark and frightening at least unfolded in the domain of the sublime and the grandiose, to our own postmodern world of dreary and degraded spaces, a world that has crossed over past tragic grandeur into grotesque smallness and corrupted humanity.

The play ends within the frame of the beginning: an old shepherd and an old blind man with a young daughter taking refuge for the night next to an old altar, a scene vaguely echoing other Greek tragedies and characters such as Oedipus and his daughter Antigone roaming the land in search of shelter and truth together with the wise seer, the blind man Tiresias. As in the beginning of the play, they talk about the desolate howls of Hecuba transformed into a she-dog. As the old blind man points out: "For as long as you will find yourself on Thracian earth you will hear during the night, the howls of Hecuba transformed into a she dog" (*PH* 72).

This play was produced with large casts and grandiose sets in two different corners of the world within contrasting if not opposing cultures, aesthetics and histories: Brazil and Japan. The Japanese production used huge puppets that convey the play's full hyperreal dimensions, while the Brazilian production used large casts in striking and colorful costumes for ritualistic song, dance and movement numbers. In both productions, the suffering of Hecuba emerges raw and troubling, earthshattering and sublime through the Brazilian and Japanese actresses, while both plays end with the overpowering screen projection of Hecuba's face and mouth uttering the endless scream reverberating through the universe: "WHY?" This astounding play about the atrocious cruelty of wars from one end of history to another, from one corner of the planet to the next, is intricately constructed in concentric circles, fractured plates of layered realities, broken theatrical walls like the walls of cities dismantled by wars throughout all of history, and around one never-ending ruthless unforgiving and strident note crossing history: the high-pitched note of pain, loss and indictment of grieving mothers hurled at all the gods and all the makers of the real theater of war in the world.

In his earlier play *The Word Progress on My Mother's Lips Doesn't Ring True* (2009; hereafter cited as *WPMML*), Vişniec grapples with the recent and brutal realities of the Bosnian war and explores them from the perspective of grieving parents who do not even have the remains of their sons. The play unfolds like his other plays in a string of uneven scenes as the only dramatic unit and is written in the semi-absurdist style in the tradition of his compatriot Eugène Ionesco. It is reminiscent of his other plays that brought him much acclaim, such as *Old Clown Wanted, Horses at the Window* or *The Human Trashcan.* The living parents and the dead son meet each other in the same house as real characters, all while the dead son carries on a useless monologue meant for his parents. Even though they cannot see or hear him, the parents keep setting up the table as if he were still alive and expected to arrive to supper any minute. Vişniec incarnates here the despairing presence of absence in a profoundly theatrical way. The first scenes of the play introduce us to the brutal annihilation of one national group by another, while representing with dark comedy the absurd reality of brother fighting against brother:

> **Vibko:** Are you still alive, you son of a bitch?
> **Stanko:** Yes.
> **Vibko:** So they haven't blown your brains out yet?
> **Stanko:** No.
> **Vibko:** You old bugger! You're not long for this life, you old bastard! Soon they'll be cutting you up into little bits, you and the other shits like you. Do you hear?
> **Stanko:** Yes.
> **Vibko:** You hear me, but you don't say anything?
> **Stanko:** I say you're a shit yourself and an old dog, and one day they'll make you swallow your own tongue.
> **Vibko:** Was it you that shot at me yesterday?
> **Stanko:** Yes.
> **Vibko:** And you knew it was me?
> **Stanko:** Yes.
> **Vibko:** You knew it was me, and you still shot at me?
> **Stanko:** Yes. And next time I'll put a bullet in your head, that's for sure.
> **Vibko:** You little shit! Have you got anything to eat over there? There's a real stink coming from your direction.... Soon you'll be eating your own shit, you and your other bastard friends.

Both Stanko and Vibko are killed, and their remains are impossible for their parents to find. The play mostly unfolds the story of Vibko and his parents, but Stanko returns at the end of the play, also as a dead man whose remains from a minefield have been scattered in the common graves. None of the sublime tragedy of Hecuba and none of the feminine psychoanalytic roller-coaster of Kate and Dorra are present in this play. Vişniec explores the multifaceted nature of the cruelty of wars, in this case modern wars with their utter lack of heroism, genocidal cruelty and cynical moneymongering through the sex trafficking of war victims and even the sale of corpses and burial remains for the consolation of bereft parents.

Vişniec notes (2014c) that the inspiration for this play came to him from "journalism and the delirium of history," and in particular from a real story he had heard about a case during the Chechen war: a mother was asked two thousand dollars to acquire the body of her son killed in battle. "In matters of horror," writes Vişniec, "reality exceeds fiction." Thus he wrote a play about "a mother who wishes for nothing more than to be able to have a decent grave for her son," which, Vişniec comments, "has become a luxury in the context of wars such as the ones in the former Yugoslavia." It is precisely because the reality of the horror of modern wars has become so unimaginable that Vişniec's style and dramatic construction of this play greatly exceeds realistic representation and moves into the realm of the fantastical, the absurd, and the grotesque. In ancient Greece at least, the burial of the dead fallen in battle was part of the basic protocol of wars and an absolutely necessary ritual as part of the heroism and honor of warriors. Whereas the common graves of today's genocides, where thousands of unidentified bodies are desacralized and thrown without a trace of respect toward their memory, have become an ordinary practice and a deliberate action on the part of nationalistic and genocidal groups or armies. Such was the case of the Serbian nationalists who, in the Bosnian war of the nineties, buried thousands of their murdered victims in the hills and forests surrounding Srebrenica.

The *Chicago Stage Review* (Zarris 2011) notes this about the production of Vişniec's play by the experimental, Chicago-based Trap Door Theatre: "The aftermath of war is realized as a purgatory of desperation where grief cannot be exorcised with the rituals we take for granted." The review notes the "hallucinatory reality" created by Vişniec and the "hauntingly astonishing vision." The reviewer also notes, "The extraordinary ensemble brings this tragic tale of death to life with strikingly stark contrasts of brutal degradation, ridiculous corruption and affecting frailty. Every actor adds a unique flavor to this dish of despair." The "production of *The Word Progress on My Mother's Lips Doesn't Ring True* is Trap Door at its finest. It gloriously takes us to a place that is as exquisite as it is overwhelming. It connects us to a part of our humanity that is almost too painful yet completely vital and it elevates theater to its most critical purpose." And the *Chicago Tribune* review (Reid 2011b) comments on the production of Vişniec's play:

Opposite: Matei Vişniec, *The Word Progress*: Trap Door Theatre; December 2011–January 2012; directed by István Szabó K. Poster: left to right: Antonio Brunetti, John Kahara and Kevin Cox. An example of the element of the grotesque in the staging of the play, and of the fantastical and disturbing visual elements meant to suggest the unnatural and dehumanizing character of the war (photograph: Michal Janicki).

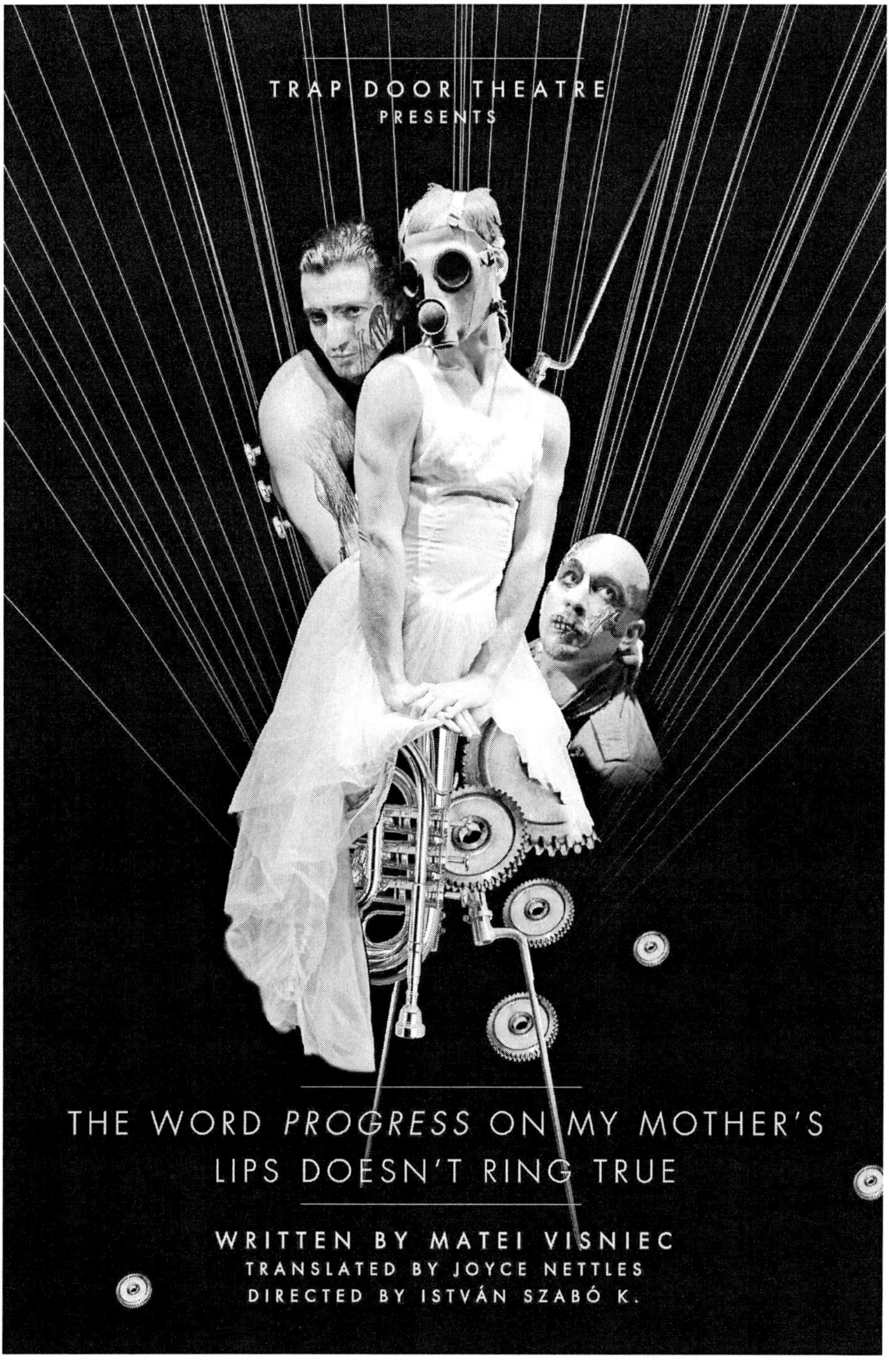
TRAP DOOR THEATRE
PRESENTS
THE WORD PROGRESS ON MY MOTHER'S LIPS DOESN'T RING TRUE
WRITTEN BY MATEI VISNIEC
TRANSLATED BY JOYCE NETTLES
DIRECTED BY ISTVÁN SZABÓ K.

> In Matei Vişniec's stunning and searing *The Word Progress on My Mother's Lips Doesn't Ring True*, now in its North American premiere with Trap Door Theatre, the lines between survivors, victims and ghosts of a nameless Balkan war are impossible to draw with any kind of moral clarity. As directed by Vişniec's fellow Romanian, Istvan Szabo K., it's a piece that unpeels and reveals itself bit by tantalizing bit, creating a series of poetic and nightmarish vignettes in which commonplace objects—broken plates, a white shirt—become stand-ins for those lost to war and genocide.

What emerges clearly from the reviews and the images of Vişniec's play is the hallucinatory and multilayered nature of the play-turned-performance. Realities that defy fiction require fiction that breaks rules, explodes conventions and creates unparalleled images that in turn engage in the exploration of the subconscious, giving shape to visceral anguishes that reconnect us to our deepest human reality. The reviewer is right to ponder: "It's a play that one feels along the nerve endings rather than comprehending in a chronological/logical way. After all, whoever can make literal sense of the betrayals and losses of endless warfare?" (Reid 2011b). This comment points to the necessity of imaginative forms that defy chronology and logic in order to explore illogical realities such as the modern genocides. In the transformation from illogical realities to surreal art, a sublimation, a new kind of cathartic movement and transformation takes place, one that might just give us sparks of understanding, and would encourage us to crisp questioning and heightened compassion towards victims of such wars. Another review in the *Chicago Tribune* by Kerry Reid (2011a) notes:

> Matei Vişniec's sorrowful exploration of the aftermath of a Balkan civil war circumvented the cerebral for a punch to the gut. Through a series of heartbreaking and darkly poetic vignettes (captured through director Istvan Szabo K.'s unforgettable stage pictures), Vişniec's script and the stellar cast channeled the voices of the dead—and walking dead—in a region where war has been a predominant fact of life for centuries.

The breaking down of recognizable, realistic structures and representations challenges the audience members to their own reinvention and possibly transformative change, even rebirth, in a world that has become uninhabitable. If the journalist and the writer are at war in Matei Vişniec, it is still the imagination of the writer, taken to its most feverish and extreme potential, that might offer us some salvation from the incomprehensible realities of war and historical violence. Unlike such realities, the artistic imagination pushed to its rawest form offers nuance and celebrates emotion, thought and individuality. Vişniec's war plays, and this one in particular, are disjointed yet hang together in a satisfying way. Vignettes, wildly

Matei Vişniec, *The Word Progress*: Trap Door Theatre; December 2011–January 2012; directed by István Szabó K. Beata Pilch in foreground, with Wladyslaw Byrdy. Hallucinatory image in which the mother in the play is experiencing a cathartic moment as she finds the remains of her son killed in battle together with the very incarnation of his ghost (photograph: Michal Janicki).

contrasting scenes and sequences of action and dialogue follow one another breathlessly, yet time seems to be suspended in circular repetitions of forward and backward movements. In the movement from page to stage it is obvious that Vişniec creates theater with its acute liveliness in mind, attentive to visual image, movement, sound, and rhythm. He creates postmodernist theater for postmodernist performances.[8] The conversation between the parents, the ritual of the table setting, the return of the dead soldier, the grotesquely carnivalesque scenes of sex trafficking of the soldier's sister and her return home alive yet unseen, repeating her brother's lines at the end of the play, the constant digging of holes in search of the son's remains, the apotheosis of the discovery of his remains—these scenes hang on a fragile string of jagged storytelling. Yet they also exist separately and independently of one another in haunting images and vignettes in a carousel of sorrow and horror, of objects that acquire animistic dimensions and humans that become objectified, of living creatures that appear dead, and of the living dead. The miracle of this dangling, fragile theatrical architecture matches the shocking reality of war from a postmortem perspective as it is voiced by the dead son:

> Be careful when you're digging, father. There are several layers of bodies in this forest... And they're in a very fragile state, father; everything could collapse at any moment.... It's as if there were layers upon layers of spiders' webs, one on top of the other, that had swallowed up a great pile of bodies.... There must be at least thirty nationalities in the bowels of this earth, but at least they get on with each other now.... Sometimes you can hear them singing, and, honestly, it's so funny: there's Serbo-Croat, Russian, German, Italian, Albanian, Turkish, Bulgarian, Greek, even Romanian.... When it rains, or when the earth shifts and the layers of bodies shift with it, you can sometimes get little presents from them, that they send for fun: boots, shields, old medals....

Frederic Jameson beautifully articulates the paradoxes of postmodern architecture in ways that could also apply to postmodern theatrical creations such as this one:

> The relaxation of the postmodern then determines not a return to older collective forms but a loosening of the modern constructions such that its elements and components—still identifiable and relatively undecomposed—float at a certain distance from each other in a miraculous state of suspension, which, like the constellations, is certain to come apart in the next minute [1991, 100].

The edifice of bodies piled up in a fragile configuration of postmortem ethnic diversity in the dead soldier's description is a beautifully ironic image, both grotesque and ethereal, that can also function almost as an *ars poetica* for Vişniec's theatrical architecture of his play. The scenes in *The Word Progress...*, like the layers of "spider webs" holding the fragile balance of the edifice of corpses of many ethnicities that "live" in an otherworldly harmony that they had never managed to achieve while alive, are indeed "suspended" like constellations, linked by delicate ties yet also quivering as if on the verge of utter collapse. The form of the play—with its suspended structures in a continuous "suspension" of belief and disbelief altogether, with its startling poetry, dizzying mixture of fantastical and starkly naturalistic images—is in itself the most powerful anti-war statement, while testifying even against the author's own hopelessness, to the power of theatrical inventiveness, image, sound, silence and color to create empathy and meaning even if these are as fragile as quivering spider webs.

Matei Vişniec's theater of war emerges from his profound, humanistic desire to raise an artistic wall against the unspeakable violence of our times and most importantly against the relentless and unstoppable will to destroy, kill and annihilate the Other that unfolds with maddening stubbornness, even after it was said with so much apparent conviction, "never again."

Vişniec notes that *The Word Progress*, written in a style different from his other ones, since characters representing the living and the dead dialogue with one another, is inspired by the tragedy of refugees who return home to find only ruin and devastation and also by the dangerous utopia of the European Union and its profound hypocrisies. "Europe, Europe," he says, "As much hope, so much deception, as much grandeur, so much disillusion!" "Europe is an open wound," continues Vişniec in his statement, "and on top of this wound the European Union is being built ... no other space on the planet is marked by such contradictions as Europe. On one hand Europe is a museum, on the other hand it is an abattoir. The most refined museums in the world are found next to some of the world's worst abattoirs (in the order of abattoirs are the two world wars, the extermination of Jews, Nazism and Communism)" (2014c). This dark but lucid and uncompromising look at Europe's violent territorial and nationalistic fervor is expressed in Vişniec's play in a reverse perspective from under the ground, or from the other worldly realm by one of the dead character who begs the father to stop digging for the remains of his son:

> **The Soldier:** You have no right! You have no right to dig here! This is the border. You don't dig holes at the border! It's a sacred place! And it's forbidden to dig holes there. And precisely what are you looking for? Are you looking for something *under* the border? You have no right to dig *under* the border. The border belongs to the people! You have no right to dig under the people's border [*WPMML* 45].

In death, however, brotherhood seems to be possible despite border squabbles. In the following climactic scene the son, the soldier and the father befriend each other across not only nationalistic but also death and life borders, just as the father finds the remains of the son and the mother experiences the catharsis of mourning and consolation. The scene merges the tragic and the comic in a grotesque carnival of grief, life, death and slivovitz.

The Son: Stop it, that's enough! Just calm down.... This is my father.... He's been looking for me everywhere for six months....

The Son and the Soldier approach the Father. They stand behind him, watching him dig with his hands.

The Son: Father ... father....

The Father stops as if he heard the Son's words. He puts his hand into his coat on the ground beside him, takes out a bottle of slivovitz and drinks.

The Son: Father, that's my friend Kokai.

The Father holds out the bottle to Kokai.

The Son: *(to KOKAI)* Kokai, tell my father how you died.

The Soldier: *(embarrassed, like a naughty child)* I stepped on a mine.

The Son: *(to the Father)* See ... he stepped on a mine.... *(To Kokai)* When was that?

The Soldier: Two days ago....

The Son: *(to the Father)* Only two days ago....

The Soldier takes a drink from the bottle then hands it to the Son.

The Son: Come on, Kokai, tell my father what happened, and how you managed to step on that mother-fucking mine...

The Soldier: Well, I was just in the middle of putting it down, and....

The Son takes a drink from the bottle then hands it to the Father.

The Son: Did you hear that, father? Stupid fucker! He stepped on his own mine!

The Soldier: Yes.

The Father takes a drink and puts the cork back in the bottle. He then puts the bottle back in his coat pocket.

The Father takes a rucksack out of the earth. The material has blackened, and it is eaten away with damp. He opens it and is immediately surrounded by a strange light.

The Father: Yasminska! Yasminska!

The Mother comes, running.

The Father: I've found it!

The Father takes a harmonica from the rucksack. He hands it to the Son. The Mother falls to her knees in front of the rucksack. The Son starts to play gently on the harmonica.

The Mother: *(crying onto the rucksack)* Vibko.... Vibko, my son! Vibko!

The Father: *(to the Son)* I've found it! I've found it!

The Mother cries with a kind of joy and relief. The Son continues to play gently on the harmonica. The Father takes the bottle out again, takes a drink and hands it to Kokai.

Balkan wars have always been about borders, territorial segmentation, ownership, and ethnic feuds among the more than a dozen ethnicities of either Slavic or Latin origins that inhabit the area stretching from the east of Bulgaria to the east of Serbia (or the Balkan peninsula), to the point where the words derived from the name Balkan, such as "Balkanic" or "Balkanization," have acquired stereotypical connotations of fragmentation, liminality, a chaotic mixture of many different cultural elements, or hybrid identities.[9] Such hybridity has in turn caused the identity crisis in the Balkans. Vişniec's play traces the skeletal anatomy or the artistic blueprint of Balkan worldviews and crises while simultaneously creating a dramatic form that is deliberately fractured into many different segments held together by fragile ties of artistic ingenuity. As it can be considered postmodernist, Vişniec's theatrical aesthetic can also be seen as mimicking Balkan territorial and cultural fragmentations, in its deliberately piecemeal organization that begs for an embracing of diversity rather than its erasure. The Balkans are in many ways a self-fulfilling prophesy in which multiethnic diversity has fueled ethnic hatred, which in turn has caused increased territorial divisions, which in turn have produced ethnic violence. Here is where the postmodernist embracing of difference and revalorizing of margins can offer healing and peaceful alternatives.

In an interview about the nature of his writing, Vişniec answered the following to my questions regarding (1) theatrical structure and (2) the impact that his plays have had or have tried to achieve in the society and world around him:

DR: Do you connect fractured or fragmented theatrical form, nonlinear structures and chronologies, dark humor and carnivalesque episodes to the theatrical form of your plays?

MV: I believe I have always had a special affinity with a certain type of dramatic text characterized by fragmentation. Many of my plays are created in sequences of "theatrical modules" that I propose to the director, leaving him the latitude to choose with how many actors he/she will work or in what order he/she will arrange the modules. I cannot imagine more freedom allowed to a director.... I was formed in the school of cultural resistance during the communist period in Romania; humor and derision play an important role in my theater. Humor, but also dark humor, derision, self-derision, irony and self-irony. I have always been fascinated by the Theater of the Absurd, but even more by the literature of the grotesque (typical to some extent to Eastern Europe) and by the oneiric movement in Romania. All these dimensions are to be found in my theater, from which poetry is never absent.

DR: Could you point to any concrete effects that your plays might have had in your community, society, world in terms of political action, awareness, increase in critical thinking, etc.?

MV: I consider that my plays do indeed have a social impact. I have observed, for instance, that they are being produced more and more by young directors. I write theater not in order to contribute to the entertainment industry but to explore philosophical issues and to bring back into discussion historical themes that have been forgotten (for example the Communist utopia).... I have always thought that literature helps us understand the human being in a more nuanced manner than all of the social sciences together. In order to understand the human being, one needs to read literature. So deep inside I have always been an optimist in writing literature and believing that the great answers are given by writers and artists. But I have also been a journalist for twenty years, and I realize that there has been a constant battle within me between the journalist and the writer. My great motto is one that keeps saying: we must act as if progress did exist. Even if progress does not exist, we must believe in it. For this reason, even my darkest plays, contain, somewhere deep inside, a ray of light [2014d].

Together with Matei Vişniec, I concur that we must act as if there is light at the end of the tunnel. The theater and art that emerge incessantly in the middle of the worst horrors of our world unfold in that same ray of light. Vişniec's plays illustrate at best the exquisite weaving of the carnival, dark humor turned grotesque, which is representative of East European cultural and imaginary proclivities; the Balkan liminal spaces; the neurosis of borders and the fragmentation that leads to violence; all wrapped in postmodernist architectural inventiveness. The creation in "theatrical modules," the controlled breaking of fourth walls, the derision and dark ironies pushed to the extreme of a theater that is obsessively turned towards the exploration of the world's harshest realities as seen by a disillusioned journalist and as processed creatively by an idealistic writer—all these illustrate a bold aesthetic that attempts to wake up audiences, the world, the dormant consciousness of those brainwashed by global utopias or reckless consumerism. It may be why his theater is so successful with the young, with audiences in France as much as in Japan or Brazil, and why theaters such as the Chicago-based Trap Door throw themselves passionately into entire Vişniec series, engaging in performative tours de force of innovative stagings that break all conventional borders and comfort zones. A refugee from a former communist dictatorship tormented by the brutality of modern wars, and generously embracing the ideal of a multicultural society, Matei Vişniec invents an unparalleled theater aesthetic that is at least as politically relevant as the philosophical textures held within its intricate form.

Biljana Srbljanović: Postwar Dystopias

Biljana Srbljanović is one of the theater stars in postwar Serbia, a winner of many awards for her plays, and also a political figure in Serbian politics who even ran for the position of mayor of Belgrade. According to some critics, she is considered to be part of Serbia's "lost generation," having earned part of her renown "due to her identity as a Serbian artist who did not flee the country during the wars" (Porterfield 2009, 83). I contend that while there is some truth to such views, she has earned her international renown mostly through the bold aesthetic of her plays that deal with postwar Serbian realities. I will discuss her first two and most successful plays, inspired by the war of the nineties as well as by the exodus of refugees that the war has caused. In the introduction to her play *Belgrade Trilogy* (1999, 5), she says that the play was "written in 1996, the year after a big emigration wave in Serbia, when young people (around 200,000), most of all, young intellectual people from Belgrade were leaving because they were against the war." Thus the themes of war and displacement are interwoven in her plays, as war usually creates refugees and displacement is one of its most disruptive and devastating effects.

The action of *Belgrade Trilogy* takes place in three different locations. It announces from the very first page and the naming of the characters, the disunity of space and the disconnectedness that we can expect from the unfolding of the plot and of the stories told in a triptych fashion. As someone who has lived through the war herself and was a courageous opponent of it, Srbljanović's style has a certain immediacy and freshness, the dialogue and plot having a crisp, open and dynamic way of rolling and including us in their unfolding. A particularly interesting award that Srbljanović received in 2007 is a European award called the New Theatrical Realities Award, which was established in 1986 with sponsorship from the European Commission and the European Parliament. The name of the award reflects a much-needed acknowledgment of the need for theater to be connected with the realities of our times and to keep reinventing itself in both content and form.

Srbljanović has had an active role in Serbian politics and was a vocal opponent of the war, like the thousands of young Serbians who fled the country soon after the war. War and exile form an ominous but tight couple, and the former usually engenders the latter. Even today, in Serbia, Bosnia-Herzegovina, and Montenegro there are over seventy thousand refugees and internally displaced people as a result of the wars of the nineties. Serbian forces were found to have been responsible for over ninety percent of the war crimes committed in the war, among which the most gruesome were the massacre of Srebrenica in the summer of 1995 and the massive rapes of Muslim Bosnian women in rape camps.[10] Vişniec's plays, which we looked at earlier, explore the horrors of war from the perspective of the Bosnian war victims. In Serbia, on the other hand, there was massive nationalistic sentiment and no widespread recognition of the fact that it was Serbian forces, particularly those gathered under the Republika Srepska and led by general Ratko Mladic, that were responsible for the war's greatest atrocities. The intellectual and artistic voices and initiatives such as the DAH Theater, which we will look at later in this book, or the political activities and theater of Biljana Srbljanović were part of a rather small minority. Although *Belgrade Trilogy* does not deal with the violence of war per se, it is representative of the effects of the war on Serbian population, particularly on the young people who did not want to participate in or support the war and who had a more lucid awareness of Serbia's role in the events of the nineties.

Unlike the plays we have discussed so far, *Belgrade Trilogy* (cited as *BT*) is written in realist style without leaps into fantastical, surrealist episodes, or carnivalesque incursions. Yet it is a highly modern play written in colloquial language and structured in a quilted form that illustrates spatial dislocation as it deals with groups of Serbian immigrants in three different parts of the world: Prague, Sydney and Los Angeles. The play is orchestrated in three well-developed scenes representing the various difficulties that each group of immigrants encounters in their newly displaced lives and the collapse of their big dreams of success and happiness as refugees. The last and fourth scene of the play is almost like a breath, a two-line sequence that takes place in Belgrade and portrays a pregnant woman sitting at a desk and a man's voice calling her. All four scenes occur on the same New Year's Eve night and combine an almost forced party atmosphere with the melancholy of broken dreams and monotonous hardships. There is no connection among the people in each of the four scenes, which unfold rather like vignettes of life, tied together by the nationality of the characters—Serbs from Belgrade—and by their status as refugees from a common geographical, historical and cultural universe. Only one thin thread ties the scene that takes place in Sydney with the last scene: Ana Simionova, the pregnant woman in the miniature scene that takes place in Belgrade, is mentioned by one of the characters who spends New Year's Eve in a Sydney apartment. She mentions Ana as an acquaintance who ended up working for a Belgrade TV station. In her own statement about the play, Biljana Srbljanović also notes, "It is also a play about the author's life—the life of a young Serbian woman in the middle of an era that nobody wants to live in" (1999, 265). Srbljanović is also something of a media celebrity in Serbia, and it is pretty clear that the almost ghost-like presence of Ana Simionova, the one who stayed in her country, the one spending New Year's Eve in Belgrade and working for TV, is inspired by the author's life and personality.

Although the play is written in the realistic mode with no leaps into absurdist discourse or fantastical images, I venture to call its dramatic style postmodernist realism. Its architecture is fractured into several modules tied to one another by fragile, almost invisible strings and suspended across several stories taking place in different corners of the world. Its colloquial language at times becoming harsh and even violent; the fast-paced action and the violent, shocking ending of the third scene bear the marks of a postmodernist edge or stridency, of a deliberate disregard for aesthetic embellishments and ornate discourse. I argue that the play is as much about war as it is about exile, or the aftermath of the war of the nineties. One of the brothers in the first scene, which takes place in Prague, mentions the army sarcastically in reference to one of the reasons for their immigration: "Or is his lordship cross perhaps, because I didn't leave him in the shit, I didn't allow him to be called up, ... to defend our wonderful Serbian identity, whose limits are known only to God, for all of five minutes before the first bullet came along to send him to St. Peter and his blessed duty free!" (*BT* 270).

In the scene that takes place in Los Angeles, the character of Jovan, a Serbian immigrant, tells Mara, also a Serbian refugee whom he has just met at a New Year's Eve party, that his reason for leaving his country was the disgust and disillusionment he felt towards his countrymen as a result of a violent incident of ethnic hatred. While he was presenting a play taken from Croatian literature with a group of fellow *commedia dell'arte* actors in a Serbian high school, he was beaten up and insulted by one of the students because of the choice of the nationality of the text. And the teacher "said we shouldn't have put on anything from Croatian literature. 'The kids are sensitive, they hate Croats, you have to understand.' This is a high school teacher talking to me. I should understand why kids want to lynch me. Nationalism isn't forbidden by law.... I was ashamed of my own people" (302). At the end of the scene Jovan ends up with a fatal bullet in his head, triggered by a first-generation American Serbian, a rabidly nationalist young man who crashes his and Mara's romantic conversation. The tentacles of war spread wide and large across the world through the attitudes of people carrying the ethnic hatred that started the war in the first place. Not even in exile can one be completely free from its devastating violence. The play's unforgiving cynicism also dictates its fractured mock–Aristotelian structure, in which the action takes place on the same evening of New Year's Eve of the same year, and virtually in the same mental and cultural landscape or space—that of forsaken "mother" Serbia among immigrants who fled from its not-so-beloved arms. The notorious Aristotelian unity of space, time and action is splintered and reinvented with great irony in the fragile architecture of this play that emerges equally from the heartbreak of war and of displacement, out of the disillusion caused by one's native country as much as by the collapse of the immigrant or American Dream, wherever on the planet that may be. The thin and almost translucent thread of the mysterious character of Ana Simionova, whose only appearance is in actual Belgrade and lasts all of one moment as she is sitting at the table "highly pregnant" and a man's voice offstage is calling her, may be precisely the only thread that holds the action of the four pieces loosely together. If Ana is indeed the character supposed to represent the author herself, then it is in this two-minute scene that the play acquires the totality of a work turned upon itself in a self-referential movement in which the author holds together the strings of all the other characters, their tragic or pathetic destinies that spread across the world while being tied to one point of nostalgia, belonging or negative memory: Serbian culture, language, and recent history of war. The exile of the three groups of characters—in Prague, Sydney and Los Angeles—illustrates what Salman Rushdie named the "ball hurled high into the air," the "paradox of looking forward by always looking back"; these exiles seem "suspended impossibly" above their "native earth" (2006, 212).

A tragic reality reflected in this play is that of the prolongation of war through the processes of exile, as its violence and the traumas caused in the country of origin itself reverberate across expanses of land and sea in the present lives of the displaced characters. Daca, the violent Serbian American who is about to rape Mara and ends up shooting Jovan in a semi-accidental manner, replays in miniature form the very war whose echoes and post-traumatic realities both characters ran away from all the way to Los Angeles, attempting to shape a timid version of their American Dream. The ethnic hatred, the sexual violence, the "nationalistic libido" of the frustrated "Balkan man," as Kate in Vişniec's play would put it, are transplanted and rekindled not only across the globe but also across generations: Daca was born in America and raised in the spirit of Serbian nationalism. Each one of the three sequences ends in a profoundly sad or tragic event or realization. The two brothers trying to make it in Prague as dancers in a night club argue and humiliate each other, as the younger brother is heartbroken by the discovery of the infidelity of his girlfriend back in Serbia and ends up hooking up with an unknown woman. The characters in the Sydney sequence, two couples who are friends and spend New Year's Eve together, end up acquiring painful realizations of failure, infidelity, and loss of love and dignity, as the husband of the host couple is having an affair with the wife of the guest couple. And the Los Angeles scene escalates in an attempted rape and a successful killing of the young Serbian man who had denounced the irrational violence caused by ethnic hatred and left his country precisely to get away from it. The play's grim message—that there is no getting away from one's national baggage of hatred, war and violence—radiates through the disjointed and almost tricky orchestration of the play as a "trilogy" that is a four-scene play, the fourth almost inexistent scene taking place in Belgrade. The even more tragic and hopeless dimension of the play's message is that the experience of exile, the attempt at grasping at some form of immigrant dream of a better life, is itself sullied by one's past especially when that past involves war. If the characters fail to be real exiles and can never actually get away, even if they find themselves at different corners of the planet far from their native country, then what is left for them other than an abyss of alienation and pointless displacement? Serbia and Belgrade are the emotional and cultural spaces but not the real, geographical spaces of the play. The famous Aristotelian unity of place is both held together and irreverently exploded into a flagrant disunity of place, while the unity of time of New Year's Eve is the core of the play's tragic irony. Not much is truly new for this New Year's Eve of immigrants attempting to preserve a sense of normality and of home away from home; rather, a lot of old baggage prevents them from actually moving away from their past, the experience of the war and the postwar society that they ran away from. In a way the play can be considered a trilogy of three failed exile experiences. The gesture of Ana Simionova in the last scene of taking her head in her hands may well suggest the author's sense of helplessness and profound disillusion at her own country and, in a self-referential way, of sadness for her own characters and their failed dreams.

An article in the *Los Angeles Times* titled "Playwright Not Ready to Exit Theater of War" from June of 1999, when NATO and UN troupes were bombing Serbia to stop its attacks on neighboring Albanians in Kosovo, analyzes with lucid understanding the drama that Srbljanović was experiencing during and after the war and the maddening dilemma of whether to stay or leave the country. This seems to be the underlying theme and psychological thread uniting the stories in *Belgrade Trilogy* and connecting them to the theatrical flash of the last scene:

> For her and others in Belgrade's Western-oriented circles, the choice between staying and leaving involves judgments about the future of a homeland that is being destroyed by countries they once admired but is still in the grip of a strongman they fear and revile, Yugoslav President Slobodan Milošević .
>
> "It's like two giants are trying to settle a private feud and the whole country is their hostage," Srbljanović said at the downtown cafe hangout of

her shrinking circle of friends. "Do I escape? Or do I stay to try to build a better society and be an optimist and a fool?" [Bourdreaux 1999].

By some estimates about one fifth of Belgrade's population of two million fled the country. Srbljanović herself visited friends in the United States and considered emigrating, but in the end chose to return and remain in her native country. "Sometime I feel I have to apologize to my friends who have left," she confesses. "Some of them get the picture that, just by staying, I'm supporting this whole thing here. Then I realize that this is an absurd position" (Bourdreaux 1999). The merging of the themes of the devastation of war on Serbian society and that of the exile and expatriation of many Serbians who were critical of the war that their country had waged against its neighboring countries accounts in part for the spatial indistinctness of the play, despite its headings that point to the chosen spaces of the characters' self-exile, be it Prague, Sydney or Los Angeles.

Srbljanović's realism also contains a postmodernist edge in its layering of ironic, self-referential and self-subversive realities, cultural constructs and geographies, disrupting conventional aesthetic norms. Aristotelian dramatic conventions seem to be ground up in the mix of dramatic vignettes of life tied together by a fragile thread of collective memory and history that refuses to let go and that keeps its protagonists hostage. Much like most theater works discussed so far, Srbljanović's theater emerges from her own experience of living in a devastated, postwar society. As she herself noted, the characters emerge from realities that are very close to her personal experience and to people she knew. Srbljanović's postmodern realism breaks with conventional realism, using an apparently ordered structure that holds an inner chaos in a mangling of the biographical and the imaginary, the lived and the created, the historical and the personal.

Srbljanović's play *Family Stories* (2002; cited as *FS*) is on the contrary written in a combination of carnivalesque absurdist and naturalist styles from the perspective of children playing adults. The play treats with unabashed directness and at times ferocity the realities of domestic violence in the larger context of the violence of war in a dystopian world that takes us to the lowest of humanity and even to the level of the subhuman. "*Family Stories* builds on the confusion in this period[11] and addresses the problems of federal disillusionment, radical nationalism, unemployment, escalation of crime, and black market economy" while simultaneously presenting a "ritualization of the traumatic" (Warner 2010, 91). The characters are eleven-year-old Nadezda, described as "a child filled with nervous tics," who plays the role of a dog and is treated like one; the twelve-year-old Vojin, who plays the abusive father; his eleven-year-old sister Milena, who plays the abused mother; and the ten-year-old Andria, who plays the son

Biljana Srbljanović, *Family Stories*: Whistler in the Dark Theater; May 2010; directed by Meg Taintor. Left to right, clockwise: Melissa Barker (Milena), Danny Bryck (Andrija, center), and Nate Gundy (Vojin). The two "children" overpowering the "father" in one of their violent games (photograph: Meg Taintor).

or, "when necessary, the daughter." The author explains the role playing that she uses for her characters in the beginning:

> All the characters in this play are children. According to the needs of the story, they grow old and re-become young. Sometimes they change their sex. Nothing unusual. On the contrary, the actors are not children. In this play, it is the adults who play children who in their turn play adults. There is nothing surprising in this either. There will be enough other reasons to be surprised [*FS* 9].

The description of the Factory Theater in Boston, which produced *Family Stories* in 2010, says the following about the play:

> In Biljana Srbljanović's haunting-yet-hilarious *Family Stories,* four children play house amid the wreckage of a bombed-out playground. Reflected in the fun-house mirror of their game is a thrilling and devastating allegory of a post-war society. Part slapstick and part tragedy, *Family Stories* examines the fear that results from living in a society without free media or civil liberties [Factory Theater 2010].

And a review of the 2008 production at the Griffin Theater in Sydney, Australia, notes:

> Biljana Srbljanović's work explores the boundaries between theatre and reality, personal and public opinion, decency, comedy and tragedy. Fiercely smart, she stunned Europe with her unique approach to expressing unbearable psychological and political anxiety following the breakdown of Serbia. With this play, she strengthened an entire culture's consciousness of their contemporary existence [Ride On Theatre, 2008].[12]

Based on these reviews there is no doubt that Srbljanović's theater has had a profound impact of the society of her time and that her theater, emerging from the devastation of her own country and the political dilemmas in her own life, has struck a chord with audiences worldwide.[13] The *Theatermania* review of the 2002 production of Family Stories at Cambridge Market Theater gives it a half-hearted, indulgent rating as it recognizes that the play is "interesting" but says that the role playing is unsuccessful:

> Although Srbljanović's re-creation of an adult world through children's eyes is not quite successful, it is interesting. And one could make the case that American theatergoers are too ignorant of Serbians to recognize a joke: A European audience might take for granted that the actors aren't portraying absurdist Serbian adults or morally ambivalent Mother Courage types. The ambitious playwright (based in New York City for a year) has tackled a serious and universal theme in exploring the ways that violence and fear in the home sustain communal violence and warfare [Elis 2002].

Indeed this reviewer is right to acknowledge that American theatergoers would very likely miss the cultural constructs referred to in the play. I argue that they would be equally impermeable to the East European Balkan carnivalesque mode and ruthless mixing of the tragic and the comic into an aesthetic of the blatantly grotesque. European audiences and critics from Germany[14] to the Netherlands to France to neighboring countries such as Romania (where *Family Stories* has been played and continues to be played in most national theaters across the country) have greatly acclaimed her plays. The Serbian theater director Milos Lazin, living and working in France, has written a compelling article in which he explores with great sensitivity the political boldness and aesthetic complexity of her theater, noting the surprising fact that "Biljana Srbljanović knew world success before knowing success in her own country" (2006, 218). This realization starts with a mean-spirited comment by one of her compatriots about her theater being "the reason for the bombardments" by NATO and UN forces. Of course this rather blinded Serbian intellectual could not possibly consider that the war crimes, brutal genocidal events waged by Serbian nationalists against Croats, Bosnians and Albanians had anything to do with the NATO, American and UN bombings that were trying to stop the sustained elimination of entire ethnic groups. For him they had everything to do with a couple of anti-war plays by a young and idealistic Serbian playwright. I would say that if anything it is precisely attitudes such as the one of this unnamed Serbian intellectual that may have fueled the fierce and blinded nationalist hatred that in turn led to the genocidal war of the nineties. Indeed, we can only hope that the power of theater is so great that Biljana's plays may have drawn some attention with her fiercely ironic words to the absurd nationalism of her countrymen and have had some role in awakening the Western world to take military initiative in support of the war victims.

Lazin places Srbljanović in the frame of what he calls "La Nouvelle écriture théâtrale" ("The New Theater Writing"), which he opposes to the "image theater" very popular in Europe in the seventies and eighties as well as part of the revival of the playwright in theater following the almost complete domination of the director. He considers Srbljanović as one of the new playwrights with a newly acquired "conscience of the world" and of reality who, much like British writers such as Sarah Kane, have created theatrically the "clinical tableau of the violence in the world" and in opposition to the postmodern "reduction of the real to mere artifact ... have renewed the sensuality of theater" (Lazin 2006, 220). In terms of its unabashed and even over-the-top stage violence, Srbljanović's theater (like her compatriot Milena Markovic's plays that I discuss later) could fit the "in-yer-face" theater aesthetic of Sarah Kane that Radmila Adamova also claims as source of inspiration. Lazin considers that one of the great reasons for the success of her plays is, besides the fact that "she was at the right moment at the right time," the distancing or alienation that she creates in her plays through the choice of space. The geographical distancing of the last scene in *Belgrade Trilogy*, in which the murder of Jovan is committed by a nationalist Serb born in Arizona, points, according to Lazin, to the deep reasons for "the atrocities committed on Yugoslav soil in the nineties: they were unfounded" (222). The mastery of the art of playwriting in her second play, *Family Stories*, moves beyond the temporal and plot linearity of the first and accomplishes the effect of alienation neither through spatial nor temporal distancing but through the artifice of using children's voices and imagination as a "magnifying glass that brings out the cruelty of the adult world to which the adults themselves have become immune" (223).

Family Stories has known international success and has been translated into and performed in twenty languages. According to Lazin this success, similar to the success of Sarah Kane, is largely part of the movement of the New Theatrical Writing of the new generation of playwrights, which has restored and reinstituted the social and political relevance of theater. I am comforted by the fact that Lazin sees the structure and form of Srbljanović's plays as relevant and representative of the movement that has created innovative theater, in terms of its reconnection to the world around it, by innovating at the level of form. This new theatrical writing has created a new kind of realism that illustrates the fragmentation of identity of the new generation through the fracturing of structure and the utilization of simulacra (Lazin 2006, 223). I would add that in conjunction with the utilization of simulacra and games, Srbljanović relies heavily on a carnivalesque aesthetic in which the grotesque, the grimace of tears melting into laughter and vice-versa, are fundamental to the overall mood and coloring of the play. In response to the claim that the New Theatrical Writing is somehow a reaction to the postmodern "reduction of the real to mere artifact," I have to disagree. Rather the theater of Srbljanović and that of Sarah Kane reflects one aspect of postmodernity while possibly arguing with another. Not all postmodern thought, theory and art is characterized by the belief in or the attempt at "the reduction of the real to artifact"; in fact a central part of postmodernist aesthetic is the reckless plunge into the real, often into the darkest, seediest corners of the real of our world. Such is the case of the authors studied here, who have boldly tackled the war and postwar realities of the Balkan world in audacious art. However, unlike authors such as Matei Vişniec, who have written plays inspired by the Bosnian war of the nineties from the outside of the country and its devastating war and have used journalistic and scholarly sources, Biljana Srbljenovic's theater is born directly from her own experiences, from the moral and intellectual agonies, the torment that she herself has undergone as one of the few artists and intellectuals who have taken a powerful stand against the Milošević regime and against the war of ethnic cleansing. Her plays are written in her own blood and tears, so to speak. This is also the reason for their fractured realism, for their uncompromising violence, for their profound impact on the international arena and theater world. As Lazin points out, she is part of a generation who has lost all traditions, has found itself in a vacuum of freedom post–1989, only to be dragged into the "madness of power" and "the spirit of a tribe in agony" and caught between two choices: "that of succumbing to indifference" and that of positioning itself as "creative subjectivity" and "real existence" (227).

The setting of the play is poignant and profoundly relevant, as it evokes the brutal realities of "a ruined country" just as the characters themselves are the "citizens of a ruined country" (*FS* 11). It evokes a dilapidated Belgrade neighborhood in the odious-looking style of "post socialist realism," filled with graffiti, trash, ravaged lawns, and a filthy pot of sand. On the stage there is also "an abandoned caravan." The ugliness and sense of discomfort that the set evokes illustrates Srbljanović's postmodernist realism. It is rough and edgy; it causes discomfort and displeasure; yet it is fascinating in its gritty and anti-aesthetic quality, transporting the audience into a dystopian world.

The same stands true for the characters, the children/adults mimicking in childish manner the violence and crassness of the adult world with a toothless grin and irrepressible cynicism. This aesthetic is postmodernist because it plunges deep into a brutal reality but comes out with broken jumbled pieces of that real, both flirting with it and removing itself from it, both grabbing the real by its hair and packaging it in ugly wrapping. Srbljanović's simulacra leave us profoundly troubled by their edgy aesthetic, cynical humor and mostly by their tenuous yet persistent relation to a real that is otherwise impossible to represent. The dystopian atmosphere of this play may well be infused with the melancholia of the postmodern individual that Jean Baudrillard attributes to the "disappearance of meaning," the "loss of history" and their replacement by simulated realities (1994a, 1–3, 43, 163). However, Baudrillard also attributes the loss of meaning, history and most importantly of the real in favor of an image or reproduction of the real to television, film and the Internet in what he calls "mediatization" and "artificial memories that efface the memory of man, that efface man in his own memory" (49). "More real than real, that is how the real is abolished" (81). Srbljanović's "in-yer-face" theater fights against the abolishment of the real as much as artistic expression is capable of doing.

An article from a July 2, 2000, issue of the *New York Times* that connects public violent occurrences in Belgrade by Serbian nationalists with the theater and political stance of Biljana Srbljanović notes the following about *Family Stories*:

> This highly theatrical, farcical psychodrama, in which adult actors play children playing adults playing house in a violently dysfunctional family, has Bertolt Brecht's fingerprints all over it, a debt Ms. Srbljanović freely acknowledges. In one scene, the play's children are told that the gravest sin, the one with the harshest penalty, is to admit to an independent thought and risk unspoken reprisals, beatings and worse [McQueeney 2000].

Even as the stories in this play are told through layers of simulation, by adult actors playing children who play adults, they never lose the throb of the real, and as Lazin has aptly noted, the artifice of the child persona and voice only exacerbates the reality of the adult world and its brutality.

The Brechtian distancing and breaking of the fourth wall catalyze our reconnection with a real that is hard to comprehend because of its violence in ways that are less mediated than the world of virtual images on TV screens or the Internet. The good thing about Srbljanović's play and about other plays that use simulation is that in the end the simulation fails and reality wins, even if broken, distorted, or presented in bits and pieces—or maybe precisely because of that. As in Lazin's apt conclusion, Srbljanović has made the choice to adopt a "creative subjectivity" and perceive herself as having a "real existence." The children's mimicking of domestic violence and family dysfunctionality on the background of nationalist violence and war brings out the recent reality of the actual devastation of Belgrade, possibly of the besieged Sarajevo, and the postwar devastation in both Serbia and Bosnia. The Brechtian alienation accomplishes what Brecht had wanted: a distancing that allows and calls for a lucid look at the actual violence that is being simulated.

Family Stories is built from eleven scenes or tableaux that portray various episodes in the life of the simulated family of Milena, Andria, Vojin and Nadezda the dog, who is a girl playing and being treated as a dog. The scenes vary from violent exchanges that mimic family bickering (in which Milena, who plays the mother and the wife, is mostly abused by the child who plays Vojin the father and the husband) to violent actions in which the son shoots his parents or sets them on fire, to violent beatings of the dog-girl Nadezda, to nightmares in which all the characters die in violent ways and then come back to life. The first scene plays out a dinner situation of Milena the mother, Vojin the father and Andria the son in which the conversation focuses on the necessity of obedience and lack of thinking while living in society; the scene ends with the appearance of the "dog" Nadezda. After the father teaches his son this lesson of blind obedience in which the definition of an intelligent man is one who "observes the rules: the head in the sand, the ass at the wall" (*FS* 18), he beats the mother, the mother slaps the son, and both Milena and Vojin hit and abuse Nadezda. At some point in the scene the son interrupts the "game" and decides he no longer wants to play:

> **Andria:** I don't want it. I don't want to always be the child and to always be beaten up.
> **Milena:** Me too, I am beaten up.
> **Andria:** It's not the same. You are a woman. It's normal.
> **Milena:** I know it. It's why I put up with it. The father beats up the mother, it's normal.
> **Vojin:** And it's normal that they both beat up the child.
> **Andria:** I don't care about what's normal. I don't want to play any longer [25].

Srbljanović achieves a double Brechtian distancing by having the characters of Milena, Vojin and Andria point ironically to their characters of mother, father and child and by referring to the game itself in a self-referential manner. Thus the enormity of their lines, the legitimation of violence and of blind obedience appear in their glaring ugliness and absurdity, and we become Brecht's epic theater spectator who thinks critically and lucidly about the play and its characters instead of emotionally. According to Brecht (1964, 20), the epic spectator says: "I'd never have thought of it—that's not the way—that's extraordinary—hardly believable—it's got to stop—the sufferings of this man appall me because they are unnecessary—that's great art—nothing obvious about it—I laugh when they weep. And I weep when they laugh." By distancing themselves from the real, these characters make the real show its ugly heads. They pretend the real and make their pretense obvious, their language being a parody of the adult language. Through this game the spectator becomes more aware of the absurdity of the adult world of domestic violence, lack of courage and lack of critical thinking that leads to more violence and more wars. The dog/girl Nadezda offers a momentary distraction, as the characters are both frightened by her apparition and abuse her with stones and a chain.[15] There is something profoundly troubling and scabrous in the degrading role of a human character treated and acting like a dog, who furthermore is also tied to a chain on stage in most productions. There are denunciations that remind one of secret police informants; saying things "against" results in the loss of a job for Milena; and the son Andria pours gasoline and sets fire to the house with the parents in it. Cruel games with the dog performed in ominous silence are interspersed with the dialogues. Illustrating their infantile roles, the characters also play with paper airplanes, type stories on a typewriter with no paper, make plans for a voyage to the center of England or to Vranje, and again Andria shoots both his parents, who end up on the floor in blood only to reappear alive, playing more games, in the next scene.

There is variety and contrast among the play's eleven tableaux, as the characters undertake to represent in the form of parody the gamut of human experiences in conditions of oppression, fear, violence and catastrophic events. Some of the scenes are more poetic and tragic, while others are grotesque and violent, alternating long and short scenes, intense stage action with rapid dialogue or storytelling. The scene following the murder of Voijin and Milena by their son consists only of stage actions in which Andria teases Nadezda with a piece of chocolate and ends up eating it without sharing. Silent stage action can have power equal to or even greater than an abundance of words on the stage, as it turns the actor's body into the only producer of meaning. The rain washes away the blood spilled in the previous scene, and at the end Milena is calling Andria as if from far away, while Nadezda "remains in the rain like a dog unaware of his misery" (*FS* 39). In another scene the characters act out a situation reminiscent of periods of food shortages during wars that could be the war of the nineties, or to use another referent common to people from Eastern European countries, the times of food shortages and rationing specific to the communist era. Voijin and Milena are counting beets, kilos of sugar and nuts. Andria plays a daughter, wearing a dress visibly on top of his boy's clothes from the previous scenes. Voijin dies again, choking on a nut while Andria is asking for her marriage dowry, and Milena sings a folkloric mourning song that subverts its own content with uncompromising irony as she asks: "Who is going to love me / Who is going to beat me / Who is going to impose his law on me?" (50). At some point the characters sing Serbian folkloric songs and mention refugees from Bosnia. One of the scenes ends with the grotesque rape of Nadezda by Andria, after which he sings a "tchetnik" song. For anybody who has lived through or has heard of the war of ethnic cleansing of the nineties, this is a troubling reference to the mass rapes of Bosnian women by Serbian soldiers. For any survivors of those events that reference is as real as it gets, and there may be spectators or critics who would argue that it does too good a job of simulating and refreshing the memory of the horror. One of the most troubling and imaginative scenes in the play is one in which the three characters recount their nightmares, which are interconnected with one another in a Luis Bunuel–type of journey through the labyrinth of subconscious realities.[16] In Andria's nightmare he is swallowed up by the melting asphalt on his way to a competition to Zagreb. Voijin's nightmare ends with him being shot dead while drowning because he was not a supporter of the "Red Star." Milena dies of heartache upon hearing of the deaths of her son and husband and particularly of the high prices of their burials. At the end of the scene, Milena and Voijin die again, this time from heartbreak because the authorities have forbidden the free sale of narcotics. At the end of each nightmare sequence the narrator announces he/she died or was killed and the others agree, creating a leitmotif with a predictable rhythm almost like a funeral chant:

> **Andria:** And then? He kills you?
> **Voijin:** He kills me, obviously.
> **Milena:** Obviously. (*All are quiet*) Oh My God, my God....
> ...
> **Voijin:** And you?
> **Andria:** ... You die?
> **Milena:** Obviously. I lie down and I die of grief....
> **Nadezda:** Obviously [*FS* 61–62].

The characters' constant hide-and-seek with death echoes the relentless presence of violence in their world with a constant mockery of death reminiscent of carnivalesque and medieval macabre humor and of Balkan attitudes towards death. Saviana Stanescu's comment about the way Balkan people deal with death is of relevance here. She "recalls being surprised that American people were afraid to laugh at death and war. 'In the Balkans there's a different sense of dealing. We survive with humor'" (Pippa 2007). Theatrically, the characters' serial deaths and resurrections create successive suspensions of disbelief that irreverently point to the falsity of the convention of stage deaths in the first place. No matter how realistic a theatrical scene may appear, a death on stage, unless an actor is actually dying—which has not been a rare occurrence in the history of theater—is the ultimate simulation. As one of the characters in *Rosencrantz and Guildenstern Are Dead* beautifully put it, "Death isn't." But a stage death, like children's games of dying, killing and being killed and then coming back to life, can offer us what the French philosopher Michel de Montaigne urged all humans to engage in: "the practice of death." "To practice death is to practice freedom," he said. "A man who has learned how to die has unlearned how to be a slave" (1993, 416, 684). In the context of a play about war and postwar societies, Srbljanović may also use this device to urge audiences to practice empathy at the relentless deaths of others in useless wars that often start like children's games and end up in apocalyptic disasters. Empathy and moving outside of ourselves towards the grief of others is also to "practice freedom."

The experience of immigration and leaving Serbia during the postwar period, a theme that haunts Srbljanović, is also present in the play in a tumultuous scene in which Voijin becomes possessed by rage at South and North America, at black people, at President Clinton. He suspects that his son is taking drugs and finds the Dominican flag that he was carrying at the beginning of the scene, returning from a demonstration. The father's language carries all the markers of hate and nationalistic language as he hurls insults:

> **Voijin:** Whose flag is this?
> *Looks at the flag and tears it up*
> Do—mi—ni....
> **Andria:** Dominican Republic
> **Milena:** Where is this?
> **Andria:** In South America.
> **Voijin:** Where there are Blacks?
> **Milena:** Blacks are notorious drug users.
> **Voijin:** Is it for the Black that you are fighting against our militia?
> **Andria:** Daddy, I haven't fought....

Voijin: Is it the Blacks who are paying you to tear up your country?

...

Voijin: You have found the means to sell yourself to South America? To put yourself under their flag? And right in the heart of Serbia, of our cradle, the Kosovo, earth of Emperor Lazar and of Dusan the Omnipotent?

Voijin breaks the flag on his knee.

I shit on their history. Let President Clinton do their politics and leave us alone.

Milena: Blacks of shit!

Andria: Mom, what shame.

Milena: What did you say?

Voijin: What did you say to your mother?...

Andria: It's not good to talk like that.

Porterfield notes that in this passage, Voijin "is meant to be the mouthpiece for the xenophobic sentiments of a significant and vocal section of the population," while also concluding that Srbljanović's "ability to appeal to international audiences lies, in part, in her willingness to remain critical of both her own government and those of its friends and enemies" (2009, 95). Again, in the spirit of my book, I would add that this appeal is due to the fact that she has ramified and incarnated her criticism into arresting, troubling, and startling structures, characters, and language. Following the exchange quoted above, Voijin brutally beats up Andria and at the end of the scene Andria strangles his parents with a chain, saying: "No choice!" No wonder that even Serbian intellectuals with the least amount of patriotic or nationalistic sentiment would consider Biljana Srbljanović a "traitor" and would be critical of her courageous stance. She takes no prisoners in her criticism of racial and ethnic hatred and of overblown patriotic pride. The uncompromising denunciation of nationalistic violence combined with domestic violence targets both sides of the war/abuse: it vindicates the victims and shames the aggressors.

At the end of yet another scene the parents die again, this time of grief as their son Andria immigrates to Norway. And at the very conclusion of the play Nadezda acquires her humanity; she talks and apologizes to Milena and Voijin as if they were her parents as well, promising to be good in the future. Nadezda and Voijin are lying like corpses "carrying all the signs of the previous deaths." At the end Nadezda throws a grenade that explodes in the distance and "Milena, Voijin, Andria and Nadezda remain frozen" (*FS* 82). The "signs of the previous deaths" written on the actors' bodies and the ending in another violent action catch us in an existential vertigo, in a carnival of life and death in which neither holds any weight; yet they seem to stare at us with the grimace of "frozen" masks whose laughter is indistinguishable from tears.

By trying to elude the real through games, dreams, a wild circus of life and death that mercilessly breaks the suspension of disbelief, Biljana's play brings out in sultry colors many shreds of the real: the loss of humanity as a result of nationalistic hatred; domestic abuse; and the devastation brought about by war, food shortages, emigration, greed, suffering, blood, and death. Whether horrific, beautiful, banal or anything in between, we need to acknowledge the real because only by facing our historical moment in all its colors and shapes can we protect ourselves from its dark sides. Srbljanović's simulacra do not produce the "liquidation of the referential"; they trigger memories and images of the referential. However, it is my contention that in artistic expression the real of our modern era is best guarded, remembered, examined or criticized through refraction and not through reflection, through oblique evocation or incorporation and not through the arrogance of creating images that pretend to be "more real than the real." It is true, as Baudrillard has articulated eloquently, that through simulation the real disappears as it gets lost in the multitude of its copies. In Biljana's theater, as in Saviana Stanescu's or Matei Vişniec's theater, the real is on the contrary testified to or simply allowed to shine through because of the distancing, the games, the carnival, the formal brokenness and even messiness. These structures refer to reality obliquely and thus paradoxically make it more obvious.

Lazin points out that "failure and the characters deprived of a reality" are specific of Biljana's style. He also points to the importance of the "game" in the Belgrade school of playwriting that Biljana has assimilated from her training (Lazin 2006, 231) while combining such devices with realistic sequences (230). Indeed her postmodernist realism is connected to the world she lives in and offers resistance to its inequities through the clever use of the game and of all the imaginative and bold Brechtian theatrical strategies, combined with her own original mark as a profoundly parodic and harshly ironic theater artist. *Family Stories* is a magnificent illustration of Linda Hutcheon's theory of postmodern parody and irony as "wholesale nudging commitment to doubleness or duplicity" (2002, 1–2), which, unlike Jameson's notion of postmodern "pastiche" (1991, 17) is not, as he believes, devoid of political relevance but on the contrary offers an important critique of society. Irony and parody unsettle all ideologies and claims to any ultimate truth (Hutcheon 2002, 93–95). According to Hutcheon "parody is doubly coded in political terms: it both legitimizes and subverts that which it parodies" (2002, 101). This statement echoes the earlier discussion of Vişniec's play *Body of a Woman* in light of Judy Little's notion of "carnivalizing the sentence," according to which the voice of authority is both imbedded in the discourse and ironically overturned. *Family Stories*, particularly in the character of the father Voijin, exemplifies the full range of reckless violence, abuse of authority and hate language specific to what Dorra in Vişniec's play has aptly coined "Balkan man," with his "ancestral" state of alcoholic melancholy. It does this through the roller-coaster of "doubleness or duplicity" beautifully embedded in the artifice of children playing adults. Furthermore, if we consider the fact that Srbljanović has written plays that are sharply critical of Serbia's nationalistic politics from within her own country and has known enormous success outside the frontiers of her homeland, we have to also admire her extraordinary courage in taking such a political stance. An exile in her own country yet engaged in its political mire with a sharply lucid spirit and a relentless creative imagination, Srbljanović demands through her brilliant theatrical work the same recognition from her own native Serbia as she has received from abroad. As her compatriot and great supporter Milos Lazin has noted, "It is of extreme importance that [Serbia] recognizes Srbljanović's choice as both a human and aesthetic act" (2006, 232) precisely in order to overcome its spirit of "cultural inferiority" and "self-sufficiency" (233) that has fueled many of its acts of nationalistic violence and which in turn is the target of much of the playwright's courageous criticism.

Biljana Srbljanović's theater works dealing with the traumas of exile and war, and in particular *Family Stories*, offer a brilliant example of postmodernist aesthetics as they engage in a political critique of the postmodern world even as they are part of it. Even as it uses simulacra, her work pierces through the shell of simulacra with the unforgiving knife of irony and parody. By distancing themselves from and pretending the real, her characters, in their linguistic and behavioral delirium, offer us the troubling yet precious gift of shards of the real grasped from a mutilated world.

Milena Markovic: Grand Guignol Horror and Dystopia

Milena Markovic is another courageous Serbian playwright writing in Serbia about her contemporary society. Her plays are quite different in form from Biljana Srbljanović's works, yet they develop similar themes and focus on the same postwar period. In an article about the plays she gathered for the festival of Eastern European women playwrights under the auspices of her Immigrant Theater Project, Marcy Arlin notes about the play that she directed by Milena Markovic, titled *The Pavillions*: "It is a play like Gorky's *Lower Depths*, 'a story about a people trapped in a ghetto; it's a suburban life in a ghetto country.' First produced about twelve years ago, the play reflects the disintegration of a society recently at war and the violent devastating economic and moral effects on Markovic's generation"[17] (2012, 54–55). That generation includes Biljana Srbljanović, and like her plays, *The Pavillions* emerges from the experience of the postwar dystopia that Serbian society became in the nineties and early two thousands and from the experience of staying in the country and dealing with the material, moral and cultural devastation of that world.

Milena Markovic's plays have also been produced abroad and within the boundaries of her country. *The Pavillions* has been produced in Germany, Macedonia, and Slovenia as well as in Japan by the Black Tent Theatre Tokyo and at La MaMa Theater in New York. It is significant that the Japanese production was done with large puppets, because *The Pavillions* is presented as a "Grand Guignol Horror." The use of large puppets is much in tune with the first examples of Grand Guignol, including Alfred Jarry's *King Ubu*, the first production of which at the *Theatre de l'Oeuvre* in Paris was done with real actors dressed like puppets and produced in Guignol style. As Erik Ehn has beautifully noted, puppets "are sites into which we can travel more deeply. We can get more lost in there, in puppets. The deeper the site (the further into it we may invest) the more specific" (2013, 91). Maybe for the same reason, Matei Vişniec's Japanese version of *Why Hecuba?* was also produced with large puppets. Eugène Ionesco remembers how as a child he developed his love of theater not from the plays of Racine or Shakespeare or even Chekhov, but from the puppet shows in the Jardin du Luxembourg, which revealed to him the fascinating spectacle of "the strangeness of the world" (1962). Indeed through the bodies of puppets, which while still bodies are yet neither alive nor human, yet offer a troubling resemblance to humans, inaccessible realities and unbearable truths may find a place where they can unfold into recognizable and graspable forms.

Milena's plays are slightly more recent than those of Biljana Srbljanović, but they are also more specific to the culture and apparently are appreciated and successful in Serbia, which is not altogether true about Srbljanović's plays. Marcy Arlin notes:

> *The Pavilions* is a Grand Guignol Horror story about sexual and physical abuse, drug addiction, and the desire for love and intimacy in a working-class housing block in Belgrade, though Markovic says "it could happen in any patriarchal family and any [*sic*] marriage .... [a] story about a boy who is a junkie and has post-traumatic war syndrome is very familiar."... The language is coarse, violent, and shocking, yet weirdly captivating and beautiful, and for the Serbian audience, extremely funny [2012, 54].

In an interview she gave me, Milena Markovic expressed radically different views from many of the authors quoted here in that she does not believe in political theater or the artfulness or the necessity of it, expressing rather a position that many East European artists hold, namely a belief in theater that is not deliberately engaged in the society of its time if not by mere coincidence. When asked by me if "the experiences of war, political instability or oppression and/or exile influence not only the content of your theater and the stories you choose but also the form and the aesthetic of your theater," she answered rather cynically:

> Every experience is important for an artist. Sometimes artists who are not gifted are taking from the well of a war and political instability because it would make them successful. Those artists are anti-war profiteers and this kind of art could survive for ten or twenty years and it is over. There is a lot of deceitfulness in this kind of so-called art. I am interested in the human soul and some archetype themes which are from the beginning of man's thinking. It could be the experience and suffering of war... [2013].

In her interview she spoke with some vehemence against the notion that the small countries like Serbia are expected by the big capitalist countries to produce "some monkey stuff" and create cultural products that are only about "war, instability, oppression and ask for help from the big, big West." There is something to be said about the fact that the interest of Western countries in the artistic and cultural products of either East European or of other parts of the world often equals an attraction towards an element of exoticism or of sensationalism such as war, oppression, or genocide. A simple love story in a neutral space or time developed in a play by, say, a Polish or Hindu artist might not be of great interest for an American or French audience. However, it is always the specific that leads to the universal, and I use universal not in the sense of an essentializing view of humanity but in the sense of a commonality of the human experience and the human condition, as illustrated in a play such as *Waiting for Godot.* Despite Milena's argument against political theater or art that moves with the times and deals with the realities of its time, her own theater still reflects the realities of her society: a devastated post-communist, postwar world troubled by sexual abuse, addiction and post-traumatic stress.

In *The Pavillions* Markovic uses the style of the Grand Guignol Horror, which involves outrageous exaggerations of violent behavior and language in a kind of exaggerated naturalism. Or rather she uses a modern parody of the Grand Guignol Horror shows. The Grand Guignol Theater in Paris, which was created by Oscar Metenier in 1897, knew its highest success during World War II and closed its doors in 1962. It indulged in staging spectacles of mutilation, cruel deaths and madness that created such strong emotions and indeed such horror on stage that audience members were known to faint or vomit during the shows.[18] It is interesting that Markovic makes use of a style that knew its highest success in between the two world wars and during World War II. Milena's style is like a rough fairytale that has been passed through the meat grinder. A critic had said about Alfred Jarry's play *King Ubu* that it was *Macbeth* passed through the meat grinder and turned into sausage. Markovic is creating what Baudrillard referred to as the imitation of an imitation from which disturbing bits and pieces of a real gone really wrong may be coming out at the other end of her imaginative grinder. However, at the same time as Markovic seems to parody the style of the Grand Guignol Horror in her crudely naturalistic depiction of the abuses, drug use and violence, her parody is also a means of social critique despite her own views against political theater. The beginning of the play, in which the husband Knez, "an old thug," insults and verbally abuses his wife Lepa, "a totally ruined beauty," is reminiscent of the beginning of Alfred Jarry's *King Ubu*, in which Father Ubu and Mother Ubu unleash exchanges of insults that seem to partake of the Bakhtinian carnival of obscenity and indulgence in "the lower bodily stratum." Through the coarse language and vulgar actions of people in power, Jarry criticized the opportunistic class of his time, who although uneducated and corrupt, or maybe precisely *because* uneducated and corrupt, managed to achieve power and money through deceit and violence. Markovic's Serbian carnival goes even farther in the use of obscenity to an R-rated form of discourse that offers the image of a demoralized and degraded humanity, the "nouveau riche" turned wealthy by scabrous and illegal means in a society where the rule of law seems to have gone haywire:

Knez: Lepa!
Lepa enters.
Knez: I wish I could figure out what you feed your fat face with, you stupid bitch. The food they gave me in the nick was better than yours, Lepa. And still you're as fat and ruddy as a fucking apple, stinking cunt....
Lepa: I....
Knez: Have problems with health.... Yeah, my dick.
Open your mouth *(she opens it)*
You haven't got a single bad fucking tooth, you're a monster....
Lepa: You want to eat?
Knez: No, like I'm gonna starve.... You've made my coffee with dishwater, fucking cunt, you want to poison me.... You just keep quiet and go on poisoning me....
Lepa: Here....
Knez: Here, here. Lepa's cheese pie, a snot pie, better said, made of leftovers that are, like, not for throwing but are only good for the bin.... You make my pie from pig's trough leftovers and a different pie for yourself, you stinking cunt. It's too much to look at you. And my Zora's cabbage smelt like cake, and cheese pie, what cheese pie it was, like you'd wish from the fairies, you hear me, you stupid bitch?

He eats.
Knez: Lepa, sweetie! This cheese pie of yours is really good, chewy like chewing gum, fucking pie.
Lepa: Thank you.
Knez: Come, let Knez give his fatso a kiss, you're a queen *(he slaps her bottom)* [2012].[19]

Dziga, "a legend, nearly former" is Knez's brother, a war veteran who "was burning houses and blowing up cows for three years." He is addicted to heroine and now works for someone called Copa the King, who is something of a mafia man. Knez is also in love with Mala, "a ruined beauty" and former prostitute. The lowest of humanity gather in this postmodern Guignol Horror in which the horror derives from the harshness of reality itself, and is represented in a naturalistic manner that is as shocking as it is fascinating. Addiction, sexual violence, and delinquency are part of the post-communist societies of many East European countries, and Serbia has the added history of a relatively recent war of aggression and ethnic cleansing.[20] The brutal gang rape of one of the acquaintances of this scary family, depicted towards the end of the play, is nothing that Serbian soldiers hadn't performed themselves. Thousands of Muslim Bosnian women were subjected to brutal genocidal rapes and forced inseminations in rape camps by Serbian soldiers of the Republika Srepska. Markovic uses the Grand Guignol Horror not, like in the original French shows in the interwar and war periods, as an escapist leap into the fantastical but as a plunge into the gruesomely real and into the life of a world that has become desensitized to violence, human pain, and even death. In her interview she answered my question about theater aesthetic with the following:

DR: Do you connect fractured or fragmented theatrical form, non-linear structures and chronologies to the theatrical form of your plays?

Milena Markovic: I am always trying to play with structure, language, form, poetry, metric, etc. Most of my plays are fragmented and open, but some of them are fragmented and very linear and focused. I have one play which is in continuity. I play. It's what I like. And first of all I write poetry, so I have this ability to play with language too [2013].

The importance of playing with language and structure fits Lazin's earlier informative commentary that the Belgrade school of drama and play writing focuses on the use and exploration of the potentialities of the game in the creation of theater and performance. One can notice similarities between the theater of Biljana Srbljanović and Milena Markovic in terms of pushing the limits of sarcastic and parodic language, of exploring the extremes of stage violence, and of the use of the carnivalesque and the playful in tackling difficult themes such as sexual and domestic violence, war related post-traumatic stress disorders, addiction and delinquency. But while Srbljanović's texts are multilayered, diverse and different from each other and engage in an unapologetic social and political critique of her time, Markovic's play *The Pavillions* rushes in one violent scene after another until the climactic moment at the end when one of the characters' girlfriends blows herself up with a gun after she has shot heroin. The play ends in "darkness and explosion." Even though the narrative is relatively linear, the structure of the play is one of broken linearity, just as Markovic said in the interview. The different scenes, or rather the rapid sequences taking place between the characters, rush rapidly without any separation or transition from one another in one continuous but bumpy ride. One moment we are in the house of Lepa and Knez, who bicker in their vulgar way; the next some older aunts or grandmothers of the family Ludmila and Dobrila are being attacked by thieves; and the next the brothers are talking about drugs, and killing people; then we are back with Lepa and Knez; then with the brothers and Copa the King, engaged in vulgar conversations about guns, drugs and brutal sex; then Mala, the girlfriend of one of them, shoots heroin and then "she shoots herself in the mouth." After the conversation about Cera's pregnancy and their future as mother and grandmother, we are back with the men talking about Fat Jolly, a woman who had been gang raped and who killed herself after the fact. The characters act as if the suicide of Mala had never happened; they talk about the gang rape as if talking about ordinary facts in a shockingly blasé manner. At some point in this back and forth of conversations, one of the thieves who had broken into the old women's house gives an absurd soliloquy:

> That's impermissible. Life is short and everyone should take care of culture and hygiene. I, for instance, don't like to talk about nonsense. I miss nothing. I'm sick of it. I like to eat well, I make sure I sleep well for that is good for your organism. Sometimes I catch some good movie, only I never remember the title. Nor do I remember the story. I don't know what my name is. Nor is it of any importance. There are so many beautiful names. My mother is a woman who smells of cinnamon. I've got a wife somewhere. I have kids too. They belong to themselves. One should not tie oneself to things. Today you're here tomorrow you're gone [2012, 3].

There is a sense of complete moral void combined with a sense of suspended time and indiscriminate place in this dystopian world where all boundaries between right and wrong have been obliterated and where the only difference is between wrong and more wrong. The male characters in particular seem entirely desensitized to the most gruesome of violent acts as they glide in and out of their drug-induced stupor or aggressiveness or a combination of the two. The women are either entirely complacent, like Lepa, or as vulgar as the men, like Mala. The playfulness is grisly rather than humorous and offers no redemption for any of the characters, whose only logical end seems to be in "darkness and explosion." If we felt sympathy for the children playing the violent adult games in Srbljanović's play and often appreciated their dark humor or even poetry, as they moved in and out of a wide range of tragic situations, no empathy is elicited by any of the characters in Markovic's play, as they seem to be entirely blind to their own moral degradation and human misery. The overlapping of conversations and broken flow of scenes without any transitions keeps us in a kind of aesthetic and psychological immobility where there is no evolution towards any significant revelations, but just an inevitable glide towards the final horror that puts an end to the series of many horrors:

> **Copa:** If somebody shoots me, the brothers go down and Kepa gets Mala. Hey, love, do you like Kepa? Look how big he is.
> **Mala:** Copa, tell them to go out. I'd never shoot at you. Never.
> **Copa:** Go out!
> **Mala:** I'd never shoot a man. I don't know how you could.
> **Dziga:** You're bullshitting.
> **Copa:** I've never shot a man either.
> **Dziga:** That dirty job is mine, brother.
> **Mala:** How many people have you killed?
> **Dziga:** I don't know.
> **Mala:** I'd like to feel it going off.
> **Dziga:** Don't fuck about.
> **Copa:** Love, give me that and come with me.
> **Mala:** I'm coming.
> *She shoots herself in the mouth.*
> *Darkness. Dziga's screams are heard* [2012].

While the original Grand Guignol was played with puppets and then with actors in overly histrionic modes, this play offers a terrifying view of humans acting like puppets in a world devoid of moral boundaries or lucid understanding. The ultimate horror is not in a nightmarish vision of reality but in a reality-turned-nightmare. In an NPR interview about his movie *Django*, which depicted the horrors of slavery, Quentin Tarantino, when asked about the extreme violence of the movie, answered that the violence depicted in the movie, as gruesome and over-the-top as it might seem to today's viewers, is nothing when compared to the actual reality of slavery. The realities from which both Srbljanović and Markovic derive the substance of their plays, the recent histories of the war of the nineties and of Serbia's part in it, are in fact much scarier than the ones portrayed on stage. I return to the scope of the present book again to note that the theatrical aesthetics of works emerging from the realities of war or postwar societies carry specific signs and markers. In the case of the two Serbian playwrights, realism is pushed to heightened degrees of intensity where it still breaks with traditional realism and changes into what I have called postmodernist realism: an aesthetics that does not fall into the fantastical, the oneiric or the absurd, but that uses game, dark humor, sarcasm, and violent discourse and actions to point to a reality that is even harsher. If in the process Biljana uses the device of children's games portraying adult situations to depict domestic abuse and war violence, and Milena uses the exaggerations of the Grand Guignol Horror to depict a dystopian society, if they indulge at times in pastiche or the imitation of imitation, they also manage to squeeze out of twisted images some of the bitter juices of the reality around them.

Milena Markovic's body of dramatic works is quite diverse, and she is true to her statement that she likes trying out different forms and experimenting with language and structure. Her play *A Boat for Dolls* is often violent in action and language but is entirely built within the structure of and with characters taken from different fairy tales. *A Boat for Dolls*, or *The Doll Ship*, was produced at La MaMa theater in New York in 2012 and advertised with the following description:

> In *The Doll Ship*, a specific collision occurs between the archetypical model of the intricate world of fairy tales, and the bare essence of a reality we know all too well—a reality freed from crumbling crusts that give an educational purpose to fairy tales as reading material. The result offered by Milena Markovic is the truth, and a painfully frightening one at that.[21]

Markovic mixes many plots and characters of different stories, including Snow White, Goldilocks, Thumbelina, Papa Bear and Mama Bear, a generic witch, princess, big sister, the frog, Sleepy, and Grumpy, and turns the utopian world of traditional fairy tales into a dystopian chaotic tale in which sexual abuse, sex between animal creatures and humans, alcoholism, and physical abuse infiltrate every corner of the plot in dark colors and a troubling theatrical universe. This play is not really about either war or exile and it is tangential to the scope of this book, but because of the weirdly dystopian universe created from bits and pieces of known fairy tales, the humor, the continuous use of pastiche and parody in the depiction of dysfunctional relations between parents and children, siblings, or spouses, it creates an original world that could be a post-apocalyptic one or a world filled with rambling exiles who travel from fairy tale to fairy tale in search of a home, a family, or an identity. The element of terror, and the frightful creatures, supernatural events and beings that fill traditional fairy tales are all further heightened, creating a threatening universe with no heroes and redeeming acts to save the day, but only anti-heroes and heroines caught in sexual games and rambling aimlessly through a world devoid of meaning. Known fairy-tale interdictions and songs are recreated and parodied in ditties with ominous forebodings, such as in the following exchange between daughters and their mother, reminiscent of a mixture of *Blue Beard*, *Goldilocks*, and *The Three Little Pigs*:

> **Little Sister:** And why can't we go into that room?
> **Mum:** The time hasn't come yet.
> **Big Sister:** And when will the time come?
> **Mum:** There are beasts in that room.
> **Little Sister:** What sort of beasts?
> **Mum:**
> One says now
> the other says no
> the third one is looking at you and grinning
> the fourth one eats the wiggling meat
> but its eyes are kind, the beast's,
> the fifth one says do it do it
> no harm in that
> the sixth one has no eyes
> the seventh one has no ears
> the eighth one has no mouth
> the ninth one is memory
> the tenth one is death [2004, Scene 1, 3].

All sexual taboos are broken; characters of known fairy tales such as *Snow White* have sex with one another and indulge in obscene language that reminds us a lot more of the unleashed, bawdy carnival language in the Bakhtinian sense than the glossy world of children's tales. It also has echoes of Sarah Kane's theater and of the "in-yer-face" theater aesthetic of stark unadorned violence:

> **Sleepy:** I can't stand it.
> **Grumpy:** Don't hit your head too much, the shelf will fall down.
> **Doc:** Let the roof fall down let the world collapse I can't stand I can't stand I can't stand how can people like that sleepy little cunt even exist.
> Do you think he can save you now if I say I feel like harassing you, you see he doesn't even see straight he's a little cunt has he asked you for money.
> He's gonna start asking you for money tomorrow [2004, Scene 2, 20].

The mythic world of fairy tales is cracked open and the archetypal figures of the lost little girl, the princess, a frog that is actually a prince, and the bad witch are all reinvented in light of the realities of our world and Freudian psychology. Thumbelina and the frog are making out, after which they sing a bawdy song as flash cameras photograph her. There is applause as if she was performing in a bar, cabaret, strip joint:

Song: "Success"
Thumbelina and the Frog:
I came to this beautiful place
And everyone was there
And everyone was looking for me
And I was there
And then I was left alone and I went
To fuck the bartender
And the bartender was quick.
Mama can you see me now
Mama it was all
For you
Mama [2004, Scene 4, 9, 36].

In her extensive study, *Postmodern Fairytales; Gender and Narrative Strategies*, Christina Bacchilega explores the many ways in which modern and postmodern writers have appropriated the fertile field of fairy tales and have reinvented and adapted old fairy tales to the questions, anxieties and realities of our times. She points out that feminist writers have "engaged the tradition of fairy tales 'to refuse to obey their authority by revising and appropriating them'" (1997, 4). Her study focuses mostly on the production of gender in postmodern, recreated fairy tales and attempts to answer the question, "What kinds of images of woman and story do these rewritings/revisions project?" (4). It is obvious that Milena Markovic's dramatic recreation of fairy tales breaks the boundaries of traditional children's bedtime stories and turns them into R-rated stories in which the images of women radically contradict the archetypal figures of the sweet princess pining for her prince, the innocent or lost little girl, the evil witch, and so on. That some of the female characters are bawdy, openly sexual and even sexually aggressive is obvious, but in what way they offer emancipated images of women that reverse and explode gender stereotypes altogether is not clear. This play is not without relevance to my present topic, as it offers an extended picture of a worldview emerging from a society broken by a genocidal war against its neighbors, devastated by the exodus of young people emigrating, and shaken by political and economic instability. Even if the female characters are willing or even eager to have sex, there are still intimations of sexual violence, as it is still largely the men starting discussions of sex or initiating it, and it is still about the rule of the father, as in Thumbelina's story.

The world of this play is a Disneyland turned on its head, in which the illusion of perfect heroes and heroines, the classic battle between good and bad with the good characters always victorious over bad witches and evil monsters, is cracked open and populated by degraded, trashy copies of Disney versions of old fairy tale characters mostly in a chase for sexual thrills. Beaudrillard considers Disneyland a classic example of simulacra and of the hyperreal, and a perfect example of the different stages of simulation: "Disneyland is presented as imaginary in order to make us believe that the rest is real, when in fact all of Los Angeles and the America surrounding it are no longer real, but of the order of the hyper real and simulation" (1994a, 262). I contend, as I did earlier in the discussion of Srbljanović's postmodernist realism, that Markovic's use of fairy tale archetypes and of Disney versions of fairy tales is a different kind of postmodernism. This theater is postmodernist *because* it mocks the postmodern presumption of a real that is "more real than the real" and that completely loses all sense of a basic reality. As noted earlier in the discussion of Srbljanović's use of pastiche, the use of fairy tales and Disney recreations of old fairy tales reveals a postmodernist art that is critical of its own artifices while making use of them. As it explodes the illusions of fairy tales and Disney magic into a multitude of pieces of raw language, lewd action, gross irony and sarcasm, Markovic's play brings us closer to the basic realities of a troubled society. The awareness of the characters as such—typical of postmodernist self-referentiality—cracks open the shell of simulation and moves beyond it back to its original model. *Boat for Dolls* carries us ruthlessly onto the hard shore of painful realities and maybe also beyond them in the final and pathetic cry of the witch begging her daddy to be reborn, a cry that is both clingy to that ultimate patriarchal figure and desperately wanting to be freed from it.

> Daddy, I wanted to ask you to make me a boat to leave on.
> ...
> Make me a boat to leave on.
> To sail on it and then you'll tell me
> Pretty stories daddy
> I want to be born again
> My daddy [2004, 66].

A symbol of exile in its solitary and definitive movement of leaving shores and countries; of journeys between countries at war; of new beginnings, as it gathers like a children's grotesque version of Noah's boat, humans and beasts of all specimens; the boat of Markovic's play is populated with sinister beings, lonely, sad princesses and witches who beg to be freed from their ancient shackles of illusions and stereotypes and to jump head first into our world, sad and scary as it might be. It is not without significance that the last words of the play are about wishing to be reborn. If we looked for a moment at Markovic's two plays, *The Pavillions* and *A Boat for Dolls*, in terms of the evolution of the author from one play to another, it would be aesthetically satisfying to consider that after the violent ending of *The Pavilions* in "darkness and explosion," suggesting complete obliteration, the ending of *A Boat for Dolls* creates the possibility of a new world, the desire for a new beginning, the only possible direction if one were to move past the finality of the complete "darkness," and if one were to consider the possibility of renewal after the destruction of war and the confusion of exile.

Motti Lerner: Playwriting as Resistance to War

The first time I met Motti Lerner, at his house in Tel Aviv on a hot and humid afternoon in July of 2012, he told me that the atmosphere in his country was becoming very radicalized, that there was little dissent left even among the most leftist liberal intellectuals and artists, and that he often felt like an exile in his own country. Instead of "dissent," there was growing "consensus," he said. He confessed he was one of the very few artists who still dared to question and at times even contradict the unequivocal pro–Israeli attitude, or to dare look at the other side as well. He was concerned about the general "consent" with the new government even among many of his intellectual friends. When his twenty-year-old daughter walked into the room, though, he announced proudly that she was just about to start army training, which all men and women in Israel have to complete for two years. Life in Israel is full at every moment of such contradictions, and no one could understand better the price and the need for peace then a parent who has to face on a daily basis the hard reality that his child might have to go to war. Though he spoke passionately of peace, he understood equally well the need for Israel to train its youth and prepare it for war, which has been a reality for Jews in that part of the world for decades now.

Motti Lerner is known as one of the pioneers of radical political theater in Israel. His plays, docudramas, television scripts, and open views on many aspects of the Israeli-Palestinian conflict, the occupation of Palestinian territories, and relations with the Jewish diaspora across the world have raised much controversy in his country. He has taught as a visiting professor at Duke University and still teaches courses at Knox College in Illinois. His plays have been produced for years in different theaters across the United States, including the Center Stage Theater in Baltimore, Chicago theaters, and most recently Theater J in Washington, D.C. For the amount of travel he does between his native Israel and the United States, he could claim himself as an American citizen as well. His play *The Murder of Isaac*, inspired by the brutal assassination of the Israeli prime-minister Ytzhak Rabin, has only recently been produced at Tel Aviv University. In

Motti Lerner, *The Murder of Isaac*: The Department of Theater Arts at Tel Aviv University; February 2014; directed by Roee Hertz-Rousso. Boris Gurlik (left) and Yael Hod (right). Yuda, the "belligerent" patient, and Shulamit, "a 38-year-old religious woman who plays a Settler," as characters in the play within the play who support the continued war (photograph: Mariela Piwnica).

2012 Lerner spoke with great chagrin about the fact that his play had not yet seen the stage lights in his own country, while it had been produced in Germany and the United States and the French version of the play had just been published. He must be one of the few writers left in Israel who still passionately believes in peace and in the necessity and power of theater to promote peace or make a change in the world. His unshakable position in the great value of political theater and of artists having the courage to ask the most difficult questions of their governments is as moving as it is inspiring. This is what he said in an article titled "*The Murder of Isaac* by Motti Lerner," before the play had been produced in Israel:

> What do I expect from the production of the play? I'm not naïve. I know that it will change neither the fate of the Middle East nor the results of the next elections in Israel. It's very difficult to change people by plays in the theatre. We must be aware of that. But nonetheless, we mustn't lose hope. Books and plays and films do create a change. Sometimes the change is very small. Sometimes the change is hidden. Sometimes the change is so deep that we can't see its traces on the surface. But even if this change is very minor, even if it's hidden, it's worth attempting [Lerner 2005].

Lerner's unshaken confidence in the importance of political theater is not a naïve or romantic dream but a lucid and well-thought-out philosophy of creating and existing in a country that has been devastated by wars, assassinations and attacks for decades, the more so as he faces significant opposition and criticism for his positions in his own country. His insistence on the importance of lucid questioning by artists of all realities, but particularly of the gruesome realities of wars, illustrates a position of great courage and integrity. The fact that in the end his play was produced at Tel Aviv University (2013) proves that holding on to the belief in the power of theater to make a difference is not a useless and hopeless endeavor and that the artist still holds a tremendous power for social and political change through relentless questioning of the status quo and of any type of monolithic thinking.

I am focusing mainly on Lerner's play *The Murder of Isaac* not only because it deals with a crucial and tragic moment in the recent history of Israel or because it has raised such controversies, but also because it does all of the above through an extremely ingenious experimental form that further illustrates the thesis of my book. This is what he said about the inspiration for the aesthetic form he chose for writing a play inspired by the subject of the assassination of the prime minister, and how finally he settled on a form after considering a couple of other alternatives:

> The idea was to write the play as if it were taking place in a closed clinic for people who suffer from shell shock—or as it is defined in the psychological literature, PTSD (Post-Traumatic Stress Disorder). These people might not have suffered physical injury, but the war trauma has hurt them so badly that it reappears daily and ruins their lives. They can't live outside the clinic because of their anxieties, aggression, and lack of concentration. I had the feeling that this place could be a great metaphor for the Israeli society, which has been suffering consistently for more than fifty years from postwar traumas. This point of view was strong enough for a start to the writing of the play. The play immediately got its basic form: The inmates of the clinic are presenting a play that they themselves wrote about the murder of Rabin. The next phase was to find the characters and start writing some scenes. Quite soon after the beginning of writing, I realized that these suffering characters have much sharper observation of the reality then I had [2005].

I will look at *The Murder of Isaac* through the lens of Lerner's own views about the power of and necessity of political theater. In an article titled "Playwriting in Wartime," (2009) Lerner offers a constructive and beautifully articulated manifesto with regards to the responsibilities and obligations of the theater artist in times of war and violence. Even though he is of course referring to the Israeli-Palestinian war in his country, his observations and reflections are of value and can apply to any country in conditions of war and to the role of the artist in society in general. As someone who grew up and has lived his entire life in a country at war, Lerner is not only haunted by the question of the utility and function of art in conditions of historical and political violence but is consumed by a search for solutions. He says: "I am not suggesting that playwrights engage in political negotiations, but rather that playwrights engage in investigation of the psychological, ideological, mythical and political infrastructure of their society, in order to prove that these other possibilities indeed exist" (1). Furthermore, he notes that the playwright in times of war "must expose the lies disseminated amongst us on the nature of war. For countless centuries we have glorified war and described it as a stage on which man's courage, his willingness for sacrifice and his stubborn will to win are revealed." He calls the poetic glorifications of war "a tissue of lies" (3) and goes on to note:

> Most people who have participated in a war remember it as a terrible, ugly and humiliating experience. When they think about it they are filled with terror, horror and disgust, not pride and not satisfaction. They know that the pain they experienced will never abate. Hundreds of thousands of us are unable to live normal lives because of our war experiences, and our neighbors, too, have similar nightmares. The playwright must remind us all of this so that those who have not experienced war will not be so eager to participate in it [2].

In line with my belief in the necessity of a theater of war that aims towards the awakening of critical thinking in the audience in the ways promoted and illustrated by Bertolt Brecht, Lerner notes that a theater of war that lucidly exposes the evils of war will act as a warning force for the audience, and therefore create, as I have contended so far, a safe space or at least the possibility of a safer space:

> The heroes of our political plays, too, will fail in their endeavors to counteract the reasons for war. They, too, will fail to prevent the titanic clashes in whose shadow we live. But their failure is a warning signal for the audience. Their failure on stage strengthens the audience to contend with the reasons for war existing in their own political reality [4].

The function of theater as a "warning signal" is in my thinking that which has the potential of making out of the theater of war a safe space, in the sense of enabling the spectators to develop strategies of resistance to war, strategies of denunciation of its injustice and futility, and furthermore, strategies of self-preservation in conditions of war and violence. In an ironic manner, the artistic theater of war must to some degree, through its reenactments, the rekindling of painful memories, the reliving of suffering and the telling of wrenching stories, inflict a form of secondary psychological trauma on the audience in order to alert them and warn them of the primary trauma of war itself and thus turn them into resisting subjects.

Even when torn by doubts about the function of the playwright in society, Lerner persists in believing against all odds in the necessity of creating art that stands up to the cruelty of war:

> Every day I awaken to new doubts, and every day I am compelled to go on fighting them in order to again believe that the playwright's influence is not an illusion. Every day I reiterate to myself that while the playwright is, perhaps, unable to bring about immediate change, he can possibly do so in the long term. Perhaps he is creating a latent stream of consciousness that is gradually spreading, gradually reaching hidden corners, and in not too many years' time we will all discover its influence [9].

It is the "latent stream of consciousness" reaching "hidden corners" that makes of political theater, and of the theater of war in particular, a safe space where audiences are being warned, awoken to and initiated into a rhythm of questioning, critical thinking, and lucid action that, even if not capable of stopping wars, is at least capable of creating a cordon of resistance and memory. For instance, the street performances of Women in Black in silent remembrance of the victims of the Bosnian War of the nineties have by now become an annual occurrence in Belgrade and are now protected by a cordon of police. Lerner's play *The Murder of Isaac* is finally being produced in Tel Aviv during a time when violence and armed conflicts between the Palestinian and Israeli forces are as worrisome as they have ever been. Its message of peace, articulated in a highly experimental theatrical form, is allowed to air itself at a time of extreme conservativism of the Israeli government.

The Murder of Isaac takes place in the Israeli Ministry of Defense rehabilitation center for post-traumatic stress disorder patients. It is structured in multiple layers of theatrical action as the patients are engaged in the production of an anti-war play that keeps getting sidetracked and distracted by the actors' personal issues and their own diverging positions towards the war. The character resembling Yitzhak Rabin is shot at the very end of the play in an oblique remembrance of the prime minister and his tragic fate. The play's language and structure are, as in Erik Ehn's observation, "splintered" and composed of collages of songs, speeches, and dialogues among the patients as patients and as the characters they are playing, of movements in and out of the audience, all in a Brechtian roller-coaster of "separation of elements" and broken fourth walls. The patients go in and out of their parts, offering comments on their own characters. They break down and they break the continuity of the play that they are expected to produce. Layer upon layer, they build a relentless denunciation of war as they are both living and playing war, as they are both remembering their own traumas and attempting to remove themselves from their memories through the parts they are playing and also not playing. In the scene quoted below, the rabbis are characters in the play that the patients try to produce, and they are attempting to find a solution to the war. The scene breaks down when one of the actors points a gun at Binder, the character who plays the prime minister. Lerner notes, "The play is constructed as a play within a play. The dialogues written and rehearsed by the patients are printed in this font, while those created as the play is staged due to the various snags and interruptions appear in this one."

Rabbi B: What do we do, Rabbi?
Rabbi C: Everything. We do everything.
Rabbi A: "Everything" meaning "everything"?
Rabbi C: (*Forcefully*) Everything. Everything. Everything. Everything.
Rabbi B: You mean really everything?
Shulamit: He said everything.
Rabbi C: (*In a rage*) Everything. Everything. Everything. Everything. Everything!
At the height of Rabbi C's ecstatic outburst Yigal pulls out a gun and aims at Binder.
Yigal: Everything! (*"Fires" three shots*) Blessed art thou, O Lord our God, who wreaks our vengeance.
Binder: (*In panic*) Ahhhhh... (*He shields his head with his arms*)
Natan: My ears are ringing, Lola.
Lola: (*To Yigal*) Sit down until it's your turn. And put that gun in your pocket. (*To Binder*) Calm down, Binder, he got confused, that's all.
Binder: Did you check everyone at the entrance? Their bags too?
Lola: Yes. (*To Avi*) Bring him some water.
Binder: Are the doors locked? Are the guards outside?
Lola: Yes. (*She wipes his nose*)
Binder: (*To the audience*) They're trying to kill me. By running me down. By poisoning me. By throwing me out of a window.
Lola: We can't continue without you, Binder.
Binder: (*To Lola*) They'll do anything so I won't remind them what war is all about. (*To the audience*) War is a sting on your shoulder. A burning sting! In the dark. Like a hornet's sting. What is it? What's this sting? I've been shot. Who dares? You shout and no one answers. You're all alone in the world. And there's another sting. On the cheek. God, what a terrible noise. And there's nowhere to run. Now there's a flash of lightning and the rumble of thunder. And you're covered in dust and smoke. And you choke and retch. You want to stand up but can't. You try again and fall down. And more lightning and more thunder. And suddenly you

feel a dull pain. And the pain slowly spreads. You look to the side. It's hard to see in the darkness. There's something lying there, right next to you. Something weird. Suddenly you understand. (*Slaps his artificial leg*) It's your leg. Your leg that has been ripped from your body. And it's still wearing your boot...

Natan: (*To Talia*) Sing, Talia. Sing your song.

Talia: (*Looks for her mother in the audience*) Where's my mother?

Natan: She's right there.

The orchestra plays, Talia sings.

If I had said the cannon needs cooling
You would have said, "Hold off!"
If I had said the rifle was jamming
You would have said, "Cease fire!"
If I had said that we're low on ammo
You would have ordered, "Halt!"
If I had said the tank blew an engine
Then you would have said, "Retreat!"
But I say our hearts are wrecked and defeated
I say our blood's frozen cold in our veins
I say our breath has grown short and weak
And you say "Fire! Fire! Fire!"
...
I say that there's no more purpose in fighting
I say that this makes no sense anymore
I pray to you, won't you please let us live
And you say "Fire! Fire! Fire!"

Binder: (*To the audience*) I sometimes go out of here. They take me to see this country of ours. I walk through the streets. I look at the passersby and don't see any pain in their faces. I see people hurrying by. I see people working. Walking. Enjoying themselves. Loving. Quarrelling. But I know. That one's brother is dead. This one's father. That one's son was blown up.... This one hasn't slept since a bomb landed next to him and ripped five people to shreds. (*Indicates Shulamit*) Her husband and two children were murdered. Pain is a danger signal. If we cover it up, we won't see the danger coming... [15–16].

Just as the patients have suffered scars and amputations, and just as the war victims have suffered blowing up, explosions, and traumas, the play's discourses and continuity, and the play within the play are all constantly splintered and blown up, broken and patched back together: an artificial leg, a broken-up line, a song, an argument among the actors/patients/war veterans, a shredding of theatrical discourse and a shredding of bodies. Yet there is a relentless and unforgiving will to create a safe space of questioning by refusing to "cover up" the pain, by refusing to pretend and act as if "we won't see the danger coming." And let us not forget that, when the play is produced in Israel, the audience lives rather close to if not precisely within the larger and real theater of war. But if there is any possibility for safety, then that is paradoxically in the courage to ask the unsafe questions, in the boldness to see and point to the "danger signal[s]." Just as in the sample above, the entire play is constructed in a relentless race and shift between the actual lives of the characters/actors/patients—such as Binder, Shulamit, Talia, and Yigel, who are all war victims—and the roles they are acting in the play that they are attempting to put together yet never manage to. Binder, the one who throughout the play is trying to promote peace and is playing the role of someone promoting peace—very much like the assassinated Yitzak Rabin—is also the one trying to alert everyone to the monstrous brokenness and abnormality of war, in a country where war has become the norm. The fact that in the end he is the one who ends up being shot by one of the actors in the play is doubly ironic and something of a *mise-en-abîme*, thanks to which the audience seems to be drawn closer and closer to the action of the play-within-the-play as well as to the action of the real war itself, while remaining within the boundaries of the theatrical production of the larger play. Was it the PTSD patient Binder or the character in the play that the patients are trying to put together who was shot? Both of them, of course. Crumbling, shredding, and breaking are not simply metaphors; they are the reality outside the theater house, and they define the construction of the play-within-the-play that never manages to come together and be presented before an audience. At the very end the patients/actors are desperately trying to keep the play running, just as it is disintegrating towards the brutal ending. They urge the orchestra to "Play, play" and the audience to "Start singing" just before one of the patients/actors fires "three real shots into Binder" (70).

When I asked Lerner if the experience of war has influenced the form of his play, this is what he answered: "If the content has to do with the experience of war or exile—the form will grow from the same experience. In *The Murder of Isaac* the form certainly grew from the experience of war" (2012a). In its brokenness, Lerner's play does its best to keep us whole and to keep its audiences safe by mercilessly waking them up from the mirage of war, from the illusion that we need war to keep peace, from the lie that there might be any heroism in war, and by reminding them that the prime minister had been killed by "real shots."

The combined use of the device of theater-within-theater and that of madness in order to deal with a raw and painful reality offers a superb example of the aesthetic of theater of war and of the distancing necessary to approach such subjects artistically. Are these devices and explorations of painful realities examples of simulations overlapped on top of simulations and reminding us of Beaudrillard's theories? Of course they are. And yet they are also something else: because they take inspiration from and refer to real historical events and hard realities of a country, they function as necessary distancing devices that evoke rather than represent, suggest rather than portray, and thus facilitate a clearer and tolerable tackling of harsh truths about this war that the audience, particularly the Israeli audience, would most likely not have been able to process otherwise. The theatrical device of madness, just like that of disguise, has a long history in the theater. From Shakespeare's clowns to the "mad scenes" of the *commedia dell'arte* actresses,[22] to nineteenth century romantic drama, to postmodern plays such as Vişniec's *How to Explain the History of Communism to Mental Patients,* to the acting of feminist "hysteria" and madness by performance artists (Aston 1999), madness has been used by theater makers as a means of telling the truth in a roundabout way, with the use of humor, playfulness, and even deviousness so that a particular truth can be made accessible or even acceptable to those who otherwise would have stayed impermeable to it. In the theater, the masking of reality is often the best way of exposing it.

Brecht suggested that in order for the public to understand historical events of the times, a theatrical performance should offer the necessary historical distance and deal with wars or other political issues taken from the past. A play about the Holocaust during the Holocaust would have been impossible to process or even watch for most Europeans at that time. Brecht's *Mother Courage,* a play about the Thirty Years' War (1618–1648), was created and presented in 1939 with the clear intention to resist and raise consciousness about the rise of fascism and in response to the occupation of Poland by Germany. The play was produced in Germany and Switzerland between 1941 and 1952 with the famous actress Helen Wiegel in the role of Mother Courage. The play is known as a great illustration of Brecht's theories of estrangement and epic theater; it consistently breaks the suspension of disbelief with scene and costume changes on stage and songs interspersed with narrative and dialogue. Lerner's play is similarly interspersed with songs, with the actors consistently going in and out of character, talking about the production within the production and addressing the audience directly. Maybe despite all the distancing devices beautifully used by Lerner in his play, the necessary distancing had not yet taken place for the Israeli audiences to be able to accept and process a work about the tragic assassination of their prime minister. It is maybe why it was close to fifteen years before the play could be produced in Israel. In a paradoxical manner, the refusal of Israeli theaters to produce this play for fear audiences would be traumatized and/or offended is a sign of success and a proof of the power of theater to move people, to create meaning, to elicit a variety of emotions and thoughts and to influence the public. And by the same token, the success of the Tel Aviv production of the play attests to the force that theater has to transform society. When asked about this production, Lerner shared the following: "The production of *The Murder of Isaac* at Tel Aviv University Theatre was very moving. I re-visited the play and revised it. I thought that the currents of madness and terror in the collective subconscious of the Israeli society have become clearer to me and I was able to interpret them through the characters more vividly. The play was received well" (2012a). As he commented in the article "Playwriting in Wartime," theater may not have the power to stop wars and change policies, but it does create an undercurrent of resistance; it touches the collective subconscious in ways that even though not always visible are conducive to change.

Recently Lerner's play *The Admission* has raised much controversy in the Washington, D.C., area and as a result its projected thirty-four-show run had initially been scaled down to a sixteen-show run presented as a "workshop." The play presents the parallel destinies of two families, one Israeli, one Palestinian, who are friends and neighbors in the old city of Jaffa and who have never been able to get closure and healing from events that happened during the 1948 Israeli-Palestinian war, when many Palestinians in a village were killed by Israeli soldiers. One of the generals partly responsible for these killings is the father in the Israeli family portrayed in the play. According to the *Washington Post*, the play provoked "a vigorous campaign mounted by a local ad-hoc group that calls itself Citizens Opposed to Propaganda Masquerading as Art to stop the presentation" and inspired the writing of e-mails such as this one: "One must ask: Why are Theater J, the DCJCC, and the Jewish Federation of Greater Washington promoting a discredited and defamatory lie against Israel?" (Marks 2013). As a result of the controversy and even though many people still supported the play, which ran to full houses, other groups of donors vowed to withhold support higher than $250,000 unless the play was cancelled. When interviewed about the controversy Lerner answered honestly and lucidly: "I didn't know that this would be so frightening and scary that it would create such a discourse in America." He added, "The play ... is trying to suggest that these historical memories have to be explored and revised continuously in order to create a solid basis for reconciliation between the two people" (Marks 2014). Peter Marks' cogent answer to the controversy is a passionate statement in support of theater's courage to ask and deal with the most difficult and uncomfortable questions in compelling artistic forms:

> Good theater does not depend on an investigative journalist's fealty to who, what, when, where and why. It succeeds when it finds metaphors that

> illuminate deeper truths, those that don't necessarily correspond to one verifiable set of facts. And the reality that *The Admission* boldly explores has to do with the opposing versions of calumny that Jews and Palestinians cultivate, competing archives of victimization that minimize the other side's scars and keep the wounds—and mistrust—forever fresh [2013].

The night I saw the play there was a small group of protesters in front of Theater J, but that did not stop the crowds that were curiously rushing to see the "workshop" of *The Admission* nor did it stop them from wholeheartedly applauding at the end of the show. If anything, the noise and controversy surrounding the play significantly increased the numbers of audiences. I do not discuss this play in detail because it does not display the features I have analyzed in my book. It is nevertheless an example of Lerner's artistic versatility combined with the unshakable courage to tackle hard truths and unpleasant historical events. And the unfolding journey of this play gives some reasons for hope. After reducing the number of productions, because of the very successful run of the first two weeks, and largely due to excellent reviews and full houses, Theater J extended it back to almost what had been planned originally. Furthermore, the play *The Admission* will be produced by Cameri theater in Tel Aviv. Lerner commented, "This is a very encouraging development that proves that the struggle to produce the play was worthwhile and I hope that this will mark the beginning of a more honest and more open discourse of the Israeli-Palestinian relationship and this in turn will contribute to reconciliation between the two nations" (2012a). Lerner's theater is living proof of the fact that the power of live theater can never be underestimated.

❧ ❧ ❧

The theater artists in this chapter travel through real and imaginary landscapes of terror, grim sites devastated by wars and circles of human suffering and degradation that make Dante's burning and freezing circles of his *Inferno* appear calm and innocent. Though it cannot be said that like Dante, at the end of their journeys they emerge unscathed with their eyes towards the stars, they do manage through their craft to guide us through dark tunnels of human agony and bring us at the other end into an eerie light—one that, although it shines over post-apocalyptic spectacles, yet does shine, allowing us to take another look at ourselves, inside ourselves, at our brothers and sisters in suffering, or in the words of the medieval French poet, at our "frères humains qui après nous vivez" ("human brothers who after us will live") (Villon 2004). It is not that they beautify trauma, genocide, war and postwar devastation through their art. It is that whether through the use of fantastical imagery, recreated ancient myths or fairy tales, macabre humor, or the artifice of madness or pastiche, these playwrights break up trauma into concrete shapes and sounds that may bear soothing and healing, that may warn us of the lies and dangers hidden behind discourses of fear and create ripples of lucid thought, authentic feeling, and stubborn resistance under the surface of dormant consciousness or convenient complacency.

Saviana Stanescu, *Aliens with Extraordinary Skills*: Women's Project Production; October 2008; directed by Tea Alagić. Nadia (Natalia Payne, right), and Nadia's boyfriend (Seth Fischer, left).

Pavel Zuštiak, *Painted Bird Trilogy*: La MaMa Theater; June–July 2013; directed by Pavel Zuštiak. This scene suggests crowd mentality, but also mass suffering (photograph: David Kamerman).

Dorota Maslowska, *A Couple of Poor Polish Speaking Romanians*: Trap Door Theatre; June 2009; directed by Max Truax. Parcha (Tiffany Bedwell) and Dzina (Kevin Cox). The two nomadic characters try to find their way, the direction of their travels, or a vehicle to take them to a faraway and vague destination. They are confused and also under the influence of alcohol and drugs (photograph by Michal Janicki).

Opposite, bottom: Matei Vişniec, *Pourquoi Hécube*: Theater Kaze, Tokyo, Japan; September 2013; directed by Sayaka Ehara. Yumiko Tsuji as Hecuba. The Japanese production was made with masks just as the ancient Greek tragedies were performed by actors wearing masks (photograph: Kaze).

Above: Matei Vişniec, *Por que Hecuba*: Teatro Vila Velha; January 2014; directed by Márcio Meirelles. In contrast with the grieving Hecuba, scenes such as this glamorous ensemble's dancing number are part of the show within the show (photograph: Márcio Meirelles).

C4

Matei Vişniec, *The Word Progress*: Trap Door Theatre; December 2011–January 2012; directed by István Szabó K. Simina Contras portrays an almost vaudevillian, tragicomic image of the daughter who returns home alive but battered, abused and traumatized (photograph: Michal Janicki).

Biljana Srbljanović, *Family Stories*: Whistler in the Dark Theater; May 2010; directed by Meg Taintor. *Above*: Nadezda (Jen O'Connor, in front with back to audience), Andrija (Danny Bryck), Milena (Melissa Barker), and Nate Gundy (Vojin). *Below*: Nadezda, the "dog" (Jen O'Connor), and Andrija, the "son" (Danny Bryck) (photograh: Meg Taintor)

C6

Adriana di Scipio's *Journey Theater*: Mazer Theatre, New York; 2003; directed by Marcy Arlin and Victor Maog. The woman whose face we see is Mayura Baweja. Masks by Liberty George Dukov (photograph: Marcia Mercadante).

Opposite: Motti Lerner, *The Murder of Isaac*: The Department of Theater Arts at Tel Aviv University; February 2014; directed by Roee Hertz-Rousso. Boris Gurlik (left) and Gilad Fridman (right) (photograph: Mariela Piwnica).

The Story of Tea: DAH Theater, Belgrade; 2006; directed by Dijana Milošević. Left to right: Sanja Krsmanović-Tasić, Aleksandra Jelić, Maja Mitić (photograph: Jovan Čekić).

The Presence of Absence: DAH Theater, Belgrade; October–December 2013; directed by Dijana Milošević; devised by DAH Theater Ensemble. Maja Vukovic (foreground), Sanja Krsmanović Tasić, Nemanja Ajdačić (man with violin, also composer of violin music) (photograph: Dijana Milojevic).

Three

Performance as Memory Keeper and Promoter of Peace

In this chapter I look at the aesthetics of art about war and exile from the perspective of performance and some concrete theater projects. While in the previous chapters I explored dramatic texts or "playscripts" and their performative possibilities in light of tackling either the theme of exile or that of war violence, I will now take three examples of theater practicum that emerged as direct response to these realities: the performance art and storytelling of Noa Baum, the theater activism and directorial work of the Immigrants Theater Project in New York and the performance work of the DAH Theater in Belgrade, Serbia. Each of these theatrical projects have developed from a desire of the artists to reach out from a comfort zone and confront creatively the fear of the Other, and the hate that escalates into war violence, and to celebrate human and ethnic diversity. As I pointed out in the introduction, the reluctance to respect and revel in diversity and the monolithic thinking of extreme forms of nationalism has often been at the very core of armed conflicts, wars and genocides. In *Violence and Difference* Andrew McKenna notes that "every crisis ... is ultimately a crisis of difference" (1992, 63), which since time immemorial humans have resolved through various institutionalized structures of violence.[1] However, "it is up to "postmodern identities to call upon the notions of plurality, difference, and heterogeneity," strive towards multiculturalism and the embodiment of diversity so that ideally "peace and harmony would reign instead of war and disunity" (Petrunic 2005, 3).

Noa Baum: Storytelling as a Way of Understanding the "Other"

It is not because of their message of peace and respect for the "Other" that Noa Baum's stories are relevant and have made a difference, but because of the specificity of the personal experiences they unravel and the details of life they evoke. Few political issues in modern history are as incendiary and prone to instant argument as the Israeli-Palestinian conflicts and the overall political situation in the Middle East. Each side has their own motivations for their actions and rhetoric, and from political figures to the common people, whether living in Israel, Palestine or as exiles in a Western country, they all have a bagful of arguments to support their side of the story. The exceptions are those who try to move beyond making the Other into a monster in order to justify the actions of their people, whether Israelis or Palestinians, and try to understand different, even opposing views. In my own travels to Israel I tried to understand the specificities of the situation beyond the media bites and propaganda in the Western world about the situation in the Middle East, and tried to listen to people's stories from one side of the wall or the other, from the Muslim quarters or the Jewish quarters of Jerusalem with its stately, ancient walls and eight majestic gates. From taxi drivers to artists, tourist guides or shopkeepers, in general people on both sides just want to get along without violence, work and feed their families, walk the streets and take public transportation without being blown up by terrorist bombs or visit family members without the restrictions imposed by the great wall and the barbed wire that now divides Israeli and Palestinian territories. It is in fact remarkable to discover how in a city that throbs in the rhythm of three different religions and has been the target of both millenary conflicts and momentous historical revelations, people actually get along on a daily basis. Beyond the differences in the celebration of the Sabbath in the Jewish quarters or the five calls to prayer in the Muslim quarters, Jews and Palestinians have much in common. It is the discovery of the commonality of experience of people from both sides in the historical context of the Israeli-Palestinian conflict through personal stories that this portion of the chapter will focus on.

Noa Baum is an Israeli storyteller and performance artist who has had the courage and creativity to attempt to understand the dreaded Other through the most ancient form of performance art, that of storytelling. A native of Jerusalem and an actor trained at the University of Tel Aviv who immigrated to the United States in 1990, Noa Baum has employed her theatrical creativity and energies to explore artistically the human complexities of her troubled part of the world and to reach out to all sides through personal narratives. She is also the daughter of survivors from

Nazi Germany, though as she tells in her story, "Everyone that didn't escape with them was gone." "The only way that things can ever change is through personal stories," she told me in a recent interview (2014). Her work as a performance artist is organically interwoven with her work as an educator and promoter of diversity.

In an article titled "Performing Oral History: the Creation of 'A Land Twice Promised,'" Baum defines clearly the need and inspiration for her work:

> The Israeli-Palestinian conflict seeps despair into the Western consciousness, with more than 60 years of war, thousands dead, and no end in sight. Yet rarely do Westerners have the opportunity to hear the stories behind the bloodshed and the headlines. Neither do most Israeli Jews and Palestinians know what it is like to live "on the other side," less than five miles away. "A Land Twice Promised" is based on the experience of dialogue and friendship between myself, an Israeli, and a Palestinian woman. Through it I share our families' stories, attempting to give voice to the parallel and often contradictory narratives of the Israeli and Palestinian peoples from a highly personal perspective [2009, 119].

Noa Baum performing *A Land Twice Promised*: Women's Studies Department, Montgomery College Takoma Park, Maryland; March 2003; directed by Loren Niemi (photograph: Don Rejonis).

The performance/show *A Land Twice Promised*, which she has created herself as both writer and performer, has brought her national and international recognition and has affected, moved, and transformed many people from all parts of the political spectrum. The show contains stories about the wars of 1948 and 1967 in Israel, told from the perspective of the nine-year-old girl that she was at the time and also from the perspective of a Palestinian friend of hers whose family lived through those wars. She has performed it in as diverse an array of venues as it would be possible for any theater artist to perform. From the World Bank to the Defense Department to synagogues, cathedrals, conferences, myriads of colleges and universities across the United States, conventional theater venues, and in a kibbutz in Israel, she has performed *A Land Twice Promised* to the most diverse audiences and has received the widest array of reactions from them. Both the multitude of performances she has given during the past decade and the multitude of reactions she has received attest to the power of the spoken word and of live performance to awaken, educate and transform. As she herself lucidly recognizes, most likely her stories will not stop the war, prevent acts of terrorism, or bring peace in the Middle East, just as probably no amount of works of art and theater will ever be able to stop the violence of our world. But ultimately this argument is irrelevant, and if politically engaged artists took it too seriously they would have stopped creating long ago. Our postmodern times are precisely characterized by an art that often emerges almost despite itself, because we can't do otherwise. This art is often created in the interstices between hopelessness and the Sisyphean existentialist position of taking responsibility of the "stone" we carry just because it is *ours.* As Camus so beautifully articulated in his essay, "we must imagine Sisyphus happy," as he looks down upon the mountain, the stone and the horizon where his destiny is inscribed and decides to responsibly take ownership of it.[2]

As she had serious doubts about the usefulness of creating a storytelling performance about the Israeli and the Palestinian experience of the war of 1967 from the perspective of two little girls, her own acting coach and director Loren Niemi, who urged her to write her stories and perform them, told her that "every bit counts." Indeed, every artistic gesture that is rooted in our reality and tries to explore the mindboggling complexities of our world and pull out of its chaos coherent stories that pulsate with the life and emotions of individual experiences creates an oasis of meaning-making that opposes and soothes the irrationality of hatred and violence.

In the interview she gave me (2014), Noa Baum admits that she never "set out to do a story telling performance," and that "it happened like all things in life, it just sort of happened," as a result of her attending a story telling conference and doing a workshop about "telling difficult stories." The workshop challenged her to reexamine her previous work, and as a result she realized that she never crossed outside of her comfort zones in her storytelling; in her own words, "I didn't take any risks in telling stories about where I actually come from." That was an important turning point in her career, which gave her the impetus to not only rummage through her own personal memories and family stories but also to gather the stories of her Palestinian friend who was three years old during the war of 1967.

She had known her friend Jumana for seven years as their sons were playmates in Davis, California. As she was wondering, "Who would want to hear my story?" she realized that she had "never heard what that war was for her or for any Palestinian." As a result she contacted her friend and asked her to share her own story of living through the war of 1967 and growing up in Israel/Palestine in the seventies and eighties. While her friend was at first reluctant to talk about her childhood and youth in Jerusalem, upon Noa's insistence she started sharing her experience of that war from the perspective of someone who was "under Israeli occupation" (*A Land Twice Promised,* hereafter cited as *LTP*). However, because she was only three at the time of the war, she called upon her mother to recount to Noa her experiences of the war of 1967, and her mother was happy to participate in the project. From then on a long creative process of sharing personal stories, comparing and writing them started for Noa, which in the end resulted in *A Land Twice Promised.*

As Baum herself stated in her interview, the overall structure of her show and the way in which her stories are tied and woven with one another is often fragmented and layered, and most interestingly it unfolds along spiraling chronologies that move back and forth between the present storytelling by the adult women to stories that go back to events in 1981, 1974 and then all the way back to 1967 and finally to 1948 in reverse temporal order.[3] In a Scheherazade-like manner Baum creates layered stories within a larger story of recovering memory and history through the blending of the three women's narratives about their experiences of the wars. She crosses the threshold between her own Israeli reality and the reality of the Other, the Palestinian woman. The story that frames the war and the occupation narratives is a meta-narrative that traces the formation of the friendship between the two women, the trust they built with one another, the process of soul-baring and story-gathering first from Jumana and then from Jumana's mother Muna, and Baum's own process of story-gathering from both her own memories and those of her mother. The starting point is curiosity about the Other and a strong desire to understand what it means to be in the Other's shoes: "I grew up with fear all my life. I grew up under Israeli occupation. And I never met an Israeli who wasn't a soldier or a settler, until I met you," Jumana told Noa at first, claiming, "I really don't have any story to tell you." "Why would you want to hear my story?" Jumana asked Noa, to which she responded: "I've never had a friend who was a Palestinian before. I want to know how it is"[4] (*LTP* 3).

Throughout history women have had a crucial role in the creation of an oral culture of storytelling, which was often transmitted from mother to daughter and which kept alive the collective memory of a community or a people from one generation to the next. Feminist theory has often stressed the importance of reclaiming and revising history through women's personal stories and autobiographical accounts in order to recover women's traditions, material histories and contributions of their passage through the world.[5] Women's storytelling techniques are often circular and follow a chronology of the lived experience and of the stream of consciousness rather than the linear chronologies of accepted historical narratives written by men.[6] In the case of Noa Baum's *A Land Twice Promised,* we not only have stories of war from the perspective of women, but also from the perspective of exiles, as both Noa and her friend Jumana left their native countries to settle in the United States. *A Land Twice Promised* is born at the confluence of the experience of war with that of exile. The intersection of the experience of war through a young girl's eyes and its telling through the consciousness of an adult immigrant woman creates a palimpsest of liminal spaces that translates into the meandering, often piecemeal, often spiraling structure of this compounded narrative of the wars of 1967 and of 1948. In *Reading Across Borders: Storytelling and Knowledge of Resistance,* Shari Stone Mediatore responds to "recent critiques of narrative and experience" while also finding "a way to engage productively with marginalized people's experiences." She notes that "despite academic critiques of experience, many social struggles ... continue to rely on stories of experience to bring public attention to their concerns" (2003, 1). As Baum herself admits, her stories and her performance will not stop the Israeli-Palestinian conflicts, but they do "bring public attention" to "stories of experience" that address the need to cross barriers of hate and stereotyping, to embrace diversity and, in Baum's view, to accept the coexistence of contradictory worldviews and of paradox in the same space. In describing the early stages in the process of gathering the stories from Jumana, she notes the following dynamics that speaks exactly of this coexistence: "I would say things that were history and truth and she would say that is propaganda and she would say things that were history and truth and I would say that is propaganda." However, Baum notes, "we never lost our compassion, even when we were listening to things that were difficult" (2014a). Whose truth was the real truth then? The stories, in their carnality, humor and sadness, in their many specific details, sense of place and emotional intensity make us understand that each narrator holds her own truth, which is that of her personal experience. This is the only authentic truth we can have access to when dealing with trauma in particular and its translation into an art form.

The first story Jumana shares is one in which she was arrested in 1981 one day when she was returning home from her university classes. In passing she gives the context of her family, who had lived under a series of occupations. Her parents lived "under British occupation and were married under the Jordanian occupation and I grew up under the Israeli occupation" (*LTP* 4). After waiting on the bus taking her home at a blockade and then being thrown in prison for no reason, waiting under the beating sun for several hours, being lined up against the wall, and then being released with a "red dot" on her ID card, Jumana returns home puzzled by the day's events, happy to find herself back in the aroma of her mother's cooking. "To this day—I still don't know what that red dot means," she concludes. In her interview Baum mentioned the incident of the red dot, telling that her friend was at first reluctant to tell her stories because she didn't think they were tragic enough. While Noa's family had suffered the tragedy of the killing of a beloved family member by Palestinian soldiers, nobody had died in Jumana's family. Yet, that was *her* story, Noa commented, and what had marked her for life: the mysterious, scary red dot on her ID. It is only in the small details of the experience that we can connect with the Other.

The second story Jumana shares is one in which the boys from her school started a protest that incited Israeli soldiers to action, namely to use tear gas, shooting and chasing after the boys. This was in 1974, when she was ten years old and in Catholic school, so she goes back in the narrative to her childhood. Jumana, her sister and her best friend tried to escape the soldiers and run home through the *suk*, which though usually throbbing with merchants and tourists now "was so quiet. All the shutters were closed, no dresses. No tourists" (*LTP* 7). At the end of this episode the girls witness in horror as a young boy is beaten to death by Israeli soldiers:

> After that we ran so fast, I don't even remember how we got on the bus. From the window, I saw a boy, 13 or 14 years old, running out of the gate. Four soldiers were chasing him. They caught him and threw him to the ground. They kicked and beat him with their rifles. When the boy stopped moving, they lifted him into a jeep, and drove away. I wanted to yell, but nothing came out. I was only a little girl, they were big with guns. But for the first time in my life I understood that word—hate. I hated them [7].

The story line is often broken by the main narrator's comments, a return to the present and the moment of the narration and then a move back into another one of their stories. We see Jumana and hear her stories both through her own voice and also through the troubled and questioning conscience of Baum. In this channeling of the narrative we get to better understand Baum's slow process of approaching the Other from a place of compassion while also claiming the truthfulness of her own story. At the end of her story, Jumana asks: "And you, how was it for you growing up in Jerusalem?" Baum thinks to herself: "How can I tell her that those soldiers, so terrifying for her, were our boys, our symbol of security; how can I explain that the soldiers that scared me were those with the black boots, the Nazis from the stories; how could I tell her that what was the beginning of the occupation nightmare for her, I remember as the first time I saw my mother cry with tears of joy.... I said: I'll tell you about my first war" (8).

The story of Baum's experience as a nine-year-old girl during the six-day war follows in a rumbling roller-coaster that is all excitement, despite the fear of the bombs and having to stay in the furnace room for the duration of the war. The narrative moves fast and the details are those that stuck to the conscience of the nine-year-old girl: piling sacks of sand against the entrances for protection, the entire family and the neighbors all sleeping together in the furnace room, the children jumping in the furnace room and yelling: "Hey, the war effort is cooool," the light bulb painted blue and blankets covering the windows, the deafening sound of the siren ending with the sound of bombs "like a thousand thunders clashing all together," the parents running outside under the bombs to get flour and oil for bread. It all ends in the apotheosis at the end of the war when the Israeli armies take back the Wailing Wall. The "adults were shaking hands in frenzy: 'Mazel tov, Mazel tov.' For the first time in days there was music on the radio and all the adults began to sing, as tears streamed down their cheeks" (10).

Then comes the story of Jumana's mother, Muna, who recounts the six days that she spent in terror of losing her children and of her whole family being killed, covering her children's bodies with her own for protection, and praying for a dignified death rather than being captured. Yet her story bears similarities to Baum's story: hiding for refuge on the ground floors, running for flour and oil to make bread for the children, and the terrifying sound of sirens and explosions. However, at the news of the Wailing Wall having been taken by Israelis, there are tears and sighs of sorrow and not of joy: "'The Jews entered Jerusalem and they are praying at the Wailing Wall.' Um Mustafa started to cry, she cupped her son's face in her hands: 'ah! Balad Sactaat—the country fell. It's a good thing your father died before seeing the old city fall!'" (13). In Muna's story, just as in Baum's, there is a moment of comic relief when a Jewish man comes to visit a friend he had known since 1948 in the neighborhood and everybody comes out of their houses and watches transfixed. Most of them had never seen a Jew before. They had only heard that Jews were "murderers, they have no mercy; they have no human heart" (13). At the height of the tension in Muna's story comes the moment of comic relief illustrating the profound need of laughter even in terrifying situations and in the most intense of narratives. As everybody is staring at him, the Jew says: "Why are you looking at me like that? I'm just like you. Look at me, I have two hands, ten fingers ... look! You can count..." We all started laughing. It was a bit embarrassing..." Muna concludes: "he didn't look like a murderer" (13).

What is remarkable from the point of view of both narrative and performance is the coexistence of contrasting experiences of the exact same event but from different perspectives. Though from the perspective of the Palestinian family the taking of the Wall of Wailing is a tragic event while for the Israeli family it is a source of joy, a common thread runs through both experiences and reveals the common humanity of all the protagonists, whether on the Palestinian or the Israeli side: the mothers' fear of losing their children, the children's fear of losing their parents, the search for flour and oil for subsistence, and the basic fear of death. In her narrative Baum condenses the specific with the universal and keeps the marks of diversity alive, while gently pulling the unifying thread of a basic humanity throughout the details. When she performs the show, she inhabits the characters without impersonating them. She made it clear in her interview that, while working on voice and gesture to suggest the cultural, age and psychological differences between the characters, she tries to bring to life real people without imitating them. She indeed does a balancing act to go beyond simulation towards embodiment and to achieve as authentic a rendition of another's voice or moods as any actor could perform.

The last story brings out the profoundly tragic dimension of the ensemble; it goes back to 1948 and gives voice to her mother Tziporah, in recounting the episode of the death of her brother. This story ends with the fall of Jerusalem to the Arab forces and for the Israeli family with the death of a beloved son and brother, a look of terror and devastation on the grandmother's face, a muted scream in the heart of the mother. If there is an example of a good Jew in Muna's story, there is an example of a good Arab in Tziporah's story. Terrified by the occupying forces yet working as a nurse for the wounded in an Armenian monastery, Tziporah is helped by an Arab soldier who even gives her a snack and offers to take her to Amman, where his sister would have taken care of her. Besides the funny episode of the Jew who shows the Arab community he is a man just like them, Jumana also remembers how in her terrified run home after the protest of the boys, an Israeli soldier lifted her and her sister over the barbed wire and smiled at them. The identity of the Other keeps shifting, depending on the voice of the narrative, and in the process, a breaking of barriers and an equalizing movement seems to take place in which there is no more Other, but only scared civilians, along with soldiers perpetrating violence and suffering violence simultaneously and exhibiting sparks of humanity and even humor in the midst of inhumane situations. The constant shift in point of view from one story to the next achieves a melting of the notion of enemy and mellows the impenetrable face of the Other into a recognizable and mirroring image of humanness. A review of *A Land Twice Promised* (Schifrin 2003) stated, "The stunning result of Baum's work is not a competition of narratives, but a consolidation of them. Or to use a musical metaphor, her alternating of Jewish and Arab stories created a point/counterpoint that feels more like a richly dissonant piece of music than a political debate."

The ending brings it all together in a stunning arrangement of the voices of the two friends, one Israeli and one Palestinian, talking to one another above the roaring din of constant war news, attacks, bombings, like a wrenching duet for peace, like a jolted dance of compassion and a colorful utopian friendship somewhere above the wars and despite the wars:

> It is 2009. Jumana and I don't live in the same city anymore. She's in California, I've moved to the east coast 3 weeks before 9/11. It seems that every time I think it can't get any worse, it just does. That spring of 2002, at the height of the suicide bombing inside Israel, when all of my most left leaning friends became angry if I even mentioned the word Palestinian, my friend called. She couldn't help think about my family. I could not stop thinking about hers. We talked. We still talk on the phone.
>
> "Noa, I heard about the bomb in Jerusalem. Is your sister all right?"
>
> "Jumana, I heard they bulldozed houses in Beit Hanina. Are your parents all right?"
>
> "Noa, there was that terrible one in Netania. I don't have words for my pain and outrage!!"
>
> "Jumana, there are tanks in Ramalla ... is your brother all right?"
>
> "Noa, my cousin was shot at the checkpoint trying to get to work. He is severely wounded, the family can't see him because of the roadblocks."
>
> "Jumana, a bus blew up two streets away from my sister."
>
> "Noa, my father said they can see the wall from their house, it's cutting them from the entire neighborhood..."
>
> "Jumana..."
>
> Jumana and I stand together on this island in the middle of a raging sea. All around us the waves are violently crashing, splashing us until we're soaking wet.
>
> But somehow we hold on. We talk above the roaring storm. We hold on to our compassion. We bake a cake with pink and white frosting and eat together under the tree. We hold on to our little peace. We have no choice.

At some point in her storytelling Baum shares her moment of skepticism about being able to move outside of oneself in order to hear the other's pain. She asks: "How can someone who lost so much still have room for the other? For their story?" Schifrin (2003) aptly notes, "Baum's answer, however oblique, is in the very existence of her performance." Even if it is only a drop of light in a sea of darkness, a breath of hope in a sea of cynicism, telling one's story does matter. What matters equally is the careful construction of the stories of war, occupation, and living with the Other, the concentric movements that contain reverse chronologies, dislocated narratives and diverse points of view by four women of different generations, related ethnicities and opposing politics. From the present of the storytelling and its slow creation, to events experienced by the Palestinian Jumana as a young girl and woman in 1974 and in 1981, to the parallel accounts of the war of 1967 from Noa's perspective and from Muna's perspective, to the tragic story of the death of Tziporah's brother in 1948 under Palestinian occupation, and returning to a more recent present than at the beginning, with an indefinite look into an uncertain future, the spectator is taken on a spiraling ride through key events in the lives of the two women and their families. At the intersection of the experience of war with that of exile, Baum's storytelling and performance emerge in a beautifully controlled disorder and chronological leaps to contain traumas of war and the melancholy distancing of the exile experience. The Israeli and Palestinian women meet and tell their stories as immigrants in America. As Baum pointed out to me in the interview, she created her show with the American audience in mind. Most likely it is the experience of America and the distancing from her native geography, culture and history that allowed her to craft her past and that of her Palestinian friend into a coherent arrangement of stories, mixed and reconsidered in the all-too-famous melting pot. And in America, she has had the most varied reactions to her shows from Jews and Arabs, Israelis and Palestinians, anything from crying with a newly acquired compassion and understanding, to someone calling her a traitor in the middle of one of her shows. She keeps performing *A Land Twice Promised* across America because she feels she "has no choice." I maintain that it is the delicate balancing of diverse points of view—the beautifully arranged disorder of the chronologies and the meticulous details of place, time, gesture and feeling—the controlled playing of different voices and characters without the caricature of impersonation but with just the right amount of changes in accent or gesture—in a word, it is the aesthetic of her stories and performance that accounts for the success of the show as much as the content of the stories. Any consummate Scheherazade knows that she has to endow her characters with life, creating meandering and captivating paths of narrative in order to save her own life with her storytelling, night after night.

Marcy Arlin and the Immigrants Theater Project: Celebrating Diversity

Marcy Arlin is the artistic director and founder of the Immigrants Theater Project in New York City. Since its foundation in 1988 she has directed scores of productions and readings by immigrant artists, often with immigrant actors from all over the world, including Beirut, Cameroun, Kosovo, Cambodia, the Czech Republic, India, Guyana, Colombia, Sierra Leone, Romania and Serbia. For her contributions to the field and her extraordinary work in promoting artistic and human diversity in the works of scores of theater artists that treat the realities of immigration, she received the prestigious Obie Award in 2003. This is a quote from the Obie citation in the *Village Voice*: "Traditional or experimental, poetic, realistic or movement-based, all these plays are at their core American. For years, one theater has been reaching into the deep humanity and individuality of people too often and too easily swept into generalities, bringing their stories, struggles and backgrounds to New York stages." New York City Arts notes, "Since its founding in 1988 the organization has presented over 250 such plays, working with professional immigrant and native-born artists from over 70 countries and ethnic groups. The project seeks to demonstrate the universality of the American experience, promote intercultural understanding and develop a new genre known as immigrant theater." Mimicking the nomadic life of immigrants themselves, Marcy Arlin's Immigrants Theater Project has performed in a puzzling variety of conventional and nonconventional theater venues, including the Brooklyn Public Library, La MaMa Theater, the Martin E. Segal Theater Center, the New York Theater Workshop, South Street Seaport, the Barrow Group Theater, various cultural centers, consulates, public schools, and the Lower East Side Tenement Museum, where Arlin and her group were housed for a while. Much like the original *commedia dell'arte* troupes or the later traveling acting troupes in Italy, France and Spain, the Immigrants Theater Project initially contained about six professional actors who for most of their existence had not had an actual theater space but had performed plays by and about immigrants in varied spaces to a wide array of audiences eager to learn about the past and the present of immigrant communities in New York and in America, about their struggles and aspirations in culturally specific colors, and to reconnect with their own family stories and past in what is the arc of the fundamental American experience.

Arlin has beautifully illustrated diversity not only in the choice of plays she has directed but in physically concrete ways by using actors of all colors, ethnicities and nationalities: African Americans, Native Americans, Hispanics, Asians, and Eastern Europeans. In every possible way the Immigrants Theater Project has embodied the immigrant experience and the cultural diversity that accounts for much of the vibrancy and liveliness of America. In her choice of plays Arlin has also connected the past to the present, keeping alive the immigrant histories and awakening the desire in young audiences to search for their own immigrant origins. Her theater group has presented over the years stories about World War II, modern issues of acculturation and assimilation to issues of prejudice, generational conflicts between those born in the United States and their immigrant parents, interracial marriages, and religious tolerance versus secularism among immigrant communities, and the stories almost always lead to the meandering paths towards the ever-illusory American Dream. As Arlin herself commented when the group started playing in the Tenement Museum, the plays she has directed present "a whole world of people that most New Yorkers don't know much about" (Chu 1999). A review from *Stage Press* on the occasion of a festival of plays by and about Muslim women organized by Arlin in 2002 at the Tenement Museum enthusiastically noted the overall scope of the theater's mission: "Here is a project with such a basic and relevant theme that it jolts us back to thinking about the foreign people whose physical and mental labors built this country and whose descendants have become so absorbed into the fabric of American life that they—we—are today's Americans" (Sarach 2002). In the program of that festival, Marcy Arlin noted the following in the director's notes: "It was crucial to illustrate how the immigrant experience has remained the same ... over 300 years of American history, and to use quality art to promote understanding and fight against intolerance and bigotry focused on newcomer immigrants" (Sarach 2002). And "quality art" is the key indeed to Arlin's work with immigrant theater, as will become obvious in the interview I had with her.

This of course brings me again to the topic of the present book, that of a theater aesthetic that is coordinate with the great diversity of the immigrant experience in America, with the pain of displacement and the excitement of new beginnings, the yearning for the lost countries and the drive to grow new and stable roots in American soil. Arlin has directed the widest variety of plays: wild and experimental, plays with puppets, surreal and absurdist, and more traditional, realistic plays. The diversity of her aesthetic choices also beautifully illustrates the multicolored nature of the immigrant experience, the wide range of immigrant communities, and their anxieties and aspirations, such as Caribbean people as in the "CaribBeing" series, the "Unexpected Journeys" series of plays about Muslim women, and the East European women playwrights' series in 2012 called "Women Write the New." The most important thing for Arlin is to create the authentic cultural color of the plays and to bring out respectfully the aesthetic universes created by the playwrights, whether that means creating an edgy experimental performance in the Grand Guignol Horror style, such as Milena Markovic's *The Pavillions*, or a postmodernist production with surreal episodes such as Saviana Stanescu's *Waxing West*, or a performance with "highly naturalistic dialogue" such as the Jovanka Bach's *Name Day*. Over its more than twenty-five years of existence the

Marcy Arlin, *Immigrants Theater Project*: Church Avenue Merchants Block Association, Brooklyn, New York and Henry Street Settlement Abrons Arts Center, NYC; 1992; directed by Marcy Arlin. *Immigration Office*, a devised piece by the ensemble of Immigrants Theater Project. Actors from left to right, clockwise, in the foreground: Alonia King, Courtney Everett, Ben-Hur Carmona, Mary Chang, Nicki Baker, Eran Bohem, and Zahid Hussein. This is another example of Arlin's creativity in directing and orchestrating devised theater productions that celebrate diversity (photograph: Marcia Mercadante).

Immigrants Theater Project has traveled the widest territories of theater aesthetic bringing flavors, sounds and colors from all corners of the world into New York or to audiences at various international fringe festivals and venues. This is a project that lives to its deepest core and sometimes to heights of delicious ironies the nomadic, transient, multicolored and jolted existence of immigrants themselves. From the relentless work that Arlin needs to engage in so that her productions or readings can take place with live actors, to props, costumes, and spaces to perform in, to the constant hopping from space to space and the multitude of types of venues and neighborhoods that she has produced her shows in, this project is as immigrant as it gets.

Arlin also practices a kind of aesthetic nomadism, as she runs the gamut of theatrical styles and genres. Though in her interview she says that she has directed many types of plays including linear, realistic plays or what are generally called "well-constructed plays," the great majority are conspicuous in their aesthetic innovations. Her most recent immigrant theater festival took place in 2012 and was titled Women Write the New. The festival featured a group of stunningly audacious women playwrights from Eastern Europe that stand out through their theatrical experimentation, such as Milena Markovic and Radmila Adamová, who have been discussed in this book. In the yearlong festival she produced works in eclectic and cutting-edge dramatic styles from the Romanian Vera Ion, the Serbian Milena Markovic, the Czech Radmila Adamová, the Hungarian Virag Erdos, and the Bulgarian Theodora Dimova. "The plays selected for the yearlong reading series, held at the Bohemian National Hall, Romanian Cultural Institute, and Bulgarian Consulate, represent a cross section of content and form" (Arlin 2013, 50). One common thread that runs through this festival is the exploration of dysfunctions in East European societies and their dystopian universes with theatrical strategies discussed in this book, such as absurdist and carnivalesque comedy: "There is an intense examination of social ills and societal stratification with outrageous humor and wit. They give a voice to those left out of mainstream theatre: women (rarely made central characters), drug addicts, victims of abuse, new immigrants, abandoned children, damaged souls" (Arlin 2012/2013, 51).

The full interview with Marcy Arlin (2013) will cast more light on her various directorial choices and philosophy, many of which reinforce my contention of the importance and necessity of political theater that engages us in discovering the complexities of the immigrant experience or the brutality of modern wars and support the experimental theatrical strategies developed by playwrights and directors in treating such issues.

DR: As a director who has created politically engaging and provocative shows, do you believe that the experiences of war, political instability, oppression, exile or immigration influence not only the content of the plays but also their aesthetic and furthermore your own directorial choices? In what ways?

MA: My company chooses play based on several criteria, most of all the quality of the play in terms of text, character development, subject matter, etc. We look for plays that tell a unique or unexplored aspect of the American or international immigrant experience. Since many people emigrate, willfully or unwillingly, because of war and oppression, along with religious or ethnic persecution and the hope of economic betterment, or as a result of trafficking/slavery, naturally the themes you mention are either overtly or covertly implicit in each play.

But there are less world-wrenching subject matters that still can lead to great theater: intercultural love, parental expectations, tradition vs. modernity, biculturalism, assimilation. These subjects can lend themselves to comedy or tragedy or some interesting combination of both. I mostly am attracted to plays that show an exile or immigrant or minority as a whole person, who happens to be dealing with a new or difficult situation, flavored by the immigrant experience. Even when directing or producing plays about genocides and other horrors, I look for a play where there is light. Otherwise, the play becomes a version of "victimology," engendering sympathy in an audience but rarely empathy. Empathy is my goal in all that I do; I want the audience to experience the story, no matter how alien or seemingly exotic, as a story of human beings, like themselves.

In terms of style of play, I subscribe to the idea that the form will determine the content. I have directed fiercely naturalistic plays and directed odd, experimental, or more poetic musicals. My personal skills lean toward farce and drama, because they ask for a great amount of directorial detail and attention to ensemble and relationships.

I go through times, like recently, where I can't direct one more sad, horrifying story about a holocaust or massacre or impending doom. Then I find a new play about immigrants from a group I have never dealt with artistically, and I am excited by how this particular group or ethnicity has lived through one of history's crazy episodes.

DR: Do you connect fractured or fragmented theatrical form, nonlinear structures and carnivalesque aesthetics to the theater and productions dealing with war, oppression or displacement?

MA: Sometimes, but not necessarily. For example a piece I recently directed had to do with the effects of the Cambodian holocaust on an individual, modeled on Haing Ngor, who survived and went on to win an Oscar for the *Killing Fields*. It moved around in time, place, and level of existence (this life, the Buddhist afterlife). While not carnivalesque at all (though there were funny scenes), it was stylistically more fragmented than a traditional narrative. I have also worked on pieces that are very naturalistic, linear, and could be considered a "well-made play," something resembling an operetta. My only caveat is to be sure the theatricalities and production values do not overrun or intimidate the story. For example, I saw a director who had to have clowns in all her work, whether or not they were mentioned in the text. It was only confusing.

Music is a very effective mechanism for portraying misery, tragedy and horror. Sound is very important, whether created on stage or recorded. Puppetry, as in *Warhorse*, can be devastating.

So I guess my answer is that the style can be dislocated, or dislocating, aesthetically, which can reinforce the meaning of the piece. Or the story/text/character relationships can. Neither is better or worse as long as the form and content meld.

The only thing I personally do not like is overly graphic violence. Sure it is scary and upsetting, but the mind tries to distance itself from that stuff, rather than engage. Though sometimes [as] in this one Irish play, the bloodiness can be funny. If the audience then goes home asking themselves why they laughed, that is great. If they just laugh and then go home and think, gee, violence is pretty funny, then I don't think the playwright/director was successful. It is enormously tricky.

DR: Do you think as an artist/theater person it is important to deal with political issues of your time and with issues of diversity and multiculturalism?

MA: As far as I am concerned the realities of diversity (national, ethnic, sexual, gender, religious), violence against women and children and the environment, are THE issues of today. If we as a species don't figure out how to live with each other equitably and fairly peaceably, without destroying our environment, we are doomed.

I like my silly escapism, don't get me wrong. But art has to deal with the tough stuff. It can be funny, too. Below is a sort of manifesto I wrote a long time ago and it really sums up my beliefs about theater:

Theatre should sometimes reflect the feelings and emotions of the audience; sometimes it should give us something to think about. Theater should aspire to changing the world; sometimes it should be for a good laugh or cry. Theatre should tell a good, clear story; or, it could be a cacophony of bizarre images that leave one totally confused. Theatre should examine the moral and social issues of its day; but sometimes a peek at the old ways helps us appreciate the new. Theatre should carefully avoid stereotypes and categorization of people by gender, ethnicity, sexual persuasion, nationality, religion, appearance and ability. Those people who belong to a particular category, by their own definition, should have the right to make fun of themselves.

Theatre should expose the whims and cruelties of the world. It can be whimsical, but shouldn't be cruel.

Everyone should have a chance to do theatre. But skill makes great theatre, as in any art or craft. It would be better if more people could make a living doing theatre and their work was considered valid by the whole society. But the times in human society when that has happened, when theatre was your day job, it made for lazy artists and too much government control.

For the next 20 years (if we live that long), it will become increasingly difficult for people to be able to think for themselves without extreme anxiety. Theatre people are, generally, by nature, rule breakers within the context of a society. They are permitted, to some extent, to speak up, to shock, awaken and penetrate a society's complacency and self-satisfaction. They are permitted, in some places clandestinely, to think of the bizarre, amoral, nonconformist, surreal, abstract, and merciful way to live life.

We must not let that permission be rescinded, by anyone, anything, anytime, anywhere. We may have to risk our lives (it's happened, you all know that), and our sanity. But we shouldn't ask anyone, including ourselves, to unnecessarily risk themselves. We may have to give up fame, fortune, recognition, and access to audiences—such as it is. We may have to go to all the non-theatre people who live in our country and world, and do theatre with them, in a garage or yard, or basement. We just have to keep going. Be creative, be funny, be tragic, and be brave [Arlin 2005].

DR: Do you see political theater as a safe space in the sense of a space where political and personal traumas can be purged, healed, transcended?

MA: Another interesting question. There is an amazing text about trauma by Judith Herman that talks about this issue.[7] An article about theater that talks about rape in the Bosnian/Serbian conflict had an interesting point with which I agree: it's all in the timing. Sometimes theater with personal trauma can be too disturbing, too raw, awakening horrific memories. There is a debate among artists in Cambodia about the healing powers of theatre. For some just seeing the theater without follow-up is too upsetting.

My personal feeling is that when creating theater with sufferers of PTSD from whatever cause, it is crucial to have a mental health practitioner present during the process. Flashbacks, suicidal thoughts, uncontrolled anger, are all possible reactions, even in a space designated as "safe..."

Theater artists, no matter how sensitive, are not therapists. I knew this when I began working with survivors of war, torture, and 9/11 losses. For all rehearsals and performances, I insisted, in my contract with the sponsoring organization, that a therapist/clinician trained in this kind of health issue always be present, just in case. I conjecture that because of the therapist's presence, we only had two incidents, neither of which was long lasting. I believe the participants felt safe and protected.

Can the traumas be healed? Yes, I believe it is possible, but it takes a long time, and it is not over once the theater event is over. Also, sometimes the benefit includes the fact that the audience may be seeing their experience for the first time, publicly. The theatrical event, being so public, may help neutralize the shame and utter despairing loneliness that many victims feel, especially in cultures where talking about bad experiences is considered a taboo, or where people who are usually oppressed: women, gays, children, minorities, are expected to suffer in silence. For some, seeing a theatrical rendition of their experience can cause a true catharsis.

DR: In which ways do you think the theater of witness can have an impact on our reality, world, history?

MA: One example is *The Exonerated*, about people on death row who were falsely sentenced and have been freed. The fact is that the show attracted celebrities as performers, made the issue very public and mainstream, which helped the former inmates and the organizations, such as the Innocence Project, gain public and financial support.

Plays about the Jewish Holocaust have changed the way this event is viewed worldwide and given a bit of solace (perhaps) to the survivors. Ideally it would create a "never again" mentality, but as we know, it is never "never again" for other populations.

In Rwanda, theater is helping the survivors (victims and perpetrators) reconcile and create a new kind of society there. I have hopes.[8]

DR: If you had complete freedom about making the production of your dreams, what would it be; how would you go about it?

MA: Amazing actors, a year to work on it. Terrific production team. Probably a new play. Or maybe something by Garcia Lorca. Or a new adaptation of *The Master and Margarita*, though that's being done. Large cast, music and puppets. Entertaining, funny and talking about the environment and animals, somehow. I love *Conference of the Birds*. Again, been done by Peter Brook. Or something adapted from Theodore Sturgeon or Margaret Atwood or Ursula LeGuin, who are these amazingly inventive, socially minded speculative fiction authors.

DR: What conscious aesthetic choices do you make in representing or suggesting or recounting violence on stage and why?

MA: The most effective and disturbing violence I ever portrayed was not really seen. As the Greek tragedians believed, the viewer can always imagine much worse than can be shown, and, more importantly, because they have to be active with their imagination, it is more likely to stick in their minds. In the play based in Cambodia, the hero, Vichear, narrates what he saw the Khmer Rouge doing to a pregnant woman. During his narration, I focused light on the actors playing the woman and the soldier, from the shoulders up. All we saw was their facial expressions and some head movement, indicating posture. We were Vichear, witnesses to the torture and murder of the woman and her unborn child, and witnesses to the joy and pleasure of the soldier who perpetrates this. It was very disturbing and moving, and the audience was in shock. Stage violence is tricky and can't have, with a few exceptions, the realism of film. So using the semiotics of violence seems to be an effective substitute. (Also, who wants to clean up all that stage blood?)

DR: What do you believe to be the most important contributions of the Immigrants Theater Project to raising consciousness about issues of immigration, the American Dream and cultural diversity?

MA: I believe our mission, to present the immigrant experience as a valid theme for theater, has come to pass throughout the world. Plays about immigrants have won Pulitzer Prizes. There are many young theater companies that either focus on an ethnicity or region. They are thriving and attracting supportive audiences and critics. On one hand my theory is that most American theater is based on some extent, with the exception of Native American theater, on the lives and hopes and dreams of immigrants or Africans who were emigrated here as slaves, for the most part.

Our casting policy of having actors of all ethnicities playing other ethnicities is now more common. Joe Papp began this. I have no trouble casting a Chinese-American actress in a Czech play (in translation). In other words, an American theater artist can look many different ways. I believe our multicultural programming has helped immigrant audiences realize that their experiences are important stories for the mainstream culture, and that the mainstream culture is beginning to comprehend that a play about a 20th century Haitian immigrant has many commonalities with an Irish refugee from the 19th century potato famine: colonialism, prejudice, poverty, hopes and ideals for a better life for their children, success or dismal failure in trying to achieve the "American dream" and the eternal reinvention that is this country.

We presented a long-planned play series, 4 months after 9/11. It consisted of plays by women influenced by or living in Muslim countries. Theater artists were: Armenian, Israeli, Nigerian, Turkish, Jordanian, Palestinian, Ghanaian, Haitian, Polish, Egyptian, Lebanese, Indonesian, Chinese, Russian. Some were born in the United States, some were immigrants. Pretty much all religions were represented. First time this ever happened. And no problems. Only a sense of relief that here, in this theater on the Lower East Side, perpetual home to immigrants, there is peace and communality.

I have included Marcy Arlin's Immigrants Theater Project in my book because of the epic and all-inclusive scope of her theatrical work. Each one of the playwrights and theater artists discussed in this book have contributed with their work to the building of an exquisitely wrought wall of resistance to violence and a vessel of remembrance and healing. However, without the generous work of directors, promoters, fundraisers, and complete artists such as Marcy Arlin or Dijana Milojevic of the DAH Theater (discussed in the following section), such plays and artistic works would not move from page to stage where the greatest impact is to be had on audiences worldwide. Anybody who has ever produced a show knows that the endeavor of bringing a text to the stage and creating public performances is a multidisciplinary undertaking requiring collaborative work, and by various degrees the existence or the creation of an institutionalized structure that deals with all the logistical aspects of the production from casting to marketing, running the house, and keeping a budget, and in the case of nomadic theater projects such as Arlin's, the finding of performance spaces. The artistic director of a small budget theater is also an administrator and a PR manager, as well as the one creating the overall vision of the theater and of the performances presented. Arlin makes the intriguing comment in the interview that "when theater was your day job, it made for lazy artists and too much government control," even though she admits it would be good to be able to make a living as a theater director or actor. She is referring most likely to European and particularly East European countries where professional actors and directors work full time for national theaters as hired employees and of course, egos are huge; and the state often meddles inappropriately in the workings, structures or even repertories of these theaters. It is true that just as the early *commedia* troupes were composed of professional actors whose imagination and creativity combined with their nomadic life and performance styles propelled them to perform anywhere from plazas and street corners to markets to theater halls to the living rooms of rich benefactors, so today some of the most artistically innovative as well as socially engaged theater work is done in small theater halls or in alternative spaces, on shoestring budgets, with actors who have to hold day jobs to make a living. As a parenthesis, however, despite common belief, the early *commedia* troupes actually did make a living from their theater art, as they were supported by wealthy benefactors and all the actors, including the women performers, held shares in the company.

Today's fringe theaters, off, off Broadway theaters, or experimental theaters function very much like a counterculture that tries to survive in the trenches as much as to subvert the corporate-run mainstream theaters that appeal to wealthy patrons and conservative boards of trustees. Theaters that produce extraordinary cutting-edge work that is highly applauded by theater critics, such as the Trap Door Theatre in Chicago, survive only due to relentless fundraising efforts by their artistic directors and are unable to pay their actors. More and more experimental theaters that produce foreign and audacious shows, such as the Boston-based Whistler in the Dark Theater, are forced to close their doors because of budgetary constraints.[9] Marcy Arlin tells the funny and sad story of the episode when the Tenement Museum Theater, where she had been housed for several years, decided to expel her theater project from their space; as a result, she found herself like a true refugee literally in the street with the theater properties and accessories of her troupe. Countries such as France or England, or even my native Romania, on the contrary support theatrical innovations and the diversity of theater arts at the level of national budgets quite a bit more than these rich and puzzling United States of America, even though it is here that some of the most innovative and bold theater projects and endeavors in the world see the footlights. Such paradoxes only make the work of theater artists working in the trenches more valuable and the need for audiences to become active supporters of their local, community or underfunded professional theaters more urgent. With each small audacious theater closing its doors a cultural, artistic and human universe disappears. With each such disappearance the scary world of plastic simulacra, of corporately supported performances that reinforce the status quo of patriarchal structures, and of mainstream white and wealthy entitlement threatens to engulf the dazzling and multicolored diversity that is the famous melting pot of America.

DAH Theater Group: Performance as Promoter of Peace and Repository of Memory

In 1991 a group of inspired and courageous Serbian women performers and directors gathered under the name of DAH Theater and created in Belgrade—just as their country was preparing to hold Sarajevo under siege and to wage war against their neighbors of centuries—both a theatrical space and a theatrical project meant to bear witness to the raging war but mostly to create a peaceful world of belonging. This was meant to be a place where there would be a real cease-fire and where the body and the soul could rest and engage in the creation of art instead of war. The DAH Theater has functioned, grown and developed ever since, bearing witness to the violence of war, keeping and channeling artistically the memories of victims and survivors, creating spaces and artistic structures of resistance and remembrance. On the website of the DAH Theater one can find the following statement regarding the beginnings of the theater and its purpose and goals:

> In 1991, when the war started in Yugoslavia, DAH Theatre immediately had to face these questions: "What is the role and meaning of theatre? What are the responsibilities and duties of artists in times of darkness, violence and human suffering?" The group decided to interrupt their work on the performance "Gifts of Our Ancestors" to begin work on a new piece that could provide them with the answers to these questions. DAH's first performance [of] "This Babylonian Confusion" was based on the

> songs of Bertold Brecht. An anti-war performance, it was presented outdoors in the centre of Belgrade at a time when it was forbidden to even mention the war. "The forming of DAH Theatre and its cry of creation coincided with the fall of ex–Yugoslavia and the general destruction that followed. Theatre directors Jadranka Andjelic and Dijana Milošević , together with the actress Maja Mitic, decided, perhaps subconsciously, to oppose the destruction with creation, to create, in the midst of a world falling apart, a micro cosmos of theatre."[10]

Later on, in parallel with the courageous work of the women of DAH Theater, a group of Serbian women opposing the war formed and took the name of Women in Black. They would gather in public spaces dressed in black and stand in silence as a sign of protest, in remembrance of the victims of war and in resistance against its absurdity and horror. The group has grown over the years, confronting many dangers, often suffering violence by regular citizens and supporters of the war. It still engages in silent anti-war performances in Belgrade, protected by a cordon of police. Recently the DAH group in collaboration with Women in Black gathered stories of Bosnian and Serbian women victims and survivors of the war, many survivors of the mass genocidal rapes waged against them by Serbian soldiers, and published them in a book titled *Women in Black: The Women's Side of War*.[11] One of DAH Theater's recent productions, titled *Crossing the Line*, has emerged from these stories. The show stages many of the accounts of women who have survived the unimaginable and yet still had the strength to tell their stories. The performance is built from an interweaving of parts of stories performed by the three main actresses of the DAH Theater in a stunning exhibit of passionate storytelling, stage movement, singing and dancing. Movie images of Bosnian women and of the war are at times superimposed on the live performance, which evokes the Brechtian techniques of collage and the postmodernist aesthetic of mixed media. At other times, depending on whether the group is performing in its own theater space in Belgrade or is traveling, the actresses coordinate their stage actions with a filmed version of the same show, creating a dizzying and overpowering effect of mirroring images reverberating into infinity and offering a larger-than-life experience.

The very processes by which the DAH Theater creates its performances, as much as their final theatrical products, are a beautiful illustration of the aesthetics of war and exile that I have been trying to articulate in this book. Reflective to a degree of the postmodernist merging of the levels of the real and the imagined, using actual footage of war and personal stories, superimposing genres and aesthetic categories, boldly taking the harshest truths and realities of their time and incorporating them in the shows, the director and performers of the group operate according to very high standards of theatrical professionalism as they stylize and transform raw stories into performance art of stunning visual quality. The techniques used in the creation of their shows are largely those of their own devising, as they mostly perform original work created in collaboration and through the merging of texts, ideas, stories and images that come from different sources. Because of the collaborative creation, the performances bear the marks of diverse artistic points of view, yet they form a cohesive theatrical entity. It is the reason for the freshness, rawness and also the unexpected quality of their performances: they emerge organically out of experience yet are creatively transformed into art under the alchemic processes of bold imaginative processes and with the performance strategies borrowed from European theater innovators such as Jerzy Grotowski and Eugenio Barba.[12] The actor's body is the ultimate producer of meaning in an intricate semiotic system in which each gesture and movement demands our attention and incites our interpretive skills. The body becomes on stage not only the vehicle for the telling of the story but the story itself, the page onto which physical pain, terror, survival and remembrance are inscribed uncompromisingly. At some point in the show one of the actresses slaps her own face in an accelerated rhythm and with increasing violence, while the others clap or stomp their feet on the ground, creating a maddening rhythm that is meant to tell the story of the violence and torture suffered by the women in the rape camps. The dancing and singing actress is enacting the story of the Bosnian woman who was able to escape from one of the rape camps held by Serbian soldiers by acting mad and singing Serbian songs all day and all night long.[13] Words and songs are superimposed over the rhythms and sounds of the beating and all culminate in a paroxistic dance by one of the actresses. The layering of the physical actions, sounds and images, effectuated by and written on the body, functions as both testimonial of the war stories and as survival, both as enactment of the story and the focus of the story itself: this is my body, this is what it has suffered and this is what it has survived. But it *has* survived to tell its story. The transformation of experience into art almost under the very eyes of the spectators is a form of victory over the experience, but it also functions as a place of belonging; as a repository of memory, of solidarity and of collective art production. At the end of their show, one of the actresses playing the part of another Bosnian woman survivor of the rape camps hands apples to the audience with ethereal and exquisite grace, drawing us in and offering us the fruit and the gift of knowledge and healing. And in a gesture symbolic of a ritual cleansing, the actresses rip open boxes of salt and pour them out on stage, forming a circle of salt. When asked about the significance of the action and of the salt itself, they note that it is symbolic of purification and cleansing following the purging of painful and traumatic experiences. In the middle of the circle of salt they place a flower. Even in the midst of horror, they find beauty, in the midst of darkness they look for light, and in the midst of devastation they create art.

The most impressive part of these theatrical endeavors is ultimately not even their perfectly wrought symbolism but their raw physicality and literality. The DAH Theater, the silent performances of Women in Black, and the merging of the two, have created in Serbia and across the world actual spaces of creation, resistance and healing. In a recent interview with Dijana Milošević , she gave the following answer to my question, "Do you see political theater as a safe space?"

> **Dijana Milošević:** Not at all. The paradox of the theater is that while being the safe space where opposite sides can meet, etc. it is at the same time the space where the provocation is high, "Pandora's box" is opened and the audience has to meet the challenge, has to face sometimes the worst fears or denial, has to confront prejudices and to question their beliefs. This is why political theater is not a safe space, but it offers the space where people could be together in their differences, could disagree and could confront each other, but not aggressively [2013].

Obviously the paradox she is talking about is that the theater is a safe space to ask unsafe questions and to face unsafe fears, challenges and confrontations in peaceful ways. And when I asked her to point to any concrete positive effects of the DAH Theater on our society, community and historical time, this is what she answered:

> **DM:** First of all our work has positive influence on ourselves, artists in DAH Theater. Speaking in my very name, our performances and the need of the audience to see our performances and their feedback kept me in my country even during the darkest times. Our audiences and communities have been influenced by our performances in various ways—but it happened not only in our community, country or city but worldwide. People were often moved, they managed to open their hearts and to see some events or facts in a different light, very often the feedback we got from the audience was that it was important to them to hear certain things publicly, that it was like opening the window for fresh air to enter. On a more concrete level, after our performances, individuals from the audience would come to us to tell us their stories, sometimes for the first time ever, and in that way our performances had a big impact on them, almost therapeutic. As we know that society consists of individuals, if individuals experience the change by seeing our performances, we have a chance to influence the community and society [2013].

I also asked Milošević the following question, which is at the core of my study: "Do you believe that experiences of war influence not only the content of your theater and the stories you choose but also the form and the aesthetic of your theater? If so, in what ways?"

And this is what she answered:

> **DM:** Each story seeks the right form; the choice of forms of our performances is always connected with the topic we are exploring. In that sense, war and the challenging political situation we live in in our country, which we used as a topic in our performances, influenced our form. For example, in the performance *The Story of Tea*, where we dealt with difficult truths, denial and missing people, languages, civilizations, the audience was seated in a way that they were mirroring each other, and the performance was taking place in the space in between. It was because my concept was that we do need to face each other because my people were trying not to look at harsh truths for such a long time, it was important to create the shared place where the audience was seating as if for a vigil together with actors. In our other performance, *Crossing the Line*, we used the proscenium stage, but the three actresses were on separate platforms, like three islands as the homes and lives of the women whose stories the actresses were telling had been [2013].

Milošević noted that *Crossing the Line* emerged from a need "to pull souls from the wreck and to remain with them in many spiritual and concrete ways." She says:

> The challenge and the responsibility was not to stay in that place, but to return this time to the company of those souls walking in the dark.... The way to reenter light, in the company of others, is actually the power and law of theater—to transform darkness of the horrific picture into a clear physical and spiritual presence on stage, to shed light on darkness. The process would pose difficult questions about responsibility, the right to deal with hard experiences of others, to encounter my own fears, and to reject truth that hurts me [DAH Theater 2011–12].

Sanja Krsmanovic Tasic, one of the three main actresses of the production, noted the following:

> I help the wars of the nineties be seen from a peephole of intimate, sometimes harsh truths, and not through the screens of one-sided TVs, or through the mouths of covetous politicians. Because only through these personal stories and immediate contacts can we encounter humanity in ourselves and realize the essence of the relation of ME and YOU, against the relationship of US and THEM [DAH Theater 2011–12].

When I asked her the question, "Do you connect fractured or fragmented theatrical form, non-linear structures and chronologies to the

***Opposite*: *Crossing the Line*: DAH Theater, Belgrade; 2009; directed by Dijana Milošević; devised by DAH Theater ensemble. Pouring salt all over the stage at the end of the production as a symbol of ritual cleansing (photograph: Dijana Milošević).**

theatrical form of your performances and shows?" Dijana Milošević answered the following:

> **DM:** Yes, I believe that time is not linear and that we do almost violence when we try to use linear storytelling in theater. We live in the reality where things are happening simultaneously, where past, future and present are entwined, where our perception creates the reality out of bits and fragments. It is very important to capture the organic quality of life in the performances, and when we work with fragments, parallel realities, different references that exist across time and space, we are closer to this genuine quality of life [2013].

The DAH Theater and performance artists delve into harsh and very specific realities of their time, into a particular historical moment that has broken their society, and they bring those realities to the stage after they have passed them through the imaginations and bodies of the performing actors as an offering to us the audience in an attempt to witness, to keep the memory and bring healing, maybe even reconciliation. Milošević 's answer to my question about the importance of the theater of witness elucidates this point even further and with more clarity than I have attempted myself:

> **DR:** In which ways do you think the theater of witness can have an impact on our reality, world, and history?
>
> **DM:** The creative theater techniques and programs could support participants in beginning and continuing the process of reconciliation. Theater creates a safe zone and safe environment for the expression of individual needs and the overcoming of traumatic experiences through creative work. In this way, theater can play a vital role in society. Also, theater done with social awareness has an important role as witness. Sometimes, it is more important just to be present, in silence, than to act. As many of the actions of Women in Black have shown us, silence can also be a powerful tool against oppression. We can think about different kinds of silence—the silence that opens the space and mind and the silence that closes it. The silence that is limiting is not always absence of sound—it could be the sound of noise that covers the truth. When we speak from the point of theater practice we encounter something that is known to skillful practitioners/artists—in executing theater actions on the stage or while we write we have to get rid of all what is not necessary, which we call noise, that covers the real theatrical action. The performer, writer or director has to "clean" all actions of what is "garbage" or noise in order to bring to life the piece of work in order to help silence speak. Finally, theater can create a space that allows memory to live in its full dignity—memory that opens the way for the truth to be heard again, that gives voice to the ones who cannot be otherwise heard [2013].

In discussing the aesthetic contributions of the DAH group to the theater of witness, we have to place them also in the context of performance art which, according to Philip Auslander, is "taken to be an intrinsically postmodern art form, both historically and stylistically" (2004, 99). Devised performance in the style of the DAH Theater Group, which includes aspects of performance art and also involves dance, song, dialogue, stage action, the balancing of silence with words, and even theory and research that are imbedded in the final performance, seems to exemplify in a holistic manner the stylistic descriptors of postmodernist theater in which text and performance merge and are created simultaneously. It is maybe this simultaneity of art forms and the interdisciplinary nature of the work of the DAH Theater Group that has made its presentations into the ideal artistic medium for keeping memory and questioning history, for witnessing trauma and also transcending it, for posing difficult questions without offering easy answers. It is the postmodernist combination of different art forms and disciplines into one cohesive presentation that seems best fitted to encompass and bear witness to the enormity of traumatic events such as the genocidal war of the nineties in Bosnia-Herzegovina.

The world created on stage by the DAH theater performances is an open world in which audiences are included, as in the example of the actress offering apples to spectators. Again, the great impact that DAH theater has on audiences both in their home country of Serbia, in the neighboring countries as well as in West European countries and the United States, where they travel often to offer performances and workshops, derives from their openness and from the engaging artfulness of their shows. These exemplify in action all the features of theater of war and exile discussed in this book: mixing personal stories with imaginative strategies, lived experience and historical data with fictional imagery and dialogue; breaking the suspension of disbelief and engaging the audience; using mixed media and fractured narratives; combining different art forms and aesthetics; and using character fragmentation in the sense described by Auslander, of characters created from fragments such as bits of personal stories, other people's words and stories, and the actors' devised dialogues (2004, 106). The DAH Theater artists also exhibit the characteristics of postmodernist performance explored by Kristin Schmidt:

> It is precisely in the moment of the breakdown in a performance, that is, when the illusion of the stage as a closed world is denied, that the audience participation can take place and the spectator moves into the center of theatrical attention. In postmodern drama, forms of meaning are created by the gaze of the spectator and can thus be conceived as the result of the free movement within what Fischer-Lichte refers to as the "time-space continuum": the spectator becomes the "master of semiosis" [2005, 51].

Indeed, with DAH Theater we become to some degree "masters of semiosis," and we are called to create our own meaning as we travel with them from story to story, from concentration camp cells to a street or an open field, or to someone's room, all suggested by minimalist props and mostly by the craft of the actors, their bodies, voices, stage action and movement. In *Crossing the Line* the only set was made from large packages of salt placed like stools. The actresses sat on them during the performance, then ripped them open and poured the salt onto the stage at the end of the performance. Everything is in constant movement and one gesture fluidly evolves from another even when the stories are overlapping or the narratives are interrupted. And we are not only "masters of semiosis" once we view and experience the performance; we are also witnesses of the stories of trauma and we are given the responsibility to hold them respectfully, pass them on gently and remember them compassionately. Beyond any academic and scholarly analysis, the experience that the DAH performances offer the spectators is one of full presentness, of life unfolding under our eyes, of theater as part of life, of actors and spectators participating together in a sacred form of togetherness like the ancient sacred performances and shamanic rituals. It is not without significance that in one of their earlier shows Sonja Tasic performed the swirling dance of a Dervish in a stunning performance that combined dance with a form of meditation and concentration specific to Sufi philosophy.[14]

The DAH Theater's most recent production is called *The Presence of Absence* and is inspired by the aftermath of wars and genocidal events focusing on the disappearance of people as a result of abductions. As stated in the program, "During the civil wars in ex–Yugoslavia over 40.000 people have gone missing. That number is drawn from: the conflicts in Croatia during two separate periods in 1992–93 and 1995. Around 5.500 persons disappeared, of which 3.380 were identified, while about 2.120 persons are still classified as missing" (DAH Theater, 2013). The DAH Theater production was devised from numerous testimonies of family members of missing people. This is how Milošević frames and describes the performance and its role in the understanding and healing processes necessary when those who were once loved and present in our lives have disappeared:

> History tells us that the only way of healing a society after atrocities have taken place is to go through the painful process of truth telling. This is still ongoing within our region. Our performance is a contribution to that effort. "People cannot just disappear, they can die of illness, or they can be killed in wars or be murdered, but they cannot just disappear." These words are said by the "Centuries Old Woman Who Saw it All" during the performance. These words were also spoken by mothers from Argentina; and we heard them from women from Đulići in Bosnia. These words demand that responsibility be taken. Where are the missing? Who took

> them? Are they alive? In whose name were they abducted? What are our own and other governments doing about it? When will families get answers? Who is responsible? When will those responsible be punished? These questions inhabit our lives, whether we are aware of them or not. These questions demand answers. At the end of the performance, while leaving, the audience will see roses beside the painted silhouettes of disappeared people on the sacks that were brought in at the beginning of the performance by the "Centuries Old Woman Who Saw it All." Roses were carried by mothers from Plaza del Mayo in Argentina, in their ongoing circling, searching for the truth about their missing.... Hundreds of roses were carried by families of the disappeared from Đulići, Bosnia, who left them on the sites of the concentration camps where their dearest had been taken and all trace of them had disappeared. Also the families of kidnapped Serbs from Kosovo carry roses when they mark the anniversary of their disappearance. In her text *Of Beauty and Justice* the Argentinian artist Claudia Bernardi writes about families of missing children from Guatemala. During the trial of a massacre where children had been abducted and killed, the families, as a sign of protest to the verdict of "not guilty," held up the roses that they had brought. Bernardi finishes with these words: "I imagine the movement of the roses, undulating gently, like a hug, like a lullaby, without words or sounds. A lament dressed in deep red for the children who perished ..." [DAH Theater 2013].

The theatrical, performative and unapologetically political work of the DAH Theater does not obscure the truth but rather fearlessly plunges into the harshest realities, using not only theatrical and performance strategies but also ethnographic and anthropological research of the events and personal histories of real victims. Their work is postmodernist because it is profoundly implanted in the here and now and not because it escapes the here and now or deforms it into so many copies that it becomes unrecognizable. The stories of women from Bosnia, Argentina or Guatemala, their anguish, their grief, their longing for missing husbands, children, brothers and their desperate desire for closure is wrenchingly real even if transported to us via actors and acting, therefore via an act of simulation. As a stubborn and respectful repository of memory, a production such as *The Presence of Absence*, with its skilled weaving of raw material and delicate artistry, is more postmodernist than postmodernism itself. Its profound impact on communities and audiences, as can be testified from interviews with the artistic director and from their large success in different parts of the world, prove that we are desperately hungry for the real and appreciative whenever artists have the audacity and aesthetic savvy to transport us to it.

The actors and the artistic director of DAH take the ethical and aesthetic responsibility of gathering, holding and retelling firsthand stories

***The Presence of Absence*: DAH Theater, Belgrade; October–December 2013; directed by Dijana Milošević. Maja Vujović in the role of "few hundred years old woman who saw it all," a mythic witness of violence, atrocity, and also repository of memory (photograph: Dijana Milošević).**

and personal accounts of trauma in their performances very seriously and are fully aware of the balance they have to keep between testifying to violence without causing more trauma by the reliving of it, and bringing about healing and closure even for audience members who have experienced similar traumas. They live the stories they gather viscerally, allowing themselves to undergo a profound spiritual and artistic conversion and transformation. This is what Sanja Krmanovic Tasic, one of the former actresses of the theater, had to say about her work and experience in performing *The Presence of Absence*:

> I would characterize work on the performance "Presence of Absence" with the following words: the state of conscious unconsciousness; half alive; the

> walk of despair; limbo; resistance, darkness, hole, cave; the ground that keeps shifting; fog that suffocates; silent screams within thoughts; silent screams of the body; suppressing life; muteness [DAH Theater 2013].

The indomitable commitment of the theater artists who create and perform the shows offers a superb example of "tragic optimism," of finding hope in the midst of desperation, of creating meaning in the midst of a terrifying world. Reminding me of the example I gave in the introduction about the camp prisoner who wrote the vituperative letter to his wife despite the fact that he could have been actually killed for it, Dijana Milošević noted the following in relation to the use of humor and the carnivalesque in their theater:

> **DR:** Do you think you are making use of carnivalesque forms, or of the blending of tragic and comic elements in your theater and if so, what do you think is their function?

> **DM:** Life is very complex as we know; there is not only tragedy or only harmony, it is all entwined. Humor could be found in the midst of the darkest moments and sometimes deep sadness could be in the heart of the biggest joys. This is why it is necessary to use both tragic and comic moments, because only by doing that can we reach the truth [2013].

Having known and worked with Milošević and having followed the progress and life of their theater for years, I know that when she says "truth," she does not mean an abstract notion of a universal one-size-fits-all kind of truth, but the visceral truth of the stories she gathers from trauma survivors, the truth found in small and large gestures, the truth evoked from years of crying over victims of wars and disappeared people and manifested in the delicate and haunting gesture of placing roses on the painting of disappeared children, or of handing apples to the audience, the truth enclosed in the silence of the victims and survivors as much as in their words of testimony. DAH Theater illustrates the painful but necessary journey beautifully described by Erik Ehn in talking of theater of witness: "Witnesses are obliged to enter the field of grief as wide open, as open architecturally and chemically as the traumatic circumstances—but biased toward creation" (2013, 77). As we shall see later on, the actors of DAH indeed enter fields of grief and emerge with creative treasures.

The lives of the actors are often directly intertwined with the development of the show they are creating, as they absorb the lives of those whose voices and stories they perform into their own lives, and vice versa, as they spill their own personal stories into the theater event they are engaged in. The following statement by Ivana Milenović Popović, one of the actresses that was supposed to be part of *The Presence of Absence*, offers a haunting perspective of this intertwining of lives and experiences, of art and reality:

Hush, son, sleep my son,
May you be tricked by sleep
A cradle, your cradle,
Has been forged by the sea...

> This is the lullaby I sang as part of the performance of *Presence of Absence*. I sang it like a mother whose child had gone missing. It was the cry of a woman speechless with despair because of the loss of what was most precious to her.... Both moments of happiness because of the discovery of a toy, and sensing the coldness of bricks that once had been their fireplace, created in me the fear of how to answer the following question: how is it to be a mother? How is it possible to live with so much pain? Is it actually happiness to have children, if the pain from their disappearance is so strong? ... Does that missing child grow older in the memory of its mother or stay unchanged as it had been at the moment of his or her disappearance? Does the mother play and talk to the child, does she laugh, does she sing the child a birthday song? The only thing I knew for certain was that she does not want to stop searching for the child, because he or she is always present. On the 24th of May 2013, the morning of the first rehearsal of the performance *Presence of Absence*, I found out that I was pregnant. Completely unplanned and unexpectedly I discovered that that evening I would be performing the role of a mother, looking for her missing child, while carrying my own in my belly ... *Hush, son, sleep son* ... I will not be part of the performance now. The materials I have developed are being used in the performance, while I myself stay absent. The loss of that role in the performance was replaced with a strange feeling—as if I had found what I was looking for... Filled with sadness and happiness at the same time, still in anticipation [DAH Theater 2013].

Such powerful statements of the organic merging between the actor's personal life and the life of the characters they play, who in turn are created from authentic stories and testimonies, beg for an interpretation in light of the intersections between the personal, the political, and the creative, which is the mark of much feminist theater and performance theory. Such interweaving between the creation of a show and the personal life of the actor also illustrates the intersection between feminist theater aesthetic and postmodernist aesthetic. Feminist performance art and feminist solo pieces or monologues unapologetically combine autobiography with fiction, with snippets of political news or intertextual references.[15] Performance art has given women the opportunity to tell their own stories in their own voices, and to direct and perform their own shows, thus allowing them to express themselves creatively in a holistic manner as complete artists.[16]

However, the artists of the DAH Theater group go well beyond their own personal experiences and having emerged in times of war with a cry of resistance against it, they encompass larger stories of women victims of wars, sexual and physical abuse, and the trauma of loss. In the Grotowski style of diluting the boundaries between the actor's life on stage and outside the stage, they absorb these experiences in their own lives, bodies and psyches, while also going in the other direction of bringing their own lives into the lives of the characters. They have created their own genre that beautifully illustrates synergistic coalitions between feminist and postmodernist aesthetic, performance art and political theater, Brechtian theater strategies and Grotowskian performance methods, the art of sound installation with anthropological research, the art of dance with political activism. Their performances offer a complete experience that addresses the senses, the intellect and the emotions of the audience.

Jugoslav Hadžić, the artist who created the sound for the performance, offers a fascinating testimonial about the production processes that went into the show from the point of view of its soundtrack:

> The following phase was to record the texts that my colleagues Sanja Krsmanović Tasić, Maja Vujović, Ivana Milenović Popović and I had written. The topic of the texts was "signs of the presence of absence." We also recorded interviews with people who were engaged with the missing persons issue, or who had tragically lost someone.... These recordings were imported into a sound manipulation computer program.... I created another rule which I followed from then on: every sound you hear must originate from the recordings that were made in the field. While I was listening to these recordings, for days, over and over again, searching for a part of a conversation—They are not missing, they were taken away—or a sound of the environment (e.g., coffee cups clattering), I realized that, with all the misfortune they have been through, both the missing persons and their families were victims of manipulation, especially political and media manipulation. This insight uncovered a field of absolute manipulation over sound. Voices were altered, taken out from their contexts, distorted, drained through various filters, and transformed into a melody that is not intended to seduce you emotionally. Quite the contrary—its task is to prepare you for the cruel truth that awaits you when entering the theater [DAH Theater 2013].

This testimonial also uncovers the aesthetic of rupture and fragmentation, of collage and layering of both experience and artistic strategies, as a viable and necessary aesthetic for dealing artistically with trauma. Because it is un-representable, any attempt to represent it realistically would only offend the victims or miserably fall short of the real events. Therefore only by what Hadžić calls "manipulation" of sound, and in the larger sense of the full show through the artistic manipulation of space, voice, and testimonials gathered, can we have a glimpse into a reality that defies representation and whose raw telling would likely refresh trauma rather than help the healing process. Through stylized form and disjointed structures that are still held together in a fragile balance, DAH Theater humbly pays homage to the victims of trauma. It might not necessarily heal, but it honors the sufferers and engages us as witnesses. Even though as spectators of a show derived from the suffering of the victims of atrocity we will never fully understand or be real witnesses of the actual violence, loss and trauma, we at least acquire the knowledge of that past, we "enter the field of grief," we are transformed by that journey. This in turn may result in two valuable achievements: (1) We acquire an empathy towards victims of war and serious traumas, which in turn may move us to undertake social and political action; (2) We develop a better understanding and appreciation of the ability of live performance to transform us and keep us real. Holding the memory of historical violence and human suffering in the exquisite receptacle of a work of art that honors it is a necessary political gesture. Such a gesture renders all of us more human and more lucid in an inhumane world whose violence defies reason. If indeed, as Erik Ehn has noted, genocides are an attempt "to forbid history—to forbid the making of meaning by barring our real and imaginative abilities to gather history" (2012, 248), DAH Theater has responded to such attempts by creating safe spaces of questioning and remembrance, of community and meaning making, and of salvaging histories.

❧ ❧ ❧

The theater makers in this chapter bring it all together: body, voice, text, space, and story. They are indeed "makers" in the larger sense of builders of architectures and worlds. Without them and hundreds like them, without the makers who bring their bodies on stage, gather funds to pay for spaces that are open to audiences, build costumes, mix sounds, gather stories from victims, design posters; without their voices, visions, and multidimensional, multidisciplinary work the texts of the artists explored in the first two chapters would most likely remain silent lines on a page. They would certainly still have value, move readers, be taught in schools, awaken empathy or critical thinking or incite to controversy, just as novels, essays, the silent but throbbing books gathered in libraries or more recently in virtual spaces have done for millennia. But most likely they wouldn't bring us out into the street, halls, small and large spaces, to form communities and experience life in its mindboggling contradictions and colors in flesh and blood. And given the nature, themes and scope of the work of these theater artists—namely the agonies of history, the violence of modern wars and the unquenched sadness of displacement—their work as makers and builders of worlds that exist in real space and time is as courageous as it is efficient: it dislocates time and space and steals from the history of wars and exilic confusion real spaces and real hours that are crafted into oases of peace, universes of color and feeling, receptacles where memory speaks its stories of horror and joy. Indeed it keeps us in a "here and now" that is equally real and unreal, as lasting as it is ephemeral. Together, the artists in the first two chapters and the ones in the last chapter are living proof that theater exists only in the collaborative work of all of them, in the integration of text and body, idea and space, and that one can't really exist without the other, if theater is to fulfill its potential for change. Maybe political theater, more than any other kind, needs this indestructible integration of all its elements and the harmonious collaboration of artists in order to better resist and maybe even shatter the architectures of hate, simulation, and indifference and rearrange the pieces into non-stagnant and inventive architectures of love, authentic thought, diversity, passion and rebellion.

Conclusion

Theater as Survival

At the end of this journey through a troubling theatrical world in constant movement and reinvention, I believe it necessary to make a personal revelation as a preface to the concluding remarks. It is one last story about the power of live theater to save us from despair and hopelessness in the face of the world's chaos, injustices and myriad forms of oppression. I grew up and was educated through my first college years in Romania's capital, Bucharest, also often called the "little Paris of the Balkans," under the heavy indoctrination of Eastern Europe's most fierce communist dictatorship and under what I consider "a pedagogy of tyranny."[1] By some fluke in the overall system of surveillance and possibly also due to the ignorance of the censors and secret police, during the seventies and eighties Bucharest's many theaters still remained vibrant places of artistic expression where experimental productions of controversial texts such as Mikhail Bulgakov's *The Master and Marguerita* or of Shakespeare's *The Tempest* under the direction of the famous Liviu Ciulei[2] played to overflowing houses and avid audiences. For Romanians of all walks of life, from sophisticated university professors to rebellious students like me, to engineers, or factory workers, the experience of live theater was not only a refuge from the daily, dreary lines for food and the police surveillance, but also a leap into a different world that through its multidimensionality renewed our spirit, enhanced our survival strategies and made us bolder in our resistance to the overall system of oppression.

During the early eighties, as a student in English literature at the University of Bucharest, I joined a countercultural student theater that functioned after the model of Jerzy Grotowski's methods of "poor theater" or

"Laboratory Theater." Ironically enough, the theater was located in the attic of the building that housed the headquarters of the Romanian Communist Youth and was appropriately called the Attic. I could say that I received almost the equivalent of another BA in acting and performance art during the two and a half years I was part of that theater before my escape from Romania in 1983. Whether we played Shakespeare's *Hamlet*, Samuel Beckett's *Happy Days*, or Romanian canonical plays, the sets and costumes were of utmost simplicity, reusable and adaptable to each new production. We played in the Attic Theater space as well as in unconventional venues including restaurants, school gyms and once even a mental asylum. We were able to establish through our intense practices and training in the Grotowski style a fluid continuum between the life we spent in the theater and the life we spent outside it, in our classes, meetings, in the streets and halls all studded with larger-than-life portraits of our Communist Party leaders. In the daily fakeness of heavy ideology and socialist realism, Grotowski's "new language of the theater," which was "primal, a language that had little to do with literal meanings," filled with "deeply felt emotions," and "unamplified, unrealistic and deeply human" (Whitmore 2012, 82) was like fresh water for the hungry traveler in a desert of literality and vacuous Party language.

Our repertoire was extremely diverse, and because of the daily indoctrination that we suffered in our various public activities, playing any modern or classical texts of recognized national and international playwrights was an act of political resistance. In fact, being imaginative in our productions and our acting, and experimenting with directorial and acting techniques in a holistic manner that involved a variety of mental and physical practices, amounted to a politics of opposition. The Attic Theater became during my college years in Romania my intellectual and artistic home in a country where I was already starting to feel like an exile. I can say without an exaggeration that it was to a large extent my belonging to that theater and being part of the group of actors and directors who rehearsed every day until the early hours of the morning that I was able to bear with some measure of dignity the daily humiliations of our lives under a ruthless dictatorship, and that I had the courage to boldly say no to the secret police officer who tried to goad me into joining the ranks of informers in exchange for material and professional favors. I could also say that the Attic Theater saved my soul from the moral labyrinth of living under a dictatorship. The last good-bye I said the day before my planned escape, as I was trying my hardest to hold back tears so as not to reveal any of my intentions, was to the director and the fellow actors of the Attic Theater. I have carried that training and that unadulterated belief in the regenerative and redeeming powers of live theater throughout my immigrant experience in America and my professional journeys as a writer, theater director, teacher and scholar. And full circle, when I returned to Romania decades later as a Fulbright teacher/scholar with a project on theater and gender, I was stunned to find out from my Romanian students that the Attic Theater still existed, that it functioned as vibrantly as when I used to be part of it under the guidance of the same passionate director, now twenty years older, that it still trained students and young people avid for theater, and that it was just as countercultural, only in a different way adjusted to the post-communist realities of Romania with its own new set of problems.

The reason for this example is not solely to illustrate the transformative value of live theater but also to point out that this value was largely due to its unconventional form, edgy training, countercultural stance, and modern aesthetic principles that allowed for the boldness to stage a Shakespeare play in Japanese Kabuki style or a German Romantic play with touches of Romanian folklore. In the monotony of state-ordered ideologies and "pedagogies of tyranny," we needed the clashing forms, the diversity of styles, and the bold leaps of the imagination for our very own spiritual survival. I learned then that form is politics just as much as politics is politics.

Holding on to the Real

In the multitude of criticisms and theoretical claims about the loss of the real, a book about theater that is about war and exile is arguably also twice removed from these actual realities; and the entire body of critical studies that are about works about things only removes us even more from the real. Such is our postmodernist urge to create concentric circles of criticism about criticism, of theory about theory, of talk about talk, in sort of a never-ending indulgence in discussions about the real instead of an engagement with the real. Faulty as it may be, I consider my book an attempt to engage with an art form that—as long as it still involves the presence of the actor's body on a stage and the presence of a live audience—exists in the sphere of the real and tries to engage us with different sides of the real. I have tried to walk the paradoxical line of a stubborn reclaiming of the real, on one hand, and the meandering roads of theatrical disguises, simulations, games, highly imaginative structures and aesthetic tropes on the other hand. And most likely, I have only managed to "fail better" in Beckett's inspired words, to fail at getting closer to the constantly moving target that is this mythical real, in some sort of Zeno's Paradox of moving closer to the finish line but never quite arriving at it. I have struggled to define and trace the shapes that theatrical art takes when it emerges from the hard-core realities of our world. Even though made to appear almost exciting and pleasurable when reverberated through the distorting lenses of the media, virtual realities, movies, and television, the traumas of war and displacement exist in different places on earth in real spaces and time and are experienced by real people in flesh and blood. Simple as that may sound, it is a good mantra to repeat to ourselves whenever we might think that these realities are out there and they do not concern us.

As an artist, critic, but also as a politically engaged citizen of the world, or "global foreigner," the best I can do as far as reclaiming the real in a book of criticism is to position myself at the meeting place between the life of theatrical creation and the existence of human suffering born out of war and displacement as well as out of the potential for joy and hope. I have tried to follow the fluid and two-way road between personal experience and art form: the interconnectedness between experiencing a war, the aftermath of war, the loss of one's country or self and the shapes that human trauma may take in the transfiguration undergone in various theatrical creations emerging in response to it. I have often gone further and pointed to the ways in which such shapes have flowed back into the unfolding of life, into the thoughts and feelings of live audiences and communities. If trauma is the "untellable" physical or psychological wound suffered by a person, community or people as a result of extreme violence or loss, it must become something else in order for the victims to become survivors. For psychiatrists such as the Bosnian concentration camp survivor Esad Boskailo, that "something else" translates into guiding victims of trauma to rediscover meaning in their lives, first by acknowledging that they suffered it and next by reestablishing relations with family, friends, places and occupations. For artists who have suffered or witnessed trauma firsthand, or who are troubled by the trauma suffered by others in their world and community, to find meaning translates into creating shapes in which others can recognize their own traumas but also move beyond them. We find meaning in creating shapes that both contain the memory of trauma and distance us from it in a healing way. By telling specific stories, we have the artistic power to connect the personal to larger communities. The shapes of the theater discussed in my book may unsettle survivors, victims, and witnesses, as a first step in the acknowledgment of trauma. However, through the journey facilitated by artistic form, humor, contrasts, paradox, character development, and suspense—that is, through the works of a creative imagination, it may allow for a productive distancing from the rawness of the actual experience by confirming that the suffering has not been forgotten and instead it has been woven into collective memories that can teach us to do and be better in the future. And for those who have not experienced such traumas, these theatrical creations have the potential to sharpen our empathy, move us to social action, and awaken our critical thinking vis-à-vis governments and political manipulations.

Quilting Theories: Postmodernity, Carnival and the Balkans

I have quilted several critical theories in the development of my study without overly relying on any single one, precisely because of the multi-layered nature of the theater art I am talking about and the complicated referents it has outside the text and the performance space. I have both embraced and contradicted Baudrillard's theories of simulacra, simulation and the hyperreal, and Jameson's theories of pastiche and imitation as measures of the realities and cultural products of our capitalist, globalized society. I have deliberately used the self-subverting, indefinite and contradictory elements of postmodern theory and claims of a postmodernist aesthetic in order to frame the theater aesthetic I have tried to define. I have relied more on the political side of postmodernism or postmodernity as a theory or aesthetic that is critical of the society it is part of while also engaging with it.[3] I have thus made use of fluid and unstable theoretical frames to contain fluid and unstable theatrical forms. From the confluence of the two some productive conclusions have been drawn, of which the first is that the theater of war and exile deliberately escapes definition and defies formulaic tropes. Despite the plurality of positions about what postmodernism really is, despite even conflicting views among its many theorists including Jean-François Lyotard, Jean Baudrillard and Frederic Jameson, there is one strain of thought that conspicuously seems to link all views and to be reflected by various degrees in the theater I explore: the rejection of the assumptions of social coherence and the embracing of indeterminacy and of a decentered and fragmented subject.

The theater of war and exile unfolds in unpredictable narrative and chronological architectures that challenge if not destroy and mock conventions of classical or realistic theater. It contains diverse, overlapping theatrical languages within the unfolding of one play or performance. It makes abundant use of games, pastiche, simulations, and irony through which two things are generally achieved: a criticism of the very simulated realities outside the world of the performance and a sharper view of that which pulsates behind simulations due to the distancing achieved as a result of such devices. These realities may be the psychological violence of loss and displacement, the confusion of living in between cultural and linguistic realities, the existential devastation brought about by wars and genocidal events, or the absence of loved ones. Throughout all the theoretical meandering, I have held tight to the thread of Brechtian theories and practice of alienation, epic theater, historicization, and the use of disparate elements that comment on one another. This thread is woven in various patterns throughout all the theater that I engage with.

Rather than looking at living things as texts, in theater we have the unique opportunity of looking at texts as living things and at live bodies in their full ontological reality but also in their semiotic potential. Rather than treating the world as text, the theater discussed here makes a world of its texts while drawing its substance from that world. It overturns simulacra on their head by absorbing testimonials, personal stories and experiences into a contained world on stage that in turn makes us more curious and aware of the life outside the stage and forbids us to be indifferent to it. I have set myself the perhaps unattainable goal of proving that political theater with aesthetically arresting forms can offer us a sanctuary from the "banality of evil." In the process of reaching this goal many of the artists' own testimonials about their creative processes, their personal stories, and their connections to the realities of exile or war have created a bridge between created and lived worlds on the way towards the safe spaces of theater.

The upside-down world of the circus and carnival has permeated many of the plays and performances chosen for the book in combination with an incorporation of Balkan liminal spaces, aesthetic and moral hybridities, a flavor of in-between worlds reflective of a self-fulfilling prophesy that both confirms and contradicts Said's discussion of orientalism. It confirms it because the Balkan world has internalized many of the Western projections that have turned it into a "Balkanized" universe in the first place, and in its efforts to also be an overly zealous "upholder of European values" it has "Othered" itself. But it contradicts it because what is typically called the Balkan world continues to be fluid and indefinable in its multitude of cultural and psychological realities that ultimately contradict any single frozen image of "exoticism" and of the "supreme fictions" (Said 1979, xvi) of an "Oriental" other. And paradoxically, since it contradicts its own stereotypes about itself, it also confirms Said's passionate plea to Westerners to move away from any such "supreme fictions" and instead be curious about specific realities.

The carnival, a form of celebration of the people, allowed people, according to Bakhtin, a "temporary suspension, both ideal and real, of hierarchical rank," and "a special type of communication impossible in everyday life" (1984, 9–19). It is worthy of mention that the theory of carnival has been developed by a philosopher and scholar living under the Stalinist terror who also happened to be condemned to exile in Siberia. His sentence was later changed to six years in Kazakhstan. Bakhtin's book on Rabelais also happened to be his doctoral dissertation, which was rejected at the University of Moscow due to its anarchic quality.[4] The huge laughter and reversal of hierarchies of the carnival described by Bakhtin is threatening to any system of oppression and thought control, as it subverts the rigidity and cruelty of arbitrary power, it offers release from suffering and subjugation, and it shows to those oppressed the possibility of change and freedom. Veteranyi's circus existence, as is refracted through the tragic lens and uncompromising voice of a terrified girl and her nomadic passage through worlds of established structures and institutions, across national borders, religions and languages, disrupts the stability of conventional bourgeois society and the excess of capitalist materialism and allows her to be her own country. Saviana Stanescu's professional clown characters demystify the terrifying seriousness of INS and immigration authorities with their ironic balloon animals and their irreverent laugh at American consumerism, laws and fake realities, while attempting to achieve their version of the American Dream. Inverted fairytales, such as in Stanescu's *Bechnya*, Markovic's *Doll Ship*, or Sbrljanović's *Family Stories*, cast a dark and unforgiving grin onto the cruel realities of war or a demoralized postwar society while exploding the fixity of taboos and stereotypes contained in traditional fairy tales. The demented ride of Maslwoska's characters through fake worlds, towards virtual realities and across landfills of post-communist, capitalist human and physical trash, their relentless humor that still "radiates" despite hopeless loneliness, urges us to reconsider the figure of the foreigner, nomad, Gypsy, or "stranger among us"[5] and casts a glaring light onto xenophobia and ethnic prejudice. Vişniec's characters take on the cruel yet pathetic authority of "Balkan man" and Balkan wars through carnivalized language, derisive song and stage action, and negotiations between the living and the dead, thus forging the way to healing from trauma and rediscovering love and meaning. Motti Lerner's theater-within-theater combined with the use of madness as a truth-telling strategy in times of war destabilizes any notion of the rightfulness or glory of war. Noa Baum's puzzle of stories of war told both from the Israeli and the Palestinian side with moments of playfulness and humor melts the demonizing of the Other into compassion and understanding. The filtering of tragic events through dark humor or through the devised, luminous theatrical art of DAH Theater allows for reversals of power between victims and oppressors, and for tragedy to be "transformed into a story of possibility" (Boskailo and Lieblich 2012, 153). Again, it is form that modifies content. The theatrical shapes chosen by my group of artists transform the heavy experiences of trauma into tellable stories. Their Balkan flair, flirtations with margins, exotic landscapes or mock orientalism, turning the Balkan resistance to diversity on its head and transforming it into cultural polyphonies, or walking the fine line "between lands" and daring to traverse the "no man's land" of liminalities, take us to places of "radical openness" that we can make our homes.

Throughout most of the plays and performances discussed there is a conspicuous presence of song and dance, some at face value and as lyrical enhancement of the theatrical experience such as in Adamová's play or in DAH Theater's devised shows; some in parodic manner, such as in Vişniec's, Stanescu's, Srbljanović's or Lerner's plays. Without knowledge of the most engaging examples of theater of war and exile emerging from these parts of the world, one would think it is a dark and humorless art form whose ultimate effect on the audience is to bring us down. Not at all. In a very primal and mythic way it is art that takes us down to the bowls of the earth and of humanity, only to bring us up towards the sun. Balkan and Israeli cultures have deep roots in an early agrarian culture of dance, song, mythical reenactments of cosmogonic events, free commerce and traveling between the realms of the living and the dead as well as colorful and exquisitely crafted attires and artifacts. "The Dancing Goddesses" and "dancing as life" have fueled Balkan and early European cultures since the "nonliterate agrarian cultures" (Barber 2013, 367). "Ritual dancers, from the Balkans to Britain, marked out territories and fought intruding bands, to the death if necessary" and the dancing of the goddesses "created life, their wrath could destroy it" (3). Even though it often appears in distorted forms throughout the theater art discussed in my book, the presence of song, dance, carnivalesque episodes,[6] obscenity, and strong colors, and the coexistence of the living and the dead, connects us to the ancestral roots of an area that has also been known as one of the cradles of civilization and allows us to reestablish our broken ties with life-affirming practices and customs (Gimbutas 2007; Biaggi 2000).

The actress portraying a violated woman hands an apple to an audience member; another actress portraying a bereft mother sings a sweet lullaby; a character inspired by the dark realities of a genocidal war dances, drinks, sings and laughs, mocking the brutality and monotonous prejudices of "Balkan Man"; a hungry refugee from a country devastated by war finds refuge in the millenary story of Gilgamesh; another refugee on the cusp of deportation makes animal balloons for birthday parties; an Israeli female character suffering from PTSD sings mocking songs that demystify the glorification of war. Beyond all theoretical talk about the "liminalities" and "in-between lands" that the Balkans may be today, or the Balkan "hybridities" overlapped on global cultural confusion, beyond its terrifying histories of war and violence up to recent times, there is also the indomitable laughter at the tragicomedy that is our journey on earth, the dance of life and death of ancient goddesses, the meticulous attention to craft and color.

Having grown up in a country at the top of the Balkan Peninsula and having travelled many of the dark and luminous territories of Balkan worlds, I have a rather carnal and less theoretical vision of the world that so many Western critics have tried to define but that artists from these parts of the world have managed to seize in captivating colors. Accordion music in the midst of a funeral cortege; a circus acrobat performing in the street next to an amputee beggar; a peasant at the head of a horse-drawn cart filled with fresh hay talking on a cellphone; a heartbreak French song playing next to a Turkish version of rap playing next to an American pop song on a crowded beach at the greenish-violet Black Sea where people dance till morning; a play by Sarah Kane in a two-hundred-year-old theater that in the previous century had been bombed by Russian, American, and German bombs; a Hungarian language school next to a Greek Orthodox church, next to a stunning view of a corner of the brooding Carpathians, in the vicinity of a Dracula castle filled with American tourists; all this doesn't even begin to sum up my version of the Balkans, where we laugh at tragedy, where peasants in the deep rural areas still sing mourning songs at weddings and joyous songs at funerals (Kligman 1988).

One of the most recent projects of the DAH theater has been the creation of a film/bus tour, titled *(In)Visible City*, of the theater troupe moving across Balkan regions searching for and celebrating the great cultural and linguistic diversity of its peoples. The bus tour, which has been in turn made into a stunning film, has managed to transform the anxiety of difference into a hymn to the colorfulness of multiculturalism. Passengers on these buses suddenly see themselves confronted with free and explosively colorful performances by DAH Theater actors who are enacting diverse histories from the Balkans and its many regions and introducing the ideas of diversity and difference as a human and cultural enrichment and not as a threat or a loss. On this bus there is constant dancing and singing of traditional songs from the various Balkan regions, and the actors wear the most diverse and colorful costumes. Towards the end of this study, as towards the end of any theatrical work that deals with the harsh realities of our world, it is worth asking again: can art make a difference? One thing is sure: those of us working in, for and towards the creation and protection of that safe space of theater of witness are going to die trying to prove that, yes, it does make a difference. "Drama of witness is patient and unforgiving" (Ehn, 2013, 78). We may have to wait longer than our own lifetimes before we see a marked difference produced by the theater of witness, or we may see it in an epiphany in the middle of a performance or storytelling episode. In the process of healing through theater we might get hurt again and heal again. Yet the very physical presence of stories of war and genocide channeled through actors' bodies stares at the world in "unforgiving" carnality and memory turned flesh. It is in the constant motion and ripples caused by the questioning, the unsettled answers, the unforgettable colors of personal narratives that we may find meaning, the real, an unexpected and restorative journey. And I for one, am getting on that theater bus tour of the (In)Visible City and am ready for that journey.

Theater and Memory; Theater and Social Change

At the most basic level, history is about what happened. The theater studied here refuses to forget what happened. The Holocaust happened, the genocide of the nineties in Bosnia happened, the Israeli/Palestinian wars happened and continue to happen, and the displacement of thousands from their homes happens every day across the world. This theater art has amassed in its creation fragments of dramatic forms from a great variety of aesthetic incarnations and styles, and yet like mosaics made from stones and pieces of different eras and regions, it makes a cohesive picture that tells of troubled journeys, yearning souls, disrupted communities and shattered lives in the process of reinventing themselves. It is not despite its fragmented nature, layering of stylistic modes, controlled disorders, reversed chronologies, mixture of high and low, self-subverting moments, dystopian darkness and clownish stridency that this theater is transformative and strangely beautiful; it is *because* all of that.

It is not only the theater of war and exile, postmodern theater and performance that rely on the presentness of the actor's body and the emotive connection with a live audience. These are of course the crucial markers of all live theater. It is that these postmodernist dramatic forms and performative acts draw particular attention to the actor's body not only as carrier of meaning but as creator of meaning in constant dialogue with the gaze of the audience. The gliding bodies of Pavel Zuštiak's dancers through tunnels of light and rows of spectators, their unpredictable choreographies of fractured movements, the abrupt transitions from individual to group scenes, produce a sense of loss, confuse our gaze and make us restless and uneasy. Yes, in the sense of their semiotic value[7] they do act like texts, but they always remain moving bodies that contradict all academic theorizing and render it superfluous. Precisely because the theatrical texts and productions that haunt my imagination emerge from experiences, memories, testimonies of loss and violence, the presence of the actor's body and the authentic connection of thought, feeling and physicality with the live audience claim themselves with utmost urgency.[8] To fill the space of loss with a breathing, feeling, thinking body in the process of becoming a work of art while still keeping its ontological plenitude of a mortal body is already a victory over loss and grief.

This theater may not change the world in the dramatic ways that a new technological discovery or a social revolution does, but it certainly changes those who are engaged in it either as creators or spectators, who in turn carry their acquired understandings and empathies further into the world; and that is as good as any change. The theater of Matei Vişniec has moved and attracted audiences of many walks of life and ages across several continents, has opened Western eyes to the horrors of the Stalinist period and Balkan wars, and has brought comfort and laughter to many of his fellow Romanians or Bosnian war survivors. The theatrical projects of the DAH Theater have brought solace to many victims and survivors of war and have raised awareness in many parts of the world of the gravity of the genocide that happened in the Balkans as well as of Balkan cultural diversity. The plays of Motti Lerner have raised heated and needed controversies and discussions in his own country and in the United States because of his courage to question the rightfulness of any war, including the Israeli-Palestinian one, and because of his boldness in exploring and bringing to the stage stories from both sides of this war. Noa Baum's soulful storytelling has softened many hardened hearts in the United States and Israel with regards to the Israeli-Palestinian wars in her attempts to reach towards the demonized Other. The plays of Saviana Stanescu have vindicated and brought solace to many immigrant souls in American cities by addressing the insecurities of their status, the tough roads they have to travel to reach their version of the American Dream, or their inevitable fall into the American nightmare. The many theatrical endeavors of Marcy Arlin's Immigrants Theater Project have brought knowledge and raised the awareness of countless audiences in the New York area about the cultures and sociopolitical issues of myriads of immigrant communities in the full color of their cultural specificities. The raucous and dark plays of Biljana Srbljanović have troubled the consciousness of many in her native Serbia about the wars of the nineties and have given courage to others with anti-war sentiments who decided to stay in their country. As I straddle several countries, cultures and languages in my exilic existence, I have created dramatic and fictional texts driven by heroines who are in a relentless chase after an idea of home, often connecting with readers and audiences of Romanian and East European diasporas in the United States and Europe.

Moving further outside the boundaries of this book, other examples of the power of live performance and art in improvised or professional frames are worth mentioning. During his yearlong stay in several Croatian concentration camps, Esad Boskailo was leading fellow prisoners to memorize and recite out loud, in corners of their squalid habitations, poetry lines from Goethe and Baudelaire as "an escape from reality" (Boskailo and Lieblich 2012, 60), which in turn allowed them to survive that reality of horror. During World War II in France, under the Vichy government Parisian theaters were filled to capacity with people of all walks of life breathing in unison as they watched what then were considered the experimental plays of Jean Anouilh or Jean Giraudoux and their modern recreations of classical plays. The famous Living Theater, established in New York in 1947 and inspired by the writings of Antonin Artaud, has intrigued, woken up from complacency, transformed and comforted thousands of people across the world in traditional and untraditional venues such as streets, markets and prisons, with their political anti-war, anti-authoritarian collaborative performances. In Poland or Romania of the communist era, thousands of desperate citizens found meaning and developed stronger strategies of survival in the theater halls where experimental shows questioned and subverted the authority of dictatorial regimes in veiled artistic forms. In fact among the most important leaders of the Romanian revolution of December 1989 were the foremost actors and poets of the country, who stood in front of millions of stunned citizens calling them to action and announcing the collapse of the former government. In pre-communist Czechoslovakia, the playwright Václav Havel led dissident, anti-communist movements with an abundance of plays in the style of the Theater of the Absurd and with ingenious political activism, from the Czech Spring to the revolutions of 1989 when he became president of Czechoslovakia. After peacefully leading the country to democracy he became the first elected president of the Czech Republic and most likely the first playwright to become the president of a country. Recently, in February of 2014, a new play opened at one of the main theaters in the capital of Lithuania, Vilnius, called *Barikados*. The play, written and directed by young theater artists, emerged from the 1991 episode in the history of Lithuania when Russian troupes took over the television and radio towers as the native population was fighting for its independence. With loss of blood and life on the part of many courageous Lithuanians, the country freed itself from the fifty-year-old Russian shackles and is now thriving, even though in constant anxiety because of their former greedy occupier and neighbor. The play opened to much publicity and sold-out houses. I was only able to see it during the final dress rehearsal and was moved both to tears and to laughter even though I understood no Lithuanian. The inventive staging, the precise acting, the carnivalesque moments that resembled a journey into one of Dante's circles of hell transcended the language of words and drew me into its complicated universe. Equally impressive was the crowd of young people breathlessly watching the artistic staging of events that they barely remembered and wanted to know about.

And of course there is always Augusto Boal, who has initiated real social revolutions and changes in policies by storming government buildings, streets and public spaces with his Theater of the Oppressed, legislative theater and Forum Theater. Boal has inspired people across the world to create "theater of the oppressed" projects dealing with social issues, political trauma or the aftermath of genocide. One such extraordinary example is the theater in post-genocide Rwanda realized by Koulsy Lamko (Kalisa 2006, 517–19). Since, as Marie-Chantal Kalisa has noted, "genocides annihilates everything, including myths, symbols and language that define a community and its people," "theater has the potential to encourage performance and the audience to envision new imagery, new language and to reconnect with rituals." Furthermore, social theater in Rwanda "becomes a theater of reconciliation, of debate and of ideas" (518). Lamko's theater projects in Rwanda combine stories and testimonials of survivors, local folklore, myths and storytelling with dialogue, poetry and chanting, thus creating a great diversity of theatrical forms. As with all other works dealing with the realities of genocide discussed in this book, Lomko's plays and devised performances performed in Rwanda for Rwandan audiences, with Rwandan actors, voice the "unsayable" in order to "accomplish the work of remembrance" (520).

The theatrical cooperative founded in 1983 by Marco Martinelli has integrated *commedia dell'arte* scenarios and characters, and classical, canonical or modern plays such as Jarry's *King Ubu* within devised productions that include real testimonials from victims of political oppression or traumatic escape and immigration experiences and comment on modern political and social issues. The famous Arlecchino has become in the recent shows of this cooperative an African immigrant, while the remake of Jarry's play under the name of *I Polacchi* has become a production commenting on contemporary wars. This show was presented in Chicago, Naples, Sarajevo, and Diol Kadd in Senegal. Most recently, in January and February of 2014, this group has performed at La MaMa, which Martinelli has called "forever a symbol of Theater that doesn't give up" (2014, 5). And his beautiful definition of this kind of theater is worth quoting here, as it fits like a glove the theater parading in my book:

> To put it in black and white terms, we can say there are two ways to do theater in the world. One is what we call show business. There is another type, though, that combines head and heart, emotion and reason, enchantment and rebellion. A theater that, following the vision of Augustine of Hippo, an African theologian of the 5th century, embraces the challenge of Hope, who is said to have two children: Scorn for the way things are, and Courage to try to change them [2014, 5].

With the power of its many bold embodiments, political theater that has pioneered new forms of expression to resist the erasure of memory and history by wars and genocides, the abusive force of authoritarian regimes, and has captured the complexities of the condition of exile continues to create oases of authentic living and feeling in a desert of simulacra.

One recent conspicuous example of fierce and transformative engagement between playwright, performance and political trauma merits added attention. In the fall of 2012 when I announced to friends and family that I was going to spend the week before Thanksgiving attending a festival of theater of genocide at La MaMa Theater in New York City, I was met with rolling eyes, skeptical smiles and a sarcastic, "Have a good time." The series of plays by Erik Ehn gathered under the title *Soulographie: Our Genocides,* mentioned several times already in this book, were performed during that week in a mind boggling marathon inspired by "our genocides," recent and past genocidal events from the Tulsa race riots in the United States to Rwanda, Uganda, El Salvador and Bosnia. Few theatrical experiences have left me so transformed, so troubled and also so exhilarated as that performative marathon. What rendered the experience both so "real" and so transformative was not the fact that I learned a lot about genocidal acts and events across the globe, which I could have learned from a history book, newspaper clippings, or online write-ups, but the fact that I was engaged artistically by a rollercoaster of the most diverse and stunning theatrical forms, which rendered the realities of "our genocides" vivid, visceral, and unforgettable, while strangely filling me with hope. The exquisite gathering of collective histories and stories from across the globe with artistry, tenderness, rawness and responsibility turned the realities of genocide into controlled performances of memory that honored victims and wove luminous threads of humanity from the depths of human darkness and desperation. In the preface to the collection of his plays, Erik Ehn confesses, "Playwriting has always been an unsolvable problem for me; genocide is an irresolvable object" (2013b, 5). However, as already noted in my introduction, he adamantly refuses to accept the notion of the inexplicable and "submit ... to the truncheons of uselessness" (6). Erik Ehn's play cycle *Soulographie* illustrates in wrenching ways his aesthetic or ethic of "invading reality" with theatrical forms that are "stripped, fragmentary, splintered description" precisely because they engage with and resist what others may consider un-approachable, or unexplainable. Through the piecing together of the many splinters and shreds of testimony, histories, and images, he weaves a quilt of meanings and an enclosure of safe spaces. He affirms that

> Soulographie is designed like a planet—it's taking on giant themes, so wants to be shaped so you can't see all of it at once; the horizon bends away from you. The too big structure is meant to suggest the unspeakabil-

> ity of genocide; ... the method of construction (widespread, collaborative) advertises an ethic of community, in redress to genocide's attempt to forbid history—to forbid the making of meaning by barring our real and imaginative abilities to gather history [248].

His plays indeed unfold like a constellation of horror made flesh, of darkness spoken in edgy strings of words, sentences, sounds, barks, and moans as meaning emerges equally in the piecing together and in the interstices between the pieces that are gathered from across the world. The play cycle creates a constellation of communities, of broken selves that are emerging from the shards. The style of his plays is raw, evocative, abounding in nouns and adjectives that acquire the heaviness of stage actions, light and sound. Like this:

> Solamente: In a small pond Peter wades and grows lotuses.
> Mazout is a genocide singer.
> The world is a small set of hills.
> An Oklahoma, a Rwanda
> An unwiped asshole.... [137].

a) Genocide Day

Child soldier is the chief puppeteer. Lellu drinks at a café; she falls in and out of sleep. This is the fighting she sees on her journeys. Friends are trained by MILITIA MAN.

Child Soldier: Boys mass on the hills.
The rain speaks
Inside the rain.
Armed boys train [*Drunk, Still Drinking,* from *Soulographie,* 138].

One of the most painful moments in the play *Dogsbody* (in *Soulographie*) is one in which child soldiers play with a human skull made into a soccer ball. The language is stripped and visceral, a concise yet broken poem, a puzzling and puzzled haiku:

Four—Man U Tee.

Storm is over.
A slow air played on bone oboes.
A dog eating something it shouldn't, pulling at it, trying to pull it from its place.
One boy, two boys, three boys, a dozen clearing the barracks.
Belle-Rose: Years later they are still young, they are sixteen, they are a soccer team, with donated Man U tees. They play soccer with a human head [230].

During one of the post-show discussions during the festival at La MaMa Theater, Ehn told his audience that he writes the stage directions and the dialogue as one continuum, undifferentiated, in one stream of storytelling, and that he deliberately leaves out prepositions, articles, and conjunctions from his sentences to capture more forcefully the essence of a situation, emotion, action, to be more truthful. To Erik Ehn, poetic expression, elliptical language, overlapping and often contrasting aesthetics that also interweave poetic rhythms and songs with dislocated chronologies and narrative lines, dialogues and monologues with polyphonic voices and perspectives are meant to express things, actions, and emotions more clearly, to take us on an easier route directly to the limits of suffering but also to the overcoming of suffering, the recording of memory and the attempts at healing. Indeed, what's the point of articles and prepositions when one tries to stage memories of genocides? Ehn articulated it best: "When writing is working it doesn't mean anything—it happens (2013, 101).

What I retain mostly and with great vividness from this festival is the great diversity of theatrical forms, colors, nuances, and sounds that in the end lifted me up above the unbearable weight of the themes and knowledge imparted in the seventeen plays. From the melancholy of object and shadow theater; from postmodernist collages of body movement, brooding silences and disturbing video projections; from riveting dance and song numbers from African American communities at the time of the Tulsa race riots, as in *Diamond Dick*; from brooding modern re-enactments of the Medea myth in *Yermedea*; from various forms of storytelling and testimonials in poetic lines; from bare stage, colorful sets and costumes from El Salvador, or a stage magically covered in tiny lights like fireflies and a troupe of "vaudevillian fairies exploited for their historical songs and dances,"[9] telling their stories in delicate movements and lacy costumes; from the heavy poetic and carnal slowness of Cordelia's story in Noh style; from puppet and mask plays from the Central American cycle, I have retained the indestructible life-and-art pair, unfolding into myriads of cultural nuances and stubbornly refusing to escape memory, to be crushed or leveled into essentializing uniformity. I have retained the relentless stubbornness of theatrical imagination to stand up to horror and oblivion. This example, like all the theater that I have embraced and journeyed through, demonstrates that only in the magical and seamless union of the physical and the spiritual, of the visible and the invisible, of message and its vehicle of transmission, can art truly make a difference. Together with Erik Ehn and his fierce commitment to witnessing the reality of genocide through his theater, we can also hope "that we can precipitate from our abstractions to actions, that our action be compassionate, and that we find in—especially in—profound ruin: the creative act" (2013, 102).

The Theater of American Politics and the Politics of Theater

In her award-winning book *"A Problem from Hell": America and the Age of Genocide,* Samantha Power meticulously and expertly weaves an overpowering argument that indicts American governments for tragic and unforgivable inaction in the face of twentieth century genocides mostly on the basis of "our national interest" (2002, 310). Genocides in Rwanda, Uganda, the Kurdish region, Bosnia, and Kosovo came and went leaving hundreds of mass graves, hundreds of miles of devastated habitations, darkness and desperation across the globe with the United States and Western Europe intervening either too late or never. Visionary and courageous politicians who spoke out in the name of justice and who had the courage to use the "g word," when genocide was committed in full daylight, ended up resigning in disgust or being replaced. The diplomat Steven Walker wrote in 1993, right before walking out on his job because of U.S. refusal to intervene in the war of ethnic cleansing against Muslim Bosnians, "I can no longer countenance U.S. support for a diplomatic process that legitimizes aggression and genocide" (Power 2002, 311). America's and Western Europe's repeated cliché line, "We didn't know," is simply "not true," as Power demonstrates convincingly (505). She eloquently proves not simply American inaction, but through lack of initiative, actual support of genocidal armies. One glaring example was the U.S. arms embargo on the Bosnian population that was attacked by Serbian nationalists, which prevented victims of the attacks, siege, and an unjust war to defend themselves. She argues:

> In an age of constant information, U.S. officials have gone from claiming that they "didn't know" to suggesting as President Clinton did in his 1998 Rwanda apology—that they "didn't fully appreciate." ... Because the savagery of genocide so defies our everyday experience, many of us failed to wrap our minds around it. We gradually came to accept the depravity of the Holocaust, but then slotted it in our consciousness to "history"; we resisted acknowledging that genocide was occurring in the present. Survivors and witnesses had trouble making the unbelievable believable. Bystanders were thus able to retreat to the "twilight between knowing and not knowing" [505].

It is deliciously ironic that Power concludes her extraordinary five-hundred-page history of American inaction in the face of twentieth century genocides with a quote from the theatrical genius that was George Bernard Shaw: "'The reasonable man adapts himself to the world. The unreasonable one persists in trying to adapt the world to himself. Therefore, all progress depends on the unreasonable man.' Therefore," she concludes, "after a century of doing so little to prevent, suppress and punish genocide, Americans must join and thereby legitimate the ranks of the unreasonable" (516).

In this light the theater people in my book are passionate members of "the ranks of the unreasonable," making "the unbelievable believable" with their courageous art and bold imagination and doing their best to pull anyone who crosses their stages from the fake and dangerous "twilight between knowing and unknowing." Power also accuses the American politicians of "a lack of imagination" (516). The artists portrayed here display an overflowing abundance of imagination and through it have the courage to face and tell the hard truths that governments, politicians and NGOS are reluctant to accept and deal with. Maybe more theater people should run for political office, as Václav Havel did in the former Czechoslovakia. Maybe also there is a deeply hidden agenda to the lack of funding, support, and spaces that political theater, in the vein discussed here, has to suffer in this country. The Trap Door Theatre space is indented inside an alley with an entrance like a trap door and a hall that holds at most seventy-five people even though their political shows receive rave reviews in mainstream American and international journals. The Whistler in the Dark Theater in Boston has closed its doors, performing its final show in April of 2014. The La MaMa Theater is hidden on a side street on the lower east side of New York, and even though the street now carries the name of its tenacious and brilliant founder, Ellen Stewart, it does not have the visibility, funding and space of Broadway theaters, nor are their actors paid the wages that Broadway actors receive. It is true that some of the most politically and aesthetically engaging theater in America is produced in the trenches, on side streets, with small budgets and unpaid actors. But maybe we should *not* get used to this reality. Maybe we should expect this kind of theater art to come out of its many closets and go mainstream without losing its edge and boldness. Mainstream theater in America, the glittery world of show biz, the orgy of Broadway productions and the millions of dollars that go into them, largely support "hegemonic political fictions" and "contain narrative elements that support uncritical forms of subjectivity conducive to the maintenance of unconscious and socially harmful capitalist relations" (Bruner 2012, 10). Maybe we should expect live theater of resistance and the "politics of aesthetics" to achieve what in America maybe only Jon Stewart's *Daily Show* or *The Colbert Report* have managed to achieve on television, namely what Bruner has referred to as "the comic, playful, and critically meta-reflective qualities theorists claim are supportive of more emancipatory aesthetic states" (10).[10]

One absence in this book should be conspicuous by now to the attentive reader: although so many of the plays and theater projects discussed here were inspired by the Balkan wars of the nineties, in particular the war of ethnic cleansing against Muslim Bosnians (1992–1995), no Bosnian playwrights or theater groups are portrayed. All plays or projects that focus on this war are either from Romania or from the aggressor country, namely Serbia. It is an absence that puzzles me as much as it may any of the readers of this book. It is not for lack of trying to find such playwrights that such an absence exists in my study, but as a result of failed searches. Though Bosnian writers, journalists, poets, scholars, psychiatrists and war survivors, including Aleksander Hemon, Esaid Boskailo, Kemae Kurspahic or Zlata Filipovic, have written novels, political accounts, anthropological and historical studies and memoirs about the devastating period of the war, the Srebrenica massacres and the three-year-long siege of Sarajevo, so far no Bosnian playwrights writing about the war have been translated into English, to my knowledge. English-speaking Westerners such as Steven Galloway have taken inspiration from the siege of Sarajevo in the moving poetic novel *The Cellist of Sarajevo*, which arose from the actual existence and musical performance of a cellist who played every day on a Sarajevo street despite sniper fires. Even Angelina Jolie found her way to postwar Bosnia, only to produce a second-rate movie inspired by the mass rapes of Bosnian women that did nothing to raise consciousness or help the healing of the traumas, but instead outraged and offended Bosnian women activists and artists, and for very good reasons. During the siege however, many professional theaters in Sarajevo closed their doors, except for one theater that was founded, just like DAH Theater, on the cusp of the beginning of the war in 1992 and took the name of Sarajevo War Theater: SARTR. This theater apparently gave over two thousand performances during the war, resisting with art the annihilating darkness of its cruelty, just like the cellist who played for several weeks on a street in Sarajevo despite continuous sniper shootings. The creators of the theater called it "theater against death," and its contributions and merit for standing up to war despite its daily brutality was recognized by the Sarajevo City Assembly. Presently the theater is flourishing and in January and February of 2014 presented a version of Euripides' *Hecuba*. The information about this theater, though, is very scarce and shrouded in some mystery. When I visited Sarajevo and talked to poets, writers and activists, nobody mentioned to me this extraordinary theater project. I interviewed at length also the hero-journalist Kemal Kurspahic, now residing in the United States and running several newspapers in Northern Virginia, and neither did he impart any knowledge about this miracle/mystery theater. Kurspahic was a hero journalist because right after the newspaper building he was working for was bombed out of existence right at the beginning of the siege, he continued daily production of the newspaper throughout the three years of the siege in a bomb shelter that had remained intact from the period of the Cold War. Sometimes, he told me, people would chose to buy the one page newspaper instead of bread.[11] Still, it has been something of a sustained failure on my part to find the works of Bosnian playwrights, at least translated into English, or extensive information about the functioning, history, repertoire of the Sarajevo Theater of War, SARTR.[12]

There is information and there are even a couple of articles about artistic, musical and theatrical events that went on during the siege of Sarajevo, but none reveal or discuss any original Bosnian plays or theater projects that might have developed or been performed during the siege. In "The Paradoxes of Wartime 'Freedom': Alternative Culture During the Siege of Sarajevo," Larisa Kurtovic notes that amidst this devastation, the Bosnian and Herzegovinian capital simultaneously witnessed a flowering of various artistic enterprises and alternative cultural scenes. It is estimated that during the siege, "some 182 theatre productions, 170 exhibits, and 48 concerts came to life in Sarajevo" (2012, 197). However, none of the "182 theater productions" that she mentions are discussed in her article. Instead she focuses on three artistic and cultural phenomena during the siege: the "founding of the independent radio ZID (The WALL)," a large-scale musical event called "Rock Under Siege," and the work of a designer group called "Trio," which "produced postcards of Sarajevo during the siege" (199). Kurtovic explores the arena of artistic life in Sarajevo under siege "as an unorthodox site of civic engagement, which in its emphasis on music and arts and the concomitant refusal of nationalist frames of reference, emerged as a unique, complicated and largely indirect site of political contention" (197). As she further argues, most of the artistic events did not even obviously illustrate what is generally thought of as political art or theater, and cannot be explained within the same frames of reference as are used in civil societies in times of peace. Rather, she argues that the power of such events and phenomena "lay in their ability to cultivate a set of sensibilities, dispositions and structures of feeling, said to be constitutive of Sarajevo's self-professed cosmopolitan identity and in radical opposition to the agenda of nationalists" (198). Very much like the countercultural theater or art taking place in the years of the communist dictatorship under which I grew up in Romania and that I briefly discussed earlier, the political edge of such events and artistic products lay in their very existence against all odds in times of war and in their offering nuanced, imaginative artistic images that opposed the monolithic and destructive forces of a war of aggression.

In "*Hair* in Sarajevo: Doing Theater Under Siege," Nenad "Neno" Pervan discusses the creative processes involved in the production of American musical *Hair* during the very first year of the siege, 1992. As he states, "one of the main themes that provoked Sarajevo's artists to choose *Hair* was the dominant anti-war sentiment developed in the original version as a response to the United States' involvement in the war in Vietnam" (2009, 183). The creation and production processes were complex and exciting as all artists involved in it were driven by the passionate will "to keep life flowing" (182) during the siege. The entire creative team displayed extraordinary ethnic diversity, as it included Bosnians, Croats, Serbs, and Jews, thus bravely contradicting the very message and motivation of the war of "ethnic cleansing" that tried to prove that diverse groups and ethnicities could not and should not live together. Because the National Theater, like other theaters in Sarajevo, was shut down, the production took place in a small theater that barely held two hundred people. The show was a huge success and played to full houses throughout the years of the siege. Audiences literally risked their lives to go to the theater. Both the theater artists and the audiences filling the theater for the production of *Hair* braved sniper bullets and mortar shells in order to come to the theater and worked and lived without water, gas, electricity. Going to the theater or attending art and musical events was, for the Sarajevans during the time of the siege, an existential need and literally a matter of life and death. And yet, *Hair* was not an original Bosnian play that might have reflected or dialogued with the realities of the Bosnian war. Nor really could it have been. This absence confirms again Brecht's intuition that a certain distancing and the lapsing of time are necessary for a community or people to be able to be receptive to or create works that speak directly to their traumatic historical moment. Instead, just as Brecht chose the Thirty Years' War as theme for his *Mother Courage* to indirectly warn against the Nazi danger, so Bosnian theater artists chose the faraway Vietnam War to deal creatively with their own immediate and real war raging outside the theater walls.

Most likely another journey to magical Sarajevo, more interviewing, and more scholarly and ethnographic research on my part is in order; maybe even another book that would honor this theater and Bosnian theater artists alone. Maybe it is still too early for Bosnian playwrights to tackle openly the painful history of this war; maybe Bosnian cultural projects within Bosnia are ghettoized and are having a harder time to reach outside its borders into Western countries and languages. Its time will come for sure. Until then, though, this mysterious silence and absence is at least partly filled with vibrant and extraordinary theatrical works by artists from neighboring countries, from Serbia and Romania, as well as by Bosnian artists and journalists living abroad or by Western scholars, playwrights and writers interested in this dark page of European history. Such artists and intellectuals have obviously identified in profound ways with the victims of this war and lived up to the urgent necessity of creating theater works that would fill the absence and the silence with vibrant embodiments of their imagination and artistic efforts.

I choose to end my theatrical journey with a quote from one of the greatest innovators of modern European theater and one who relentlessly played with the notions of the real and the fictional in his own plays: Luigi Pirandello. At the end of *Six Characters in Search of an Author*, the father and the manager have the following exchange after the girl and the son in the unfinished play within the play are both dead:

> **The Manager** [*pushing the* actors *aside while* they *lift up the* boy *and carry him off*]: Is he really wounded?
> **Some Actors:** He's dead! dead!
> **Other Actors:** No, no, it's only make believe, it's only pretense!
> **The Father** [*with a terrible cry*]: Pretense? Reality, sir, reality! [1998, 74].

The character of the father has a point: for the characters in the play-within-the-play, that is *their* reality and who's to say otherwise? Only they would know. Pirandello creates a fictional labyrinth in which it is hard to find our way towards reality or the truth, but he also leads us towards some version of the real. And that version is the deep truth about the human condition and our humanity that strangely shines through in the "pretense" of theater whenever the ineffable magic and the synchronicity of thought and emotion between the actors' delivery and the public's openness to it takes place in the space of a theater hall. Sure, the theater of war and exile that forms the subject of this book is all "pretense." But it is "pretense" that takes us on a troubled and transformative journey towards the reality of human suffering, the agony of loss or the desperation caused by violence and teaches us the hard lessons of survival even while making us laugh, dream and hope.

Chapter Notes

Preface

1. See Joe Kelleher's *Theater and Politics* (2009), in which the author looks not only at theater emerging from political concerns and events, but also at the theatricality of politics itself, the dynamic dialogues between the two, and at the importance of political theater to deal with the theater of politics. See also Richard Boon and Jane Plastow's *Theater Matters: Performance and Culture on the World Stage*, which presents extraordinary examples and testimonials of "theater of witness" projects that have made a difference in the lives of communities affected by political traumas and wars in such places as Brazil, Argentina, Nigeria, Eritrea, South Africa, India and the Caribbean.

2. In the same preface, Skloot, quoting Helen Frein, says that "'any strategy to defend human rights which empowers individuals and associations and restricts the state from exploiting its monopoly of force without internal checks or external sanctions is a strategy to prevent genocide.' That strategy includes the theater" (2009, 24).

3. Quoted in Bruner's 2012 *Repressive Regimes, Aesthetic States, and Arts of Resistance*, p. 2.

4. Bruner's term for all art that opposes the hegemonic state, regime and status quo. He offers a beautiful and extensive analysis of the arts of resistance mostly at the level of theater starting with Ancient Rome and ending with early modern France and Germany and the present United States and television.

5. Nadal and Calvo are quoting trauma theorists such as Caruth 1996 and Luckhurst 2008. Trauma theory developed in the 1990s and has become an extensive field of study that explores concerns about memory, ethics, and representation.

6. Leys' work is an excellent exploration of trauma and the history of trauma studies from Freud to the present. See also the seminal study by Cathy Caruth, *Unclaimed Experience: Trauma, History and Narrative.*

Introduction

1. See the seminal study *Towards a Poor Theater* by Grotowski, in the new edition edited by Eugenio Barba and prefaced by Peter Brook, in which the Polish theater director describes his theories, experimental practices, work with the actors, training the body and the mind, and diluting the lines between theater and life, the actor's and the character's lives. His practice consisted of extensive physical exercises, even acrobatics, that brought the actor to a state of exhaustion and exhilaration, and a holistic blending between spiritual and physical energies.

2. A term used by Marc Silberman.

3. See the seminal study of Frederic Jameson, *Postmodernism and the Cultural Logic of Late Capitalism*, and the studies

of Jean Baudrillard, *Simulacra and Simulation, America,* and *The Consumer Society: Myths and Structures.* Jameson discusses the emergence of postmodern culture in tandem with capitalist values and structures. He develops the notion of pastiche and imitation as fundamental for postmodern thinking. Baudrillard has developed extensive and influential theories on the notion that all our reality has become a compound of imitations and of copies of copies that have lost all connection to the original model, to the "real," history or nature, and that because of the media and the virtual realities we are engulfed in, the imitations have become more real than the real, and they precede reality.

4. See Steven Connor's *The Cambridge Companion to Postmodernism* and Auslander's article "Postmodernism and Performance," as well as Auslander's book *Presence and Resistance: Postmodernism and Cultural Politics in Contemporary American Performance.* Here Auslander discusses the term *performance* in a broader sense to include "experimental theater, performance art, and stand-up comedy" (1994, 3) and agrees that "no monolithic description or evaluation is possible, for postmodernism as a historical configuration or structure of feeling has given rise to mutually contradictory, antagonistic, and just plain different manifestations" (7).

5. In his seminal study *Theater and Its Double,* Antonin Artaud developed the manifesto of Theater of Cruelty, by which he meant a radically physical and stylized theater in the tradition of Eastern theater such as Balinese performance that moved and shocked the audience, that relied much more on movement, stage action, sound, light, and costume than Western theater, which in his opinion relied too much on language. He thought that theater needs to keep a tight relationship with "reality and danger" and to "break through the language in order to touch life."

6. See the distinctions made between the terms *exile, émigré* and *expatriate* as well as the cultural variations between exiles from East and Central European countries in relation to their host country in the study *The Exile and Return of Writers from East Central Europe,* edited by John Neubauer and Borbála Zsuzsanna Török.

7. See the study on dance and folklore from the Balkan regions titled *The Dancing Goddesses: Folklore, Archeology and the Origins of European Dance* by Elizabeth Wayland Barber.

8. See *Performance, Exile and America* edited by Sikvja Jestrovic and Jana Meerzon, and in particular the article "'An American Mile in Other's Shoes': The Tragicomedy of Immigrating to Twenty-First Century America," by Diana Manole, in which she analyzes two of Saviana Stanescu's plays in light of immigrants being "different" and "not so different" with regard to their adoptive cultures, noting also that "exilic theater requires a double effort of translation and adaptation of both authors and audiences" (2009, 66). She also points to the differences between "immigrants" and "exiles" in ways that are similar to my own delineation of these concepts.

9. Said's conception of exile is a tragic one that tries to encompass not just the experience of intellectual exiles and émigrés such as Nabokov or Joyce but also a deromanticized understanding of the large masses of undocumented immigrants, the suffering of refugees and victims of wars and disasters, and the consequences of this phenomenon for our society. His view is that whatever achievements the experience of exile may claim, these are obtained at the expense of an irreparable loss.

10. See Brecht's seminal theoretical work *Brecht in Theater: The Development of an Aesthetic,* in which he develops his theories of epic theater, breaking the fourth wall, distancing, and alienation, as necessary aesthetic developments to contain the new ideas of the times and have a transformative effect on audiences.

11. As Kellner remarks, the purpose of the theatrical techniques used by Brecht was "to produce an experience of curiosity," astonishment, and shock, raising such questions as "Is that the way things are? What produced this? It's terrible! How can we change things?" (Brecht 1964, 42, 86–87, 104, 134, 139, 198–205).

12. Brecht promoted and created an aesthetics of rupture and dislocation with the purpose of initiating his spectators to social action: "in his separation of the ele-

ments," where "each aesthetic component retains its autonomy and 'comments' on the others, often in contradiction, to provoke thought and insight" (Kellner 2010, 33).

13. Brecht's postmodernism has been largely disputed, and while some critics have gone to extreme lengths to place his work within a postmodern aesthetic, critics such as R. Friedrich dismiss such claims as "fads" and as part of the desire of literary critics to give new names to old forms or to appropriate anything under the vague and ever-evolving term of postmodern. Friedrich considers that only the "mature" Brecht may share some traits with postmodernism and discards the following claims to postmodernism made by various critics: "the concept of the 'epic theatre' becomes an instance of the *leveling of genre-distinctions*; the estrangement effect is said to *negate identity* and call attention to the *fictionality of the texts*; the montage-structure of epic drama translates into the *celebration of discontinuity* and *rupture*; the open-endedness of the plays is made to signify *refusal of closure* pointing to the *indeterminacy* and *undecidability of meaning*; in Brecht's concept of 'alienated acting' the postmodern theorist discerns *differentially constructed meaning*: that which is done and shown by the actors connotes that which is not being done and shown" (1999, 44–64). Marc Silberman on the other hand finds postmodernist theory quite fruitful in looking at Brecht's work in terms of discovering paradigms of change. He states that "Postmodernist theory enables us to look at Brecht in a new way because, like all fruitful theoretical debate, it refocuses our attention. Postmodernist theory specifically offers powerful descriptions of the contemporary condition, tools for exposing the enabling conditions of cultural discourse, and a conceptual vocabulary for the problematics of representation that allows the critic/reader to establish relations between diverse spheres of activity and perception" (1993, 2).

14. See *Simulation and Simulacra*, *The Illusion of the End*, and *Art After Modernism* by Jean Baudrillard.

15. See Baudrillard's chapter "On Nihilism" (1994a, 161–163) from *Simulacra and Simulation*.

16. I would correct the use of "postmodern" to "postmodernist" in this context and instead use Philip Auslander's clarifying terminology that differentiates between the notion of the postmodern as a "periodizing" one and that of postmodernist as "a stylistic descriptor," or as an aesthetic category.

17. See also the book *Humor and Social Protest*, edited by Dennis Bos and Marjolein t'Hart, which uses Bakhtin's carnival theories to trace various forms of political actions across the centuries.

18. See Bickis and Shields (2013) regarding Lyotard's theoretical views as well as Lyotard's own books, in which he articulates his theories on postmodern theory and aesthetics, such as *The Postmodern Condition* or *La Stridence.*

19. See Boal's revolutionary works *Theater of the Oppressed* and *The Aesthetic of the Oppressed*, in which he develops his theories of the socially transformative power of theater and his innovative practices such as the Forum Theater.

20. Auslander further discusses the complex issues of "politics as representation" (2007, 31) while developing his thesis on postmodern art and its presentness as a form of "resistance."

21. It is the term Erik Ehn uses as subtitle to his theater series inspired by modern genocides, *Soulographie.*

22. See Erik Ehns' article "Channel of Witness: Space, Abstraction, and the Commemoration of Genocide" (2013a) in which he discusses the various ethical and aesthetic complexities of his plays about genocide.

23. See again Ehn, 2013a. He claims, "A theater of witness presents facts in a way that gives them life as questions" (69) and leads to "fact-shaking" "starting with repetition, persistence, and rhythm" (70).

24. See the distinction between the two made by Linda Hutcheon in *The Politics of Postmodernism* (2002). Postmodernism refers to the period, while postmodernity refers to aesthetic traits of the cultural products of this period.

25. Petrunic notes that the term and notion of "Balkans" is looked at "as *living between two* (Antić, 2003), a *transitory character* (Kiossev, 2002), and *being neither here nor there* (Bjelić, 2002)" (Petrunic 2005, 2).

26. This collection, edited by Gina Landor, also contains the play by Matei Vişniec discussed in chapter 2, *The Body of a Woman as a Battlefield in the Bosnian War.*

27. Petrunic notes, "Cultural essentialism is detrimental to understanding the development of individual and collective identity formation. In place of a Balkan identity, Balkan differences melt into sameness and essentialized identities pervade. Whether orientalizing the other (Said, 1979) or politicizing the mode of representation (Bjelić, 2002), cultural essentialism negates the idea that space becomes a place with meaning thereby creating a location in which identities are shaped and to which acts of identification are formed. This is to say that particular places create narratives to which entire communities and individuals are tied" (2005, 2).

28. See of course the seminal work by Edward Said, *Orientalism*, which critically deconstructs Western assumptions and stereotypes about the "Orient" and in particular the Middle East.

29. All quotes in the previous sentence are from this same book by the same author at page ix. See also the edited collection of essays by Valentina Glajar and Domnica Radulescu, *Amazons, Wretches and Vampirettes: Western Representations of East European Women*. The introduction and the essays in the collection deftly analyze the various projections, stereotypical images and forms of cultural marginalizing of East European women in culture, literature, and society at large by writers, artists and cultural products from Western Europe or the United States.

30. See Laughlin and Schuler's *Feminist Theater Aesthetics*, as it offers an excellent exploration of the various aesthetic strategies developed by feminist playwrights and theater artists. Also see the collection of essays *Feminism and Postmodernism*, edited by Ferguson and Wicke, on the many synergistic relations and collaborations between postmodernist theory and aesthetics and feminism.

31. See also Linda Nicholson's *Feminism/Postmodernism (Thinking Gender)*.

32. See studies on the *commedia dell'arte*, oral and street performance and their innovative and politically subversive forms, such as Taviani and Schino's *Il segreto della Commedia dell'Arte: la memoria delle compagnie italiane del XVI, XVII e XVIII secolo* (1982), Henke's *Performance and Literature in the Commedia dell'Arte* (2002), Gordon's *Lazzi: The Comic Routines of the Commedia dell'arte* (1983), and Burke's *Popular Culture in Early Modern Europe* (1978). See also my article "Caterina's Colombina: The Birth of a Female Trickster in Seventeenth Century France" (Radulescu 2008a) and my book *Women's Comedic Art as Social Revolution* (2012).

Chapter One

1. This is a reference to the quote given in the introduction from Said's *Reflections on Exile*.

2. See Jean Francois Lyotard's *Signed: Malraux* (2000), in which he develops his theory of "stridence" as a mark of postmodernist aesthetic and syncopated subjectivity.

3. In an interview in *Cinema Without Borders* (Tehrani 2013), the director gives a beautiful description of how she created the movie while trying to follow the spirit of Veteranyi's book. She notes that the girl who played the young Aglaja could not read, so she had to teach her the lines, and that the actresses who played the little girl and the teenage Aglaja often practiced by looking at each other in a mirror; both situations show uncanny resemblances to Veteranyi's own early illiteracy and the mirror imagery in the novel.

4. Such authors are Ion Tepeneag and Virgil Tanase. See the study by Laura Pavel on Romanian alternative literatures: *Dumitru Tsepeneag and the Canon of Alternative Literature* (2011).

5. The reviewer added the following: "And what can American writers learn from Romanians? To our own chagrin, it may be a sharper sense of humor—although Saviana might not say that outright. She recalls being surprised that American people were afraid to laugh at death and war. 'In the Balkans there's a different sense of dealing. We survive with humor.'"

6. The concept of chronotope was developed by Bakhtin in his article "Forms of the Chronotope in the Novel: Notes Towards a Historical Poetics." He defines the chronotope as "the intrinsic connect-

edness of temporal and spatial relationships that are artistically expressed in literature" (2002, 84).

7. It is useful here to consider Matei Calinescu's theory, in *Five Faces of Modernity*, that the postmodern mind, theory and era, heralded as early as the works of Michel Foucault, has no regard for humanism in the first place, seeing the very concept of human being and human nature as épistèmes, or constructs of knowledge or "discursive formations" (1987, 280) and not as actual realities. For Ihab Hassan, postmodernism is "a mutation in Western Humanism" (280).

8. *Train to Trieste* is winner of the 2009 Library of Virginia Award for Best Fiction.

9. It is worth evoking here the memorable notion coined by the Romanian philosopher of religions Mircea Eliade in his *Myth of the Eternal Return: Cosmos and History* (2005), which has touched the philosophical and aesthetic makeup of many Romanian artists and thinkers.

10. Terms used by R. Friedrich (1999) to point to postmodern interpretations of Brechtian techniques.

11. This comment by one of the contributors, Laura-Ceia Minjares, is made in relation to the recounting of an episode when the famous French Armenian singer Charles Aznavour visited Romania in 2004 for the filming of a remake of *Père Goriot*. In the encounter between Aznavour and the Romanian president, the French singer noted that the contributions of Romanian artists to the French patrimony are so important that they are now "considered completely French." Minjares interprets this attitude of superiority as a proof that "attitudes towards and perceptions of Romania (and other 'peripheries' for that matter) have not changed much since the nineteenth century" (2006, 3).

12. See Jon Whitmore's comments on Serban's directing as an example of postmodernist performance in which Serban develops experimental ways of using the actors' voices, bodies, the stage and the relation with the audience (2012, 73, 81).

13. Here too Bakhtin's discussion of "chronotopes" and the ways in which the representations of the relations between time and space vary in works of literature is relevant.

14. Chosen as runner-up for the Jane Chambers Playwriting Award of the Association of Theater in Higher Education, June 2013.

15. The play *Naturalized Woman* was presented as a staged reading at Nora's Playhouse in New York City in 2010 and as a full production at Thespis Theater off, off Broadway in 2012, directed by Kimberly Jew.

16. See Lyotard's *The Postmodern Condition* (1984) and the introduction to this book, as well as his book *The Postmodern Explained to Children* (1982). See also Nouvet, Stahuljak and Still's *Minima Memoria: In the Wake of Jean-François Lyotard* (2006), which discusses the great impact Lyotard had on modern thinking, and his criticism of grand narratives and embracing of personal stories and local events as a way of retelling history.

17. I am referring here to Said's claims that exile literature defies any humanistic purpose, mentioned earlier in the chapter.

18. See Day 2, Story 5, of the *Decameron* which tells the story of Andreuccio.

19. Stokes develops the notion of "fault lines." These lines are: 1. "the line that separates Orthodox Christians from Catholics"; 2. "The line that separates the Ottoman cultural area from that influenced by the great Christian empires"; and 3. "The line that divides the socio-economic conditions of Western Europe from those of Eastern Europe" (1999, 16). In relation to the wars in the Balkans of the nineties, which are a source of inspiration for much of the theater studied in this book, see Ramet's study *Thinking about Yugoslavia: Scholarly Debates About the Yugoslav Breakup and the Wars in Bosnia and Kosovo* (2005).

20. See Griffin and Braidotti's *Thinking Differently: A Reader in European Women's Studies* (2002), an excellent study on the line of Said's *Orientalism* that discusses the stereotypical constructs and "othering" of East European populations and individuals by Western European ideologies and cultural constructs as the "foreigner among us," or semi-exotic, familiar-yet-distant stranger. The authors look at this "othering" from the perspective of gender differences and the treatment and views of East European women by Westerners.

Chapter Two

1. *Merriam Webster Dictionary*, s.v. "theater of war."

2. Feminist theaters and performance theories over the past three decades have been focused on subverting the theatrical canon, on exploding realistic or mimetic modes of representation that have over the centuries enforced the status quo of patriarchy and marginalized women. The notions of a specifically feminist theater aesthetics is treated at large in all its controversial facets in *Theater and Feminist Aesthetics*, edited by Laughlin Schuler (1995). See in particular Gillespie's "Feminist Theory of Theater: Revolution or Revival?" in that volume. See also the seminal collection of essays *Upstaging Big Daddy: Directing Theater as if Gender and Race Matter*, edited by Donkin and Clement (1993), and *Acting Out: Feminist Performances*, edited by Hart and Phelan (1993).

3. Many feminist theoreticians of humor and performance theorists have analyzed humor in terms of gender and have noted that women's humor, both in society and in works of art, tends to be different than that of men or of male writers. Gray's *Women and Laughter* (1994), Regina Barecca's *Last Laughs: Perspectives on Women and Comedy* (1988), Philip Auslander's "Brought to You by Fem Rage," in *Acting Out: Feminist Performance* (1993), Mahadev Apte's *Humor and Laughter: An Anthropological Approach* (1985), and Judy Little's *Comedy and the Woman Writer* (1983) all contain substantive and valuable studies on women's humor, the cultural differences between men's and women's humor, the marginalization of women's humor in the sphere of mainstream comedy, and women's humor and comedy as forms of resistance to and subversion of oppressive social structures.

4. In *Inventing Ruritania: The Imperialism of the Imagination*, Goldsworthy develops the thesis that Western culture has performed, over the last two centuries, a form of imperialism of the imagination, in casting the world of the Balkans and of Eastern Europe in two dichotomic and stereotypical molds, while using the folklore, nature, and culture of that world as inspiration for many of its own literary works. These two molds are that of the "barbaric" and the "exotic." She notes also that the populations of the Balkans themselves have often seen themselves as upholders of European values, largely from an inferiority complex vis-à-vis their Western neighbors.

5. See also Adorno's *Minima Moralia: Reflections from Damaged Life* (2006), in which he deals with trauma from a philosophical perspective as well as offering extraordinary insights into modern culture.

6. The traveling letter and all that it signifies has become a trope much analyzed in psychoanalytic criticism by writers such as Jacques Lacan and Barbara Johnson. The discussion started with the analysis of Edgar Alan Poe's *The Purloined Letter* and has moved into trying to demonstrate that the letter becomes a signifier without a signified. In this case the traveling letter has a signified: Dorra's future life plans and her child.

7. See Matei Calinescu's *Five Faces of Modernity*, in which (as I mentioned in chapter 1) he discusses the progression from modernism to postmodernism as simultaneous with the disappearance of the belief in humanism that according to him started with Michel Foucault.

8. See Auslander's discussions in *Presence and Resistance* (1994) about postmodern play scripts, postmodern performance, classical texts produced in postmodernist ways, or as in Vişniec's case, postmodernist texts produced with postmodernist means.

9. As Ana Petrunic (2005) has noted, the piecemeal nature of Balkan identity is both the cause and the effect of the continuing Balkan crisis in a political context where instead of working towards the harmonious integration of ethnic groups and multicultural communities, the main tendency is towards domination, ethnic violence and in the worst cases, wars of ethnic cleansing.

10. For documentation on the Balkan wars of the nineties see Mojzes' *Balkan Genocides* (2011), Machek's *Sarajevo Under Siege: Anthropology in Wartime* (2011), and the moving diary by Filipovic titled *Zlata's Diary: A Child's Life in Wartime Sarajevo* (2006).

11. "This period" meaning the escalation of the nationalist conflicts in Serbia, Montenegro, and Kosovo in 1998.

12. See also "Kevin Jackson's Theater Diary" page on the site of the production on October 31, 2008. http://www.kjtheatrediary.com/2008/10/family-stories-belgrade.html.

13. See also the review by Caroline Burlingham Ellis (2002); the review by Carolin Clay (2002); Aleksandar Lukac (2004).

14. Where she was awarded an important prize at the Bonn theater festival.

15. The use of the dog/Nadezda as a scapegoat for the characters' own frustrations and inadequacies is reminiscent of the Schmurz character, a subhuman being dressed in rags and band-aids and always tormented by the characters in the absurdist surrealist play of the fifties *Les Battiseurs d'empire,* by Boris Vian. The Schmurz, whose name derives from the German word for pain, is a literal incarnation of the scapegoat or punching bag that the characters kick, hit, spit at and abuse in a variety of ways whenever they are frustrated with their own reality. The play denounces with the means of the Theater of the Absurd the vacuousness and insensitivity of the postwar bourgeois and middle class generation whom Boris Vian considers largely responsible for the devastation of the war.

16. In the movie *The Discreet Charm of the Bourgeoisie,* by Luis Bunuel, the characters' dreams are sometimes woven with one another and the recounting of dreams reaches a point where it is hard to know what is dream and what is reality or who is dreaming about whom. Violent war and guerrilla scenes also unfold as part of the dreams or the main narrative of the movie.

17. Marcy Arlin organized and directed in 2012 a theater festival titled Women Write the New, which introduced for the first time to American audiences plays by various East European women writers.

18. See Gordon's *The Grand Guignol: Theatre of Fear and Terror* (1997). See also the newer studies on this theatrical phenomenon in France, which reached its peak during the two world wars and particularly during the Second World War: Hand and Wilson's *Grand Guignol: The French Theater of Horror* (2002) and Hunter's *Chapel of Gore and Psychosis: The Grand Guignol Theater* (2012).

19. All quotes from this play and the next one are from the unpublished versions kindly shared by the author.

20. See the interesting study by Marc Morje Howard titled *The Weakness of Civil Society in Post-Communist Europe,* which explores at length the complexities and problems encountered by post-communist countries in establishing democracies and civil societies following Leninist and Marxist regimes. See also Rasna Karklin's *The System Made Me Do It. Corruption in Post-Communist Societies:* an excellent study on corruption in post-communist societies at the level of the press, NGOs, and the overall cultural structures and governmental institutions.

21. La MaMa theater site. November-December 2012.

22. The "mad scenes" were performative stepping stones for the *commedia* actresses that allowed them to display the virtuosity of their acting and improvisational skills. They were also a form of artistic and political emancipation for female performers as it allowed them to express ideas and realities they would not have otherwise been able to when playing a role at face value. The most famous actress of the early Renaissance, Isabella Andreini, achieved her greatest artistic fame playing a mad scene in a play titled *La Pazzia d'Isabella* (*The Madness of Isabella*). A detailed witness account of this memorable performance was given by Pavoni (1589).

Chapter Three

1. McKenna (1992) engages in a complicated yet necessary discussion of the origins of violence in humanity in light of René Girard's theory of "violence and the sacred," of the sacrificial victim chosen by a community as scapegoat in order to contain the spread of violence, and of Jacques Derrida's notion of difference.

2. Camus' philosophical essay *The Myth of Sisyphus* (1985) ends with the sentence "Il faut imaginer Sisyphe heureux" ("We have to imagine Sisyphus happy").

3. In the article "Performing Oral History" (2009), Baum describes the different phases in the creation of her text, which ultimately led to the production of *A Land Twice Promised.* She divides this creative process into the following stages: "The

Story Begins," "Creating Performance," "Telling the Story of the Other in the First Person," "Creating a Sense of Place," "Creating the Picture/Images," "Creating Emotional Resonance," and "Truth vs. Fact."

4. Interestingly, during the interview, some of the things Baum told me about the making of this story closely resembled lines in the text. This is a beautiful example of life and art; the author's life and recreation of it through art are almost seamlessly merged.

5. See for instance Hemmings' *Why Stories Matter* (2011) and Hesford's "Storytelling and the Dynamics of Feminist Teaching" (1990) in *Feminist Teacher*. See also Burke's *Popular Culture in Early Modern Europe* (1978) for a cohesive discussion of the role of women in the development of an oral culture in early modern Europe.

6. In *Coming to Writing* (1992) and "The Laugh of the Medusa" (1981), Hélène Cixous develops at length her theory of "feminine writing," which explores the organic relations between women's sexuality and creativity. Cixous talks about the specifically feminine ways of writing from the body, in swoops and circles that move and flow in the rhythms of the woman's consciousness and sexual life simultaneously, without the traditional bipolar Platonic divisions between mind and body.

7. She is referring to Judith Herman's book *Trauma and Recovery: The Aftermath of Violence—from Domestic Abuse to Political Terror.*

8. On the topic of the use of theater in the post-genocidal Rwandan society, see Kalisa's "Theater and the Rwandan Genocide" (2006). Kalisa notes that theater is present in Rwanda and is perhaps the most visible form of artistic expression. The subject matter often relates to the question of reconciliation as well as other economic, health, and social issues in post–1994 Rwanda. The idea of enacting genocide raises ethical questions such as how you "create a spectacle" based on disastrous events. It appears, however, that theater for the sake of recovery has become a natural tool in conflict and post-conflict areas. Such is the case of South Africa where a large body of dramatic expression exists in connection with the ongoing process of "Truth and Reconciliation." In Rwanda, many of those who initially produced written testimonials, novels, and films have felt compelled to adapt their work on stage. "It is not uncommon to see theatre used during the April commemorations of the genocide in Rwanda, as well as among Rwandan communities in the Diaspora" (515–16).

9. Whistler in the Dark is the theater that produced Blijana Srbljanovic's *Family Stories* and, as of this writing, is closing in April of 2014.

10. Dubravka Kenezević is being quoted here, from "Till the Last Breath," *SCENA* no. 5/6 (September/December 1995).

11. The book consists of a large collection of firsthand narratives by actual survivors of the Bosnian War and of the rape camps, told in the first person and largely unedited. It circulates almost anonymously for fear of reprisal and it is hard to obtain. I personally was able to obtain the book with the help of Dijana Milošević, the artistic director of DAH, who put me in touch with one of the members of Women in Black in Belgrade.

12. See the techniques used by Jerzy Grotowski and Eugenio Barba. Grotowski, like Barba, developed a theater practice that made the actor and the actor's body the very center of the theater experience often subjecting actors to strenuous physical work and use of the body on stage. See Barba 2005, and Barba and Savarese 2009.

13. This story is told by the survivor herself in the *Women in Black* volume.

14. See also Eliade's *Images and Symbols* (1991) and *The Myth of the Eternal Return: Cosmos and History* (2005). In the latter book Eliade develops the theory of myth reenactments in early societies as a form of reliving and recreating the original creation of the world, the sacrifice of the hero and his return to life in a continual circle of life, death and resurrection.

15. With regards to performance art, Auslander has noted that it is "often taken to be an intrinsically postmodern art form, both historically and stylistically rather than an art form with postmodern manifestations" (2004, 99).

16. See Elwes' "Floating Femininity" (1990) and her discussion of the importance of performance art for women in terms of allowing them to express themselves in a variety of ways. See also

Swindells' *The Uses of Autobiography* (2013).

Conclusion

1. See my 2007 article "Winnie in the Attic: Towards a Feminist Awakening in Beckett' s *Happy Days*," in which I theorize about my experience of playing the character of Winnie from Beckett's *Happy Days* and how that experience influenced all my subsequent work in the theater and the classroom.

2. Ciulei was artistic director of the Guthrie Theater in Minneapolis in the eighties and had lived in the United States since the seventies, but he often returned to Romania to direct plays.

3. As mentioned in Chapter Two, this view of postmodernity as both critical of and engaging with its time, as well as the distinction between postmodernism as a periodizing term and postmodernity as the set of philosophical and aesthetic markers, has been extensively articulated by Linda Hutcheon.

4. See the excellent biography and study of Bakhtin's works and influence by Katerina Clark and Michael Holquist titled *Mikhail Bakhtin*. In it they show at length Bakhtin's lack of recognition during his lifetime as a brilliant scholar, with the exception of the last seven years of his life.

5. See Braidotti and Griffin's *Thinking Differently: A Reader in European Women' s Studies* (2002), in which Braidotti develops the theory of "the stranger among us," referring particularly to East European women, seen by Western eyes as neither fully European nor exotic enough to be of much interest. See also Braidotti's book *Transpositions: On Nomadic Ethics* (2007), in which she takes issue with the universalism and globalism of our society, the highly technologized and mediatized world we live in, which lead to a form of "schizophrenic capitalism" to which she opposes a nomadic ethics that negotiates political emancipation.

6. According to Barber the carnival was also a way for the agrarian and rural societies to preserve their connection to nature and fertility rites for their survival and despite the Church's severe and consistent attempts at destroying those beliefs and rituals.

7. See Ubersfeld's *L'école du spectateur* (1996), in which she articulates the semiotic systems that are at play on stage in the production of live theater, from objects to all the nuances in body language. See also the chapter "Semiotics Defined" in Whitmore's *Directing Postmodern Theater* (2012).

8. See Whitmore's chapter "Audience" in *Directing Postmodern Theater* (2012) and Grotowski's discussion of the relation between actor and the audience in *The Poor Theater* (2002).

9. From the program of *Soulographie*, Sunday November 18, 2012.

10. Bruner is actually discussing Jon Stewart's show as one such example of "emancipatory" comedy.

11. See Kurspahic's extraordinary account of journalistic experiences during the war of the nineties, *Prime Time Crime: Balkan Media in War and Peace* (2003).

12. The name offers of course a wonderful and most likely not accidental pun, as it sounds just like the name of the French existentialist philosopher and playwright, a passionate political activist of the left, Jean-Paul Sartre.

Bibliography

Adamic, Louis. 1940. *From Many Lands*. New York: Harper and Brothers.

Adamová, Radmila. 2012. *The Alluring Little Shop*. Manuscript, courtesy of the author.

_____. 2013. Interview with author. May.

Adorno, Theodor. 1973. *Negative Dialectics*. Trans. E. B. Ashton. New York: Seabury.

_____. 1998. *Critical Models: Interventions and Catchwords*. Trans. Henry W. Pickford. New York: Columbia University Press.

_____. 2006. *Minima Moralia: Reflections from Damaged Life*. New York: Verso.

Alighieri, Dante. 1995. *The Divine Comedy*. Trans. Allen Mandelbaum. New York: Everyman's Library.

Apte, Mahadev. 1985. *Humor and Laughter: An Anthropological Approach*. Ithaca: Cornell University Press.

Arendt, Hannah. 1976. *Eichmann in Jerusalem: A Report on the Banality of Evil*. New York: Penguin.

Arlin, Marcy. 2005. *Oldish Woman Leaves Earth*. In *Man.In.Fest*. Cluj, Romania: Babes-Bolyai University.

_____. 2013. Interview with author. August.

Arlin, Marcy, and Gwynn MacDonald. 2012/2013. "East European Playwrights. Women Write the New." *Slavic and East European Performance* 32, no. 1: 50–61.

Arlin, Marcy, Gwynn MacDonald, and Daniel Gerould. 2009. *Czech Plays: Seven New Works*. New York: Martin E. Segal Theater Center.

Armstrong, Elizabeth, and Kathleen Juhl, eds. 2007. *Radical Acts: Theatre and Feminist Pedagogies of Change*. San Francisco: Aunt Lute.

Artaud, Antonin. 1994. *Theater and Its Double*. Trans. Mary Caroline Richards. New York: Grove.

Aston, Elaine. 1999. *Feminist Theatre Practice: A Handbook*. New York: Routledge.

Auslander, Philip. 1994. *Presence and Resistance: Postmodernism and Cultural Politics in Contemporary American Performance*. Ann Arbor: University of Michigan Press.

_____. 2004. "Postmodernism and Performance." In *The Cambridge Companion to Postmodernism*, ed. Steven Connor, pp. 97–115. New York: Cambridge University Press.

Bacchilega, Christina. *Postmodern Fairy Tales: Gender and Narrative Strategies*. Philadelphia: University of Pennsylvania Press, 1997.

Bahun, Sandra Radunovic, and Marinos Pourgouris. 2006. *The Avant-Garde and the Margins: New Territories of Modernism*. Newcastle Upon Tyne, UK: Cambridge Scholars.

Bakhtin, Mikhail. 1984. *Rabelais and His World*. Trans. Hélène Islowski. Bloomington: Indiana University Press.

_____. 2002. "Forms of the Chronotope in the Novel: Notes Towards a Historical Poetics." In *Narrative Dynamics: Essays on Time, Plot, Closure and Frames*, ed.

Brian Richardson, pp. 15–25. Columbus: Ohio State University Press.

Barba, Eugenio. 2005. *A Dictionary of Theater Anthropology: The Secret Art of the Performer*. New York: Routledge.

Barba, Eugenio, and Nicola Savarese. 2009. *On Directing and Dramaturgy: Burning the House*. Drama and Theater Studies. New York: Routledge.

Barber, Elizabeth Wayland. 2013. *The Dancing Goddesses: Folklore, Archeology and the Origins of European Dance*. New York: W. W. Norton.

Barreca, Regina. 1988. *Last Laughs: Perspectives on Women and Comedy*. New York: Gorgon and Breach.

Baudrillard, Jean. 1994a. *Simulacra and Simulation*. Trans. Sheila Faria Gaser. Ann Arbor: University of Michigan Press.

_____. 1994b. *The Illusion of the End*. Stanford: Stanford University Press.

_____. 1998. *The Consumer Society: Myths and Structures*. New York: Sage.

_____. 2010. *America*. New York: Verso.

Baum, Noa. 2002. *A Land Twice Promised*. Manuscript, courtesy of the author.

_____. 2009. "Performing Oral History: The Creation of 'A Land Twice Promised.'" *Storytelling, Self, Society* 5: 119–136. New York: Routledge.

_____. 2014. Interview with the author. March 24.

Beckett, Samuel. 1984. *Westward Ho*. New York: Grove.

_____. 2011. *Waiting for Godot*. New York: Grove.

Bhabha, Homi. 1994. *The Location of Culture*. New York: Routledge.

Biaggi, Cristina. 2000. *In the Footsteps of the Goddess*. Manchester, CT: Knowledge, Ideas, and Trends.

Bickis, Heidi, and Rob Shields. 2013. *Rereading Jean-François Lyotard: Essays on His Later Works*. Burlington, VT: Ashgate.

Bilic, Bojan, and Vesna Jankovic. 2012. *Resisting the Evil: (Post)Yugoslav Anti-War Contention*. Baden-Baden: Nomos Verlagsgesellschaft.

Birringer, Johannes. 1993. *Theater, Theory, Postmodernism*. Bloomington: Indiana University Press.

Boal, Augusto. 1985. *The Aesthetics of the Oppressed*. New York: Routledge.

_____. 2008. *The Theater of the Oppressed*. London, UK: Pluto.

Boccaccio, Giovanni. 2003. *The Decameron*. Trans. G. H. McWilliam. New York: Penguin.

Boon, Richard, Jane Plastow, and Wole Soyinka. 1999. *Theater Matters: Performance and Culture in the World Stage*. Cambridge: Cambridge University Press.

Bos, Dennis, and Marjolein t'Hart. 2008. *Humor and Social Protest*. New York: Cambridge University Press.

Boskailo, Esad, and Julia Lieblich. 2012. *Wounded I Am More Awake: Finding Meaning After Terror*. Nashville, TN: Vanderbilt University Press.

Bourdreaux, Richard. 1999. "Playwright Not Ready to Exit Theater of War." *Los Angeles Times*, June 2.

Boym, Svetlana. 2001. *The Future of Nostalgia*. New York: Basic.

Braidotti, Rossi, and Gabrielle Griffin. 2002. *Thinking Differently: A Reader in European Women's Studies*. London: Zed.

_____. 2007. *Transpositions: On Nomadic Ethics*. Cambridge, MA: Polity.

Brecht, Bertolt. 1964. *Brecht on Theater: The Development of an Aesthetic*. Ed. and trans. John Willet. New York: Hill and Wang.

Bruner, Lane. 2005. "Carnivalesque Protest and the Humorless State." *Text and Performance Quarterly* 25, no. 2: 136–155.

_____. 2012. *Repressive Regimes, Aesthetic States, and Arts of Resistance*. New York: Peter Lang.

Burke, Peter. 1978. *Popular Culture in Early Modern Europe*. New York: Harper and Row.

Calinescu, Matei. 1987. *Five Faces of Modernity: Modernism, Avant-garde, Decadence, Kitsch, Postmodernism*. Durham, NC: Duke University Press.

Camus, Albert. 1985. *Le Mythe de Sisyphe: Essai sur l'absurde*. Paris: Gallimard.

Caruth, Cathy. 1996. *Trauma in Contemporary Literature: Narrative and Representation*. Baltimore, MD: Johns Hopkins University Press.

Chu, Kathy. 1999. "Performances of Things Past by Immigrant Theater." *Newsday*, June 1.

Cixous, Hélène. 1981. "The Laugh of the Medusa." In *New French Feminisms*, ed. Elaine Marks and Isabelle de Courtivron, pp. 245–64. Brighton: Harvester.

_____. 1992. *Coming to Writing and Other Essays*. Trans. Deborah Jenson. Cambridge, MA: Harvard University Press.

Clark, Katerina, and Michael Holquist. 1986. *Mikhail Bakhtin*. Cambridge, MA: Belknap.

Clarke, Laurie-Beth. 2010. "Always Already Again: Trauma Tourism and the Politics of Memory Culture." *Encounters 1*, Department of Tourism and Transnational Studies, Dokkyo University, 65–74.

Clay, Carolin. 2002. "Babes in Belgrade: *Family Stories* Isn't Child Play." *Boston Phoenix*, May 29.

DAH Theater. 2011–2012. *Crossing the Line*. Performance program.

_____. 2013. *The Presence of Absence*. Performance program, designed by Nesa Paripovic. December.

Dolan, Jill. 2005. *Utopia in Performance*. Ann Arbor: University of Michigan Press.

Donkin, Ellen, and Susan Clement. 1993. *Upstaging Big Daddy: Directing Theater as if Gender and Race Matter*. Ann Arbor: University of Michigan Press.

Ehn, Erik. 2012. *Soulographie: Our Genocides*. New York: 53rd State.

_____. 2013. "Channels of Witness: Space, Abstraction, and the Commemoration of Genocide." *Journal of Dramatic Theory and Criticism* 27, no. 2: 67–104.

Eisner, John Clinton. 2010. Introduction to *The New York Plays* by Saviana Stanescu. New York: No Passport.

Eliade, Mircea. 1991. *Images and Symbols*. Princeton, NJ: Princeton University Press.

_____. 2005. *The Myth of the Eternal Return: Cosmos and History*. Trans. Willard R. Trask. Princeton, NJ: Princeton University Press.

Ellis, Caroline Burlingham. 2002. "*Family Stories*: A Slapstick Tragedy." *Theatermania*, April 26.

Elwes, Catherine. 1990. "Floating Femininity." In *Women's Images of Men*, ed. Sarah Kent, Jaqueline Morreau, and Sheila Kitzinger, pp. 164–193. Ontario, Canada: Pandora.

Evans, Sian, and Cheryl Robson, eds. 1999. *Eastern Promise: 7 Plays from Central and Eastern Europe*. London: Aurora Metro.

Factory Theater. 2010. "*Family Stories*, by Biljana Srbljanovic." May 20.

Ferguson, Margaret, and Jennifer Wicke. 1994. *Feminism and Postmodernism*. Durham, NC: Duke University Press.

Filipovic, Zlata. 2006. *Zlata's Diary: A Child's Life in Wartime Sarajevo*. New York: Penguin.

Fisher, Barbara. 2008. "Short Takes. *Train to Trieste*, by Domnica Radulescu." *Boston Sunday Globe*, August 17.

Fortier, Mark. 2002. *Theory/Theater: An Introduction*. New York: Routledge.

Frankl, Viktor. 2006. *Man's Search for Meaning*. Boston: Beacon.

Friedrich, Reiner. 1999. "Brecht and Postmodernism." *Philosophy and Literature* 23:1.

Gimbutas, Marija. 2007. *The Goddesses and Gods of Old Europe: Myths and Cult Images*. Los Angeles: University of California Press.

Glajar, Valentina, and Domnica Radulescu. 2005. *Amazons, Wretches and Vampirettes: Western Representations of East European Women*. Boulder, CO: East European Monographs.

Glajar, Valentina, and Domnica Radulescu, eds. 2008. *Gypsies in European Literature and Culture*. New York: Palgrave MacMillan.

Goldsworthy, Vesna. 1998. *Inventing Ruritania: The Imperialism of the Imagination*. New Haven, CT: Yale University Press.

Gordon, Mel. 1983. *Lazzi: The Comic Routines of the Commedia dell'arte*. New York: Performing Arts Journal Publications.

_____. 1997. *The Grand Guignol: Theatre of Fear and Terror*. Cambridge, MA: Da Capo.

Gray, Frances. 1994. *Women and Laughter*. Charlottesville: University of Virginia Press.

Griffin Theater. http://www.rideontheatre.com/shows/from-before/family-stories.

Grotowski, Jerzy. 2002. *Towards a Poor Theater*. New York: Routledge.

Hand, Richard, and Michael Wilson. 2002. *Grand Guignol: The French Theater of Horror*. Exter, UK: University of Exter Press.

Hart, Lynda, and Peggy Phelan, eds. 1993. *Acting Out Feminist Performances*. Ann Arbor: University of Michigan Press.

Hassan, Ihab. 1982. *The Dismemberment*

of Orpheus: Toward a Postmodern Literature. Madison: University of Wisconsin Press.

Hemmings, Claire. 2011. *Why Stories Matter: The Political Grammar of Feminist Theory.* Durham, NC: Duke University Press.

Henke, Robert. 2002. *Performance and Literature in the Commedia dell'Arte.* Cambridge, MA: Cambridge University Press.

Herman, Judith. 1997. *Trauma and Recovery: The Aftermath of Violence—from Domestic Abuse to Political Terror.* New York: Basic.

Hesford, Wendy S. 1990. "Storytelling and the Dynamics of Feminist Teaching." *Feminist Teacher* 5, no. 2 (Fall): 20–24.

hooks, bell. 1994. *Teaching to Transgress: Education as the Practice of Freedom.* New York: Routledge.

_____. 2002. *Yearning, Race, Gender and Cultural Politics.* Cambridge, MA: South End.

_____. 2001. "Eating the Other: Desire and Resistance." In *Media and Cultural Studies,* ed. Meenkashi Gigi Durham and Douglas Kellner, pp. 424–438. Malden, MA: Blackwell.

Hunter, Jack. 2012. *Chapel of Gore and Psychosis: The Grand Guignol Theater.* UK: Creation.

Hutcheon, Linda. 1988. *A Poetics of Postmodernism: History, Theory, Fiction.* New York: Routledge.

_____. 2002. *The Politics of Postmodernism.* New York: Routledge.

Ionesco, Eugène. 1962. *Notes et contre-notes.* Paris: Gallimard.

Jackson, Kevin. 2008. "Biljana Srbljanovic: *Family Stories.*" *Arts Hub,* October 31.

Jameson, Fredric. 1991. *Postmodernism, or the Cultural Logic of Late Capitalism.* Durham, NC: Duke University Press.

Jankovic, Mirka, and Stanislava Lazarevic. 2007. *Women in Black: Women's Side of War.* Trans. Dubravka Radanov. Belgrade: Women in Black.

Jenkins, Keith, ed. 1997. *The Postmodern History Reader.* New York: Routledge.

Jestrovic, Silvia, and Yana Meerzon. 2009. *Performance, Exile and America.* New York: Palgrave Macmillan.

Johnson, Barbara. 1987. "The Frame of Reference: Poe, Lacan, Derrida." In *The Purloined Poe: Lacan, Derrida and Psychoanalytic Reading,* ed. John P. Muller and William J. Richardson, pp. 213–252. Baltimore: Johns Hopkins University Press.

Kalisa, Marie-Chantal. 2006. "Theater and the Rwandan Genocide." *Peace Review: A Journal of Social Justice* 18, no. 4 (October): 515–521.

Karklin, Rasna. 2005. *The System Made Me Do It: Corruption in Post-Communist Societies.* New York: M.E. Sharpe.

Keen, Suzanne. 2010. *Empathy and the Novel.* New York: Oxford University Press.

Kelleher, Joe. 2009. *Theater and Politics.* New York: Palgrave Macmillan.

Kellner, Douglas. 2010. "Brecht's Marxist Aesthetic: The Korsch Connection." In *Bertolt Brecht. Political Theory and Literary Practice,* ed. Betty Nance Weber and Hubert Heinen, pp. 29–43. Atlanta: University of Georgia Press.

Kligman, Gail. 1988. *The Wedding of the Dead.* Los Angeles: University of California Press.

Kurspahic, Kemal. 2003. *Prime Time Crime: Balkan Media in War and Peace.* Washington, D.C.: United States Institute of Peace.

Kurtović, Larisa. 2012. "The Paradoxes of Wartime 'Freedom': Alternative Culture During the Siege of Sarajevo." In *Resisting the Evil: (Post)Yugoslav Anti-War Contention,* ed. Bojan Bilic and Vesna Jankovic, pp. 197–224. Baden-Baden: Nomos Verlagsgesellschaft.

Lacan, Jacques. 1972. "Seminar on the *Purloined Letter.*" *Yale French Studies* no. 48, French Freud: Structural Studies in Psychoanalysis, 39–72.

Lang, Berel. 1986. "Postmodernism in Philosophy: Nostalgia for the Future, Waiting for the Past." *New Literary History* 18, no. 1 (Autumn): 209–223.

Laughlin, Karen, and Catherine Schuler. 1995. *Theater and Feminist Aesthetics.* Madison: Farleigh Dickinson University Press.

Lazin, Milos. 2006. "To What Is Owed the Success of Biljana Srbljanovic?" *Revue des études slaves* 77, no. 1–2: 217–243. Translations from the French by Domnica Radulescu.

Lee, Ronald. 2008. Introduction. In *Gypsies in European Literature and Culture,* ed. Valentina Glajar and Domnica Radulescu, pp. 2–28. New York: Palgrave Macmillan.

Lerner, Motti. 2005. "*The Murder of Isaac* by Motti Lerner Not Yet in Israel." *All About Jewish Theater*. http://www.jewish-theatre.com/visitor/article_display.aspx?articleID=869.

_____. 2009. "Playwriting in Wartime." Unpublished essay, courtesy of Lerner.

_____. 2012a. Interview with author. July 18, 2012, and October 16, 2012.

_____. 2012b. *Isaac Assasiné*. Paris: Editions Théâtrales.

_____. 2012c. *The Murder of Isaac*. Unpublished English trans. by Motti Lerner. Manuscript, courtesy of Lerner.

Leys, Ruth. 2013. *Trauma: A Genealogy*. Chicago, IL: University of Chicago Press.

Lindor, Gina, and Cheryl Robson, eds. 2000. *Balkan Plots: Plays from Central and Eastern Europe*. London: Aurora Metro.

Little, Judy. 1983. *Comedy and the Woman Writer*. Lincoln: University of Nebraska Press.

_____. 1994. "Humoring the Sentence: Women's Dialogic Comedy." In *American Women Humorists: Critical Essays*, ed. Linda Morris, pp. 19–32. New York: Garland.

Lockwood, Allan. 2011. "Laugh till You Don't: Dorota Maslowka's *A Couple of Poor Polish Speaking Romanians*." *The Brooklyn Rail*, February 3.

Loraux, Nicole. 1985. *Façons tragique de tuer une femme*. Paris: Hachette.

_____. 1990. *Le Mères en deuil (Mothers in Mourning)*. Paris: Seuil.

_____. 1998. *Né de la terre*. Paris: Seuil.

Lorino, Philippe, and Benoît Tricard. 2012. "The Bakhtinian Theory of Chronotope (Time-Space Frame) Applied to the Organizing Process." In *Constructing Identity in and Around Organizations*, eds. Majken Schultz, Steve Maguire, Ann Langley, and Haridimos Tsoukas. Oxford Scholarship Online: pp. 201–235.

Luckhurst, Roger. 2008. *The Trauma Question*. London: Routledge.

Lukac, Aleksandar. 2004. "Invitation to an Exorcism." *Toronto Slavic Quarterly* 9: http://sites.utoronto.ca/tsq/09/lukac09.shtml

Lyotard, Jean-François. 1984. *The Postmodern Condition: A Report on Knowledge*. Trans. Geoff Bennington and Brian Massumi. Minneapolis: University of Minnesota Press.

_____. 1992. *The Postmodern Explained to Children*. Minneapolis: University of Minnesota Press.

_____. 2000. *Signed: Malraux*. Minneapolis: University of Minnesota Press.

Machek, Ivana. 2011. *Sarajevo Under Siege: Anthropology in Wartime*. Philadelphia: Pennsylvania University Press.

MacMaster, Kayt. 2013. "La MaMa Moves! Dance Festival Presents Pavel Zuštiak + Palissimo Company's *'The Painted Bird' Trilogy* Cycle." BWWDanceWorldwww, July 9.

Manole, Diana. 2009. "'An American Mile in Other's Shoes': The Tragicomedy of Immigrating to Twenty-First Century America." In *Performance, Exile and America*, ed. Jestrovic, Silvia and Yana Meerzon, pp. 66–93. New York: Palgrave Macmillan.

Markovic, Milena. 2004. *A Boat for Dolls*, or *Doll Ship*. Manuscript, courtesy of the author.

_____. 2012. *The Pavillions*. Manuscript, courtesy of the author.

_____. 2013. Interview with the author. May 15.

Marks, Peter. 2013. "Theater J Scales Back Plans to Stage Controversial Play *The Admission*." *Washington Post*, October 9.

_____. 2014. "Wrenching Israeli Drama *The Admission* Opens at Theater J." *Washington Post*, March 26.

Martinelli, Marco. 2014. *Noise in the Waters*. Trans. Thomas Simpson. New York: Bordighera.

Maslowska, Dorota. 2008. *A Couple of Poor, Polish Speaking Romanians*. Trans. Lisa Goldman and Paul Sirett. London: Oberon Modern Plays.

McKenna, Andrew J. 1992. *Violence and Difference: Girard, Derrida and Deconstruction*. Chicago: University of Illinois Press.

McQueeney, Joan. 2000. "Theater: A Voice for the Outsiders." *New York Times*, July 2.

Mediatore, Shari Stone. 2003. *Reading Across Borders: Storytelling and Knowledge of Resistance*. New York : Palgrave Macmillan.

Milošević, Dijana. 2013. Interview with author. June.

Minjares, Laura-Ceia. 2006. "Opting in,

Opting out: The Radical Melancholy of the Modernist Margin, or Tristan Tzara Places a Double Bet." In *The Avant-Garde and the Margins: New Territories of Modernism*, ed. Sandra Radunovic Bahun and Marinos Pourgouris, pp. 1–23. Newcastle upon Tyne, UK: Cambridge Scholars.

Mojzes, Paul. 2011. *Balkan Genocides: Holocaust and Ethnic Cleansing in the Twentieth Century.* Lanham, MD: Rowman and Littlefield.

Montaigne, Michel de. 1993. *The Complete Essays.* Trans. A. M. Screech. New York: Penguin.

Morje, Marc Howard. 2003. *The Weakness of Civil Society in Post-Communist Europe.* New York: Cambridge University Press.

Morris, Linda. 1994. *American Women Humorists: Critical Essays.* New York: Garland.

Nadal, Marita, and Monica Calvo. 2014. *Trauma in Contemporary Literature: Narrative and Representation.* New York: Routledge.

Neubauer, John, and Borbalia Zsuzsanna Török. 2009. *The Exile and Return of Writers from East Central Europe.* Berlin: De Gruyter.

New York City Arts. "Immigrants' Theatre Project." http://www.nyc-arts.org/organizations/1877/immigrants-theatre-project.

Nicholson, Linda. 1989. *Feminism/Postmodernism (Thinking Gender).* New York: Routledge.

Nouvet, Claire, Zrinka Stahuljak, and Kent Still. 2006. *Minima Memoria: In the Wake of Jean-François Lyotard.* Stanford: Stanford University Press.

Pavel, Laura. 2011. *Dumitru Tsepeneag and the Canon of Alternative Literature.* Trans. Alistair Ian. Champaign, IL: Dalkey Archive.

Pavoni, Giuseppe. 1589. *Diario. Delle feste celebrate nelle solennissime nozi delli serenissimi sposi, il sig. Don Ferdinando Medici, & la sig. Donna Christina di Loreno gran duchi di Toscana. MDLXXXIX.* Bologna: Giovanni Rossi.

Pervan, Nenad. 2009. "Hair in Sarajevo: Doing Theater Under Siege." In *Portrayals of Americans on the World Stage*, ed. Kevin Wetmore, pp. 179–191. Jefferson, NC: McFarland.

Petrunic, Ana-Marija. 2005. "No Man's Land: The Intersections of Balkan Space and Identity." *History of Intellectual Culture* 5: 1.

Pippa, Cristina. 2007. "Fair Trade: Saviana Stanescu's *Waxing West*." *The Brooklyn Rail*, April 2.

Pirandello, Luigi. 1998. *Six Characters in Search of an Author.* Trans. Eric Bentley. New York: Signet.

Porterfield, Melissa Rynn. 2009. "Srbljanovic's Ugly American: Simultaneously Constructing Serbian and American Identities." In *Portrayals of Americans on the World Stage*, ed. Kevin Wetmore, pp. 83–98. Jefferson, NC: McFarland.

Power, Samantha. 2002. *"A Problem from Hell": America and the Age of Genocide.* New York: Harper Perennial.

Radulescu, Domnica. 2007. "Winnie in the Attic: Towards a Feminist Awakening in Beckett's *Happy Days*." In *Radical Acts: Theatre and Feminist Pedagogies of Change*, ed. Elizabeth Armstrong and Kathleen Juhl, pp. 27–45. San Francisco: Aunt Lute.

_____. 2008a. "Caterina's Colombina: The Birth of a Female Trickster in Seventeenth Century France." *Theater Journal*, March, 87–113.

_____. 2008b. *Train to Trieste.* New York: Knopf.

_____. 2010. *The Romanian Reunion: A Country That Devours Its Own.* Manuscript.

_____. 2012. *Women's Comedic Art as Social Revolution.* Jefferson, NC: McFarland.

_____. 2012. *Naturalized Woman.* Manuscript, produced at Cabrini Theater, New York, October 10–12.

_____. 2013. *The Town with Very Nice People.* Manuscript.

_____. 2014a *Exile Is My Home.*. Manuscript, rehearsed staged reading at TheaterLab, New York, October 20–21.

_____. 2014b. "How I lost My Memory and Never Got It Back." *European Journal of Life Writing* 3 (June): C55–C59. http://ejlw.eu/article/view/111/194.

Radulescu, Domnica, ed. 2002. *Realms of Exile: Nomadism, Diasporas and East European Voices.* Lanham, MD: Rowman and Littlefield.

Radunovic, Sanja Bahun, and Marinos

Pougouris, eds. 2006. *The Avante-Garde and the Margins: New Territories of Modernism.* New Castle, UK: Cambridge Scholars Press.

Ramet, Sabrina. 1999. *Eastern Europe: Politics, Culture and Society Since 1939.* Bloomington: University of Indiana Press.

_____. 2005. *Thinking About Yugoslavia: Scholarly Debates About the Yugoslav Breakup and the Wars in Bosnia and Kosovo.* New York: Cambridge University Press.

Reid, Kerry. 2011a. "Best of Chicago's Fringe Theater Scene." *Chicago Tribune,* December 21.

_____. 2011b. "Searching for a Lost Son in Spellbinding 'Progress'; Worthy Opus." *Chicago Tribune,* December 14.

Ride On Theatre. 2008. "Family Stories." http://www.rideontheatre.com/shows/from-before/family-stories.

Robson, Cheryl. 2002. Foreword. In *Balkan Plots: New Plays from Central and Eastern Europe.* London: Aurora Metro.

Rushdie, Salman. 2006. *Midnight's Children.* New York: Random House.

Said, Edward. 1979. *Orientalism.* New York: Vintage.

_____. 2002. *Reflections on Exile.* Boston: Harvard University Press.

Samuel, R. Lawrence. 2012. *The American Dream: A Cultural History.* Syracuse, NY: Syracuse University Press.

Sarach, Marian. 2002. "Unexpected Journeys at the Immigrant Project." *Stage Press,* February 1.

Schifrin, Daniel. 2003. "Blood Relatives." *Special to the Jewish Week,* November 28.

Schmidt, Kerstin. 2005. *The Theater of Transformation: Postmodernism in American Drama.* Amsterdam: Rodopi.

Seibert, Brian. 2013. "On a Harrowing Journey, No Matter Who You Are: Pavel Zuštiak's 'Painted Bird' Blurs Insiders and Outsiders." *New York Times,* July 2.

Siebers, Tobin, ed. 1994. *Heterotopia: Postmodern Utopia and the Body Politic.* Ann Arbor: University of Michigan Press.

Silberman, Marc. 1993. "A Postmodernized Brecht?" *Theater Journal* 45, no. 1 (March): 1–19.

Skloot, Robert, ed. 2009. *The Theater of Genocide: Four Plays About Mass Murder in Rwanda, Bosnia, Cambodia and Armenia.* Madison: University of Wisconsin Press.

Solomon, Alisa. 2003. Immigrants' Theatre Project OBIE Award citation. *Village Voice,* May.

Srbljanović, Biljana. 1999. *Belgrade Trilogy.* In *Eastern Promise: 7 Plays from Central and Eastern Europe,* ed. Sian Evans and Cheryl Robson, pp. 256–311. London: Aurora Metro.

_____. 2002. *Histoires de famille (Family Stories).* In *La Trilogie de Belgrade.* Translations from the French by Domnica Radulescu. Paris: L'Arche.

Stanescu, Saviana. 2007. *Waxing West.* In *roMANIA After 2000: Five New Romanian Plays,* ed. Saviana Stanescu and Daniel Gerould, pp. 169–247. New York: Martin E. Segal.

_____. 2010. *The New York Plays.* New York: No Passport.

_____. 2013. Personal communication to author, taken by Stanescu from a collage of interview answers, reflections and confessions.

_____. 2014. *Bechnya.* Manuscript, courtesy of Stanescu.

Stanescu, Saviana, and Daniel Gerould, eds. 2007. *roMANIA After 2000: Five New Romanian Plays.* New York: Martin E. Segal.

Stokes, Gale. 1999. "Eastern Europe's Defining Fault Lines." In *Eastern Europe: Politics, Culture and Society Since 1939,* ed. Sabrina Ramet, pp. 15–35. Bloomington: University of Indiana Press.

Stoppard, Tom. 1994. *Rosencrantz and Guildenstern Are Dead.* New York: Grove.

Swanee, Hunt. 2004. *This Was Not Our War: Bosnian Women Reclaiming the Peace.* Durham, NC: Duke University Press.

Swindells, Julia, ed. 2013. *The Uses of Autobiography.* New York: Routledge.

Taviani, Fernando, and Mirella Schino. 1982. *Il segreto della Commedia dell'Arte: la memoria delle compagnie italiane del XVI, XVII e XVIII secolo.* Firenze: La casa Usher.

Tehrani, Bijan. 2013. "Aglaya at Hungarian Film Festival." *Cinema Without Borders,* November 7. http://cinemawithoutborders.com/conversations/3527-aglaya-hungarian-film-festival-la.html

Ubersfeld, Anne. 1996. *Lire le théâtre II. L'école du spectateur*. Paris: Belin.

Veteranyi, Aglaja. 2012. *Why Is the Child Cooking in the Polenta?* Trans. Vincent Kling. Champaign, IL: Dalkey Archive.

Villon, François. 2004. "Ballade des Pendus" ("Ballad of the Hanged"). In *Lais, testament, poésies diverses*. Paris: Champion classiques.

Vişniec, Matei. 1997. *The Body of a Woman as a Battlefield in the Bosnian War* [*BWB*]. Manuscript version, first performed at the Studio des Champs-Elysées, Paris, November 1997. Directed by Michel Fagadau.

_____. 2000. *How to Explain the History of Communism to Mental Patients*. Paris: Lansman.

_____. 2002. *The Body of a Woman as a Battlefield in the Bosnian War* [*BWB*]. In *Balkan Plots: New Plays from Central and Eastern Europe*, ed. Cheryl Robson, 14–66. London: Aurora Metro.

_____. 2009. *The Word Progress on My Mother's Lips Doesn't Ring True*. Manuscript, courtesy of Vişniec.

_____. 2014a. "How I Write." Unpublished essay, courtesy of Vişniec. Trans. Domnica Radulescu.

_____. 2014b. *Pourquoi Hécube?* Manuscript, courtesy of Vişniec. Translations from the French by Domnica Radulescu.

_____. 2014c. "Who Am I?" Unpublished confessional essay, courtesy of Vişniec. Translations from the French by Domnica Radulescu.

_____. 2014d. Interview with the author. February 2. Translation from the Romanian by Domnica Radulescu.

Wallis, Brian, and Marcia Tucker, eds. 1984. *Art After Modernism: Rethinking Representation*. Boston: David R. Godine.

Warner, Vassela. 2010. "Post-communist, Postmodern, Postmortem: Images of Dogs, Women, and Children in the Drama of Biljana Srbljanovic." *Serbian Studies: Journal of the North American Society for Serbian Studies* 24, no. 1–2: 91–107.

Wetmore, Kevin. 2009. *Portrayals of Americans on the World Stage*. Jefferson, NC: McFarland.

Whitmore, Jon. 2012. *Directing Postmodern Theater*. Ann Arbor: University of Michigan Press.

Zarris, Venus. 2011. "The Word Progress on My Mother's Lips Doesn't Ring True: Review." *Chicago Stage Review*, December 30.

Index